lonely planet

BEST ROAD TRIPS
CANADA

ESCAPES ON THE OPEN ROAD

JOHN LEE, RAY BARTLETT, OLIVER BERRY, GREGOR CLARK,
SHAWN DUTHIE, STEVE FALLON, CAROLYN HELLER, ANNA KAMINSKI,
ADAM KARLIN, JOHN LEE, CRAIG MCLACHLAN, LIZA PRADO,
BRENDAN SAINSBURY, REGIS ST LOUIS, PHILLIP TANG

Contents

TERRITORY ACKNOWLEDGEMENT

Lonely Planet would like to acknowledge and pay respect to the Indigenous people throughout this country. This guide was written on and is written about land which includes their traditional lands, unceded territories and Treaty territories. We also recognise the ongoing efforts of Indigenous peoples for reconciliation, justice, and social, cultural, and economic self-determination. We hope you can use the opportunity of your travels to connect with the people and learn about Indigenous culture and society.

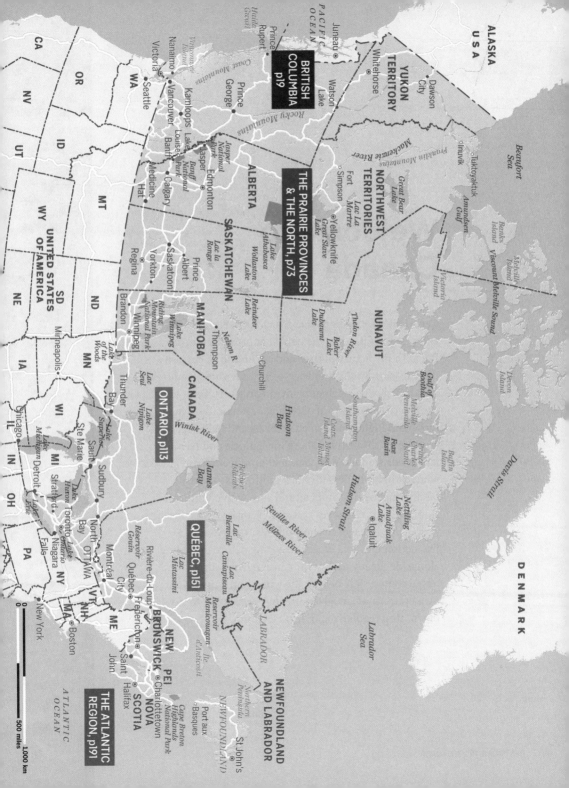

PACIFIC OCEAN

Haida Gwaii

ALASKA
USA

CA
OR
NV
UT
ID
WA
MT
WY
NE
SD
ND
MN
WI
IL
IN
OH
PA
NY
VT
NH
MA
ME

UNITED STATES OF AMERICA

Juneau

Prince Rupert

Coast Mountains

Whitehorse

YUKON TERRITORY

Dawson City

BRITISH COLUMBIA p19

Watson Lake

Prince George

Rocky Mountains

Victoria
Vancouver Island
Nanaimo
Seattle
Vancouver
Kamloops
Louise Park
Banff
Jasper National Park
Jasper
Edmonton
Calgary
Medicine Hat

THE PRAIRIE PROVINCES & THE NORTH, p73

ALBERTA

SASKATCHEWAN

Prince Albert
Yorkton
Saskatoon
Regina
Brandon
Riding Mountain National Park
Winnipeg

Lac La Ronge
Lake Athabasca
Wollaston Lake
Reindeer Lake

Great Bear Lake

NORTHWEST TERRITORIES

Franklin Mountains

Mackenzie River

Fort Simpson
Fort Martre
Lac La Martre
Great Slave Lake
Yellowknife

Inuvik

Tuktoyaktuk

Beaufort Sea

Amundsen Gulf

Banks Island

Melville Island

Victoria Island

Viscount Melville Sound

Devon Island

Dubawnt Lake
Baker Lake
Thelon River

NUNAVUT

Southampton Island

Coats Island
Mansel Island

Gulf of Boothia

Boothia Peninsula

Prince Charles Island

Baffin Island

Nettilling Lake
Amadjuak Lake
Iqaluit

Davis Strait

DENMARK

Lake Winnipeg
Nelson R.
Thompson

MANITOBA

CANADA

Churchill

Hudson Bay

Foxe Basin

Hudson Strait

Labrador Sea

Minneapolis
IA
MI
Lake Michigan
Chicago
Lake of the Woods
Thunder Bay
Lake Superior
Ste Marie
Sault
Sudbury
Lake Nipigon
Lake Seul

ONTARIO, p113

Winisk River

James Bay

Belcher Islands

Lac Bienville
Feuilles River
Mélèzes River

Lac Minto

Lac Caniapiscau

LABRADOR

Northern Peninsula

NEWFOUNDLAND AND LABRADOR

NEWFOUNDLAND

Labrador Sea

Detroit
Lake Huron
Lake St Clair
Stratford
Toronto
Lake Erie
Niagara Falls
North Bay
Lake Ontario
OTTAWA
Montréal

Reservoir Gouin
Québec City

QUÉBEC, p151

Lac Mistassini

Reservoir Manicouagan
Île d'Anticosti

New York
Boston
Riviere-du-Loup
Fredericton
Saint John
NEW BRUNSWICK
PEI
Charlottetown
NOVA SCOTIA
Halifax
Cape Breton Highlands National Park
Port aux Basques
St John's

THE ATLANTIC REGION, p191

ATLANTIC OCEAN

0
500 miles
1,000 km

Welcome to Canada

Canada is so enormous that flying between its towns and cities has become the default approach to travel. But with the luxury of time and a trunkful of curiosity, driving is by far the best way to encounter this country's wondrously diverse, highly inviting regions. Feast your eyes on clifftop views of glittering oceans and drive mountain highways flanked by bears and bald eagles. Explore jellybean-hued shoreline hamlets and friendly farmlands studded with artisanal producers. Lose yourself in boundless mystical rainforests and visit fascinating historic and cultural sites with countless stories to tell. Wherever you go in Canada, two constants prevail: locals eager to show off their regions and a live-action diorama of awe-inspiring nature unfolding alongside. Ready to dive in? Choose from our 32 road-tested routes, slide behind the wheel and launch your own epic Canadian adventure. Just remember to slow down, stop regularly and drink it all in.

Grizzly bear, Banff National Park (p61)
BGSMITH/SHUTTERSTOCK ©

Our Picks

BEST SCENIC DRIVES

Canada offers a drive-through diorama of jaw-dropping scenery that makes you want to pull over and take photos around almost every corner. From the colossal ice-streaked peaks of BC and Alberta to the glittering, forest-fringed lakes of Ontario, and from the dramatic borealis-framed far north to the brightly painted villages of the Atlantic coastline, soul-stirring panoramas can make a well-chosen driving trip into a picture-perfect visual odyssey here.

TAKE IT SLOW

Schedule extra time for famously scenic drives so you can slow down, savor the views and make frequent photo stops.

 02

Sea to Sky Highway

Savor cliffside ocean views alongside tumbling waterfalls, towering old trees and mountain-studded backcountry vistas.

P28

 15

Dempster Highway

Encounter the vast boreal forest en route to the Arctic Circle, northern lights (hopefully) included.

P106

 26

The Saguenay Fjord & Lac St Jean

Slide into a wonderland of dense forests, cliffside promontories and possible whale sightings.

P178

 32

Icebergs, Vikings & Whales

Face down Newfoundland's ruggedly beautiful coastline and snap countless photos of charming shoreline communities.

P218

 20

Southern Ontario Nature Loop

Drink in the tranquility of quiet coves, mirror-calm lakes and lofty, landscape-hugging lookouts.

P218

CORINA LARDELLI / 500PX/GETTY IMAGES ©

Northern lights, Dempster Highway (p108)

Opposite: Trinity (p221), Newfoundland

LOCAL RADIO

Tune the car radio to local stations for the regional vibe plus weather reports and road-condition updates.

HIKES

Research some short hikes in the area and add one or two of these to your scenic-drive itinerary.

VIEWING SPOTS

Pulling over to watch animals blocks traffic. Wait for designated viewing spots instead.

SAFETY

If you're planning a backcountry hike, learn how to safely encounter animals such as bears and wolves.

Our Picks

BEST WILDLIFE-WATCHING DRIVES

Watch silently grazing moose and salmon-munching grizzly bears. Glimpse inquisitive raccoons and rare lynxes and wolverines. Spot soaring bald eagles and feisty little hummingbirds. And look to the coast for lolling walruses on the shore and humungous humpback whales sliding regally through the sea. Canada is a tooth-and-claw wonderland of wildlife, offering the chance for breathtaking, humbling and spine-tingling nature encounters destined to become the highlights of any visit.

STAY BACK
Never approach wildlife for close-up photos. Stay in your vehicle and use your camera's zoom function.

Vancouver Island's Remote North

Slow down on the island's wilder end and watch for black bears, orcas and even cougars.

P46

Circling the Rockies

Hike under vast, cathedral-like skies and look for elk, eagles and much more.

P60

WIRESTOCK CREATORS/SHUTTERSTOCK ©

Orca, Vancouver Island (p40)

Icefields Parkway

Experience a drive-through safari teeming with bears, bighorn sheep and mountain goats.

P82

The Kawarthas

Delve into this woodland haven of moose, coyotes and utterly brilliant birdlife.

P136

The Cabot Trail

Hop out and hike an iconic, nature-hugging region famed for its shoreline whale-watching.

P206

Opposite: Rocky Mountain elk, Banff National Park (p61)

Our Picks

BEST FOOD & WINE DRIVES

Canada has a full menu of taste-tripping regions ripe for exploration, with everything from celebrated fresh-catch seafood to just-picked fruit piled high at friendly farmers markets. Still hungry? Cities such as Vancouver, Toronto and Montréal have renowned restaurant scenes always worth diving into. Wine fans should also weave around bucolic, vine-striped areas in BC and Ontario, while cool craft distilleries and microbrew beer producers are always ready to tempt adventurous sippers.

KNOW YOUR WINES

Research the country's surprisingly diverse wines and wine regions at winesofcanada.com.

 01

Vancouver & the Fraser Valley

Drop by farm producers, boutique wineries and Vancouver's celebrated international restaurant scene.

P22

 06

Okanagan Valley Wine Tour

Weave between tasting rooms, orchards and farm-to-table restaurants in this lakeside wine region.

P52

 23

Eastern Townships

Treat yourself to artisanal cheese, chocolate and much more in this region's charming countryside.

P160

 21

Thousand Island Parkway

Discover local producers, regional delicacies and gourmet indulgence on this leisurely drive.

P146

 31

Two Islands, Three Provinces

Meet the locals while discovering tasty craft ales and Canada's freshest lobster dishes.

P212

Musée du Chocolat de la Confiserie Bromont (p161), Bromont

Opposite: Lobster supper, Prince Edward Island (p215)

LOCAL EATS

Try some of Canada's favorite foods, including poutine, bannock, lobster rolls, butter tarts, Nanaimo bars and ketchup-flavored potato chips.

FARMERS MARKETS

Plan visits to local farmers markets (typically operating from May to October) during your trip.

Our Picks

BEST HISTORY DRIVES

Canada has a rich and sometimes tumultuous backstory that history-minded visitors love to explore. Here you'll find a deep well of tales and timelines, encompassing dramatic prehistoric sites, profound Indigenous heritage, bloody colonial battlefields, tough pioneer characters and gritty gold-rush yarns that take you right back to the rough-and-tumble 1880s. Close your eyes (not while you're driving) and slide into the fascinating stories that shaped the nation.

DISCOVERY PASS

An annual Parks Canada Discovery Pass includes admission to more than 80 sites, including many historic properties.

 07

Haida Gwaii Adventure

Learn a deep and ancient Indigenous story in this exploration of Haida heritage and contemporary culture.

P56

 10

Dinosaurs, Hoodoos & the Wild West

Commune with prehistoric critters, discover ancient petroglyphs and visit a World Heritage Indigenous site.

P76

 14

Klondike Highway

Follow in the footsteps of fortune-seeking pioneers and discover remarkable gold-rush heritage sites.

P100

 17

People & Culture Loop

Uncover the stories behind a Mennonite village and a community of escaped enslaved people.

P122

 29

South Shore Circular

Weave through the Maritimes on this delightful route, historic communities and region-defining museums included.

P200

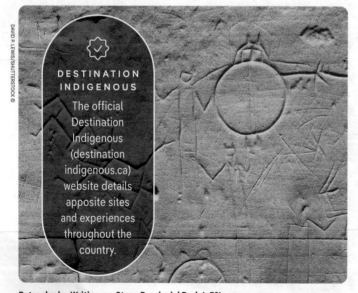

DESTINATION INDIGENOUS

The official Destination Indigenous (destination indigenous.ca) website details apposite sites and experiences throughout the country.

Petroglyphs, Writing-on-Stone Provincial Park (p78)

Our Picks

BEST ADRENALINE-RUSH DRIVES

It's a beauty, but Canada's spectacular natural side isn't just for gazing at. There are countless ways to experience the great outdoors and work up a sweat while you're here. Remarkable hikes, breathtaking kayak adventures, jelly-legged suspension-bridge walks and downhill biking fun – your next adrenaline-rich activity is just around the next curve in the road. Build some extra time into your driving schedule and dive right in.

WINTER FUN

Canada offers a snow-dusted cornucopia of wintertime sports and activities. Research regions, resorts and more at skicanada.org.

 Vancouver & the Fraser Valley

Tackle zip lines, suspension bridges and ocean-viewing hikes at the edge of BC's biggest city.

P22

 Around the Kootenays

Explore backcountry hiking routes, thrilling bike trails and whitewater rafting in this rugged mountain region.

P66

 PARKS CANADA

Check out a wide array of hiking, biking and wildlife-watching opportunities at the Parks Canada website: parks.canada.ca.

Zip-lining, Grouse Mountain (p24)

ALL CANADA PHOTOS/ALAMY STOCK PHOTO ©

The Kawarthas

Step into a nature-lovers' wonderland striped with amazing hikes, especially in beloved Algonquin Provincial Park.

P136

Up to the Laurentians

See where Montréalers get away from it all via life-affirming hiking, biking and canoeing adventures.

P154

Central Nova Scotia

Choose from surfing, rugged hikes and island-hopping ocean kayaking on Canada's super-scenic east coast.

P194

When to Go

Late spring, summer and early fall are optimum for Canadian driving trips, with inviting weather, great festivals and fully open attractions.

May and June are when Canada's spectacular nature springs back to life. It's also when the weather transitions from relentless cold and rain, and attractions extend their opening hours for the upcoming peak season. This window is also just before the summer crowds arrive and school vacations start – key considerations for savvy travelers. September and early October offer similar appeal, alongside the camera-worthy spectacle of epic autumnal foliage. Summer has the highest temperatures, of course, plus long, blue-sky days and countless festivals. But it can also be uncomfortably hot (especially in July and August) and wildfires can be a major challenge if you're driving.

Accommodations

Prices and availability vary considerably by season. In summer, campsites can be fully booked, while hotel room rates – especially in big cities and hot-spot destinations – rise sharply. In many areas, just-off-peak months such as June and September deliver considerable savings without hugely sacrificing on favorable weather.

WILDFIRES

Recent years have seen devastating summer wildfires whipping up in Canada, especially in the western provinces of BC and Alberta. During wildfire season, communities may be evacuated, cities subjected to smoky skies, and drivers re-routed away from burn areas.

Weather Watch (Toronto)

JANUARY	FEBRUARY	MARCH	APRIL	MAY	JUNE
Avg daytime max: -1°C	Avg daytime max: -0.5°C	Avg daytime max: 4°C	Avg daytime max: 10°C	Avg daytime max: 16°C	Avg daytime max: 22°C
Days of rainfall: 8	Days of rainfall: 7	Days of rainfall: 7	Days of rainfall: 8	Days of rainfall: 8	Days of rainfall: 8

SENTURKSERKAN/SHUTTERSTOCK ©

Winter Carnival, Québec City

ICE PARTIES

Many Canadian communities celebrate their chilly winters with spectacular festivals. Despite freezing temperatures, the Québec Winter Carnival in Québec City is reportedly the oldest and largest of its kind in the world, complete with concerts, ice sculptures and cheery snowman mascot Bonhomme Carnaval.

Big Events

The toe-tappingly brilliant **Montréal International Jazz Festival** is a two-week citywide party of amazing, mostly free concerts, many of them on alfresco stages in the downtown core. **June**

North America's biggest fringe theater bash, the **Edmonton Fringe Festival** serves up a cavalcade of creativity with 1600 performances taking place on more than two dozen stages. **August**

The perfect way to hang out with locals in Ontario, Toronto's carnival-like **Canadian National Exhibition** offers all the charms of a vast state fair, complete with concerts, midway rides and quirky food trucks. **August**

A 10-day celebration of East Coast food culture, the **PEI Fall Flavours Festival** is a stomach-stuffing showcase of lobster rolls, oyster shucking and great kitchen parties. **September**

LOCAL FESTIVITIES

With a grand backdrop of ocean-fringed mountain peaks, Vancouver's summer-long **Bard on the Beach Shakespeare Festival** offers spectators four sparkling plays in a tented park complex. **June to September**

Feast on a rich slice of regional heritage at New Brunswick's sparkling **Acadian Celebration**, which sees the town of Caraquet host a gigantic party of performers, traditional cuisine and rich French-influenced culture. **August**

Join Alberta's nerd-forward celebration of stars, astronomy and space: Jasper's delightful **Dark Sky Festival** hosts lectures, parties, guided walks and much more. **October**

JULY	AUGUST	SEPTEMBER	OCTOBER	NOVEMBER	DECEMBER
Avg daytime max: **26°C**	Avg daytime max: **25°C**	Avg daytime max: **22°C**	Avg daytime max: **15°C**	Avg daytime max: **8°C**	Avg daytime max: **2°C**
Days of rainfall: 7	Days of rainfall: 7	Days of rainfall: 7	Days of rainfall: 7	Days of rainfall: 7	Days of rainfall: 8

Get Prepared for Canada

Useful things to load in your bag, your ears and your brain.

Clothing

WATCH

Atanarjuat: The Fast Runner
(Zacharias Kunuk; 2001) Epic Inuit movie that retells an ancient legend in a spectacular Arctic setting.

Bon Cop, Bad Cop
(Eric Canuel; 2006) Hugely popular comedy-drama that showcases anglophone and francophone cultural differences.

Maudie
(Aisling Walsh; 2016) Moving biopic profile of Nova Scotian folk artist Maud Lewis.

Schitt's Creek
(various directors; 2015–20) Six-season TV comedy created by Canadian actors (and father and son) Eugene and Daniel Levy about a formerly wealthy family adjusting to small-town life.

The Sweet Hereafter
(Atom Egoyan; 1997) Quietly devastating small-town drama starring Sarah Polley.

Layers: Canada's summertime peak temperatures might make shorts and a T-shirt the perfect attire for an evening out, but for most of the year, and in most regions, you'll also want something warmer to slip on as the sun drops. Layers are the key to successfully packing for a driving trip here. Even in summer, jeans and light sweaters are handy options, while jackets in spring and fall are key. In winter, you'll need a proper coat, especially in colder regions where snowfall is the norm.

Waterproof jacket: Whatever season you visit, a waterproof outer layer could make the difference between a great day and a miserable

one. Keep it in your car (a light waterproof is fine for much of the year, while an insulated one is perfect for winter).

Boots/shoes: Since you'll also be hopping from the driver's seat to explore destinations on foot, good footwear is essential. Soft hiking shoes (waterproof ones are recommended) are ideal for most visitors, especially if you're just planning some urban exploring or light trail walking. For rugged hikes, make sure you bring proper hiking boots, and that they are properly worn in.

Tombstone Territorial Park (p106)

LISTEN

As It Happens
Canadian perspective on current affairs and international issues, hosted by national public broadcaster CBC.

Fully Completely
(The Tragically Hip, 1992) The first album from Canada's favorite band is a great soundtrack for a cross-Canada drive.

Le Voyage
(Paul Piché, 1999) A superb accompaniment to a Québec visit from this old-school francophone singer-songwriter.

Words (English/French)

Convenience store/dep: Smaller stores with long opening hours that sell snacks, food, drinks and more. The French word is short for 'dépanneur.'

Eh/hein: Commonly added to the end of almost any sentence; it means 'Right?'

Gas/essence: Petrol.

Give'r/donnes-en: To give it your best shot/go for it.

Hydro/hydro: Term used by many Canadians for electricity, deriving from the hydro-dam method widely used to generate electricity in Canada.

Klicks/klicks: Slang term for kilometers.

Loonie/huard: Slang term for a $1 coin. And a $2 coin? It's a toonie/toonie, of course.

Parkade/garage de stationnement: A parking garage, usually for pay parking and often pricey in major city centers.

Service station/station-service: Facilities where gas is sold; these are most common in suburban areas.

Timmies/Timmies: The ubiquitous Tim Hortons fast-food chain is easy to find along highways and in suburban areas. Its stores serve coffee, doughnuts, lunches and more.

READ

A Number of Things: Stories of Canada Told Through 50 Objects
(Jane Urquhart; 2016) Quirky stories about random historic items.

How to Be a Canadian: Even If You Already Are One
(Will Ferguson and Ian Ferguson; 2007) Humorous introduction to Canadian foibles.

Souvenir of Canada
(Douglas Coupland; 2002) Esoteric essays and photos from a celebrated writer and contemporary artist.

JOSEF HANUS/SHUTTERSTOCK ©

Georgina Point Lighthouse, Mayne Island (p42)

British Columbia

Explore

British Columbia

A drive-through diorama of ancient forests, island-studded coastlines and an ever-present backdrop of glittering peaks, British Columbia (BC) is the epitome of back-to-nature exploration. But it's not just about spectacular panoramas here. Wildlife fans love the abundant opportunities to spot whales, bears, bald eagles and more in their natural habitats. Culinary adventurers enjoy discovering the celebrated farm-to-fork dining and advanced winery scenes. And culture-cravers never exhaust the rich Indigenous heritage and colorful historical sites located around almost every corner. Wherever you go, slow down, head off the beaten track and find a grand West Coast sunset to call your own.

Vancouver

BC's biggest city, this glass-towered metropolis is framed by mountain peaks and fringed by the Pacific Ocean. Most visitors to the province arrive at the international airport here (actually located in neighboring Richmond), and spend at least a few days exploring Vancouver at the beginning or end of their trip. Don't miss the celebrated dining scenes in neighborhoods such as Kitsilano, Main Street and Granville Island. Be sure to explore on foot in historic Gastown and shoreline-hugging Stanley Park. And save time to slake your thirst in Canada's finest craft-beer scene. On the activities front, there's everything from urban beaches and quirky guided tours to kayaking excursions and Indigenous-themed

museums and galleries. And there's a full roster of hotels, hostels and other accommodations (although booking far ahead for the summer peak is essential).

Victoria

Historic BC capital Victoria is your gateway to Vancouver Island, and most visitors spend a few days here before hopping on the highway to the rest of the region. The city's camera-ready Inner Harbour is fringed by grand heritage buildings, and walking along main thoroughfare Government St brings you to Canada's oldest Chinatown. Boutique shops and independent restaurants line the rest of the downtown core, but be sure to strike out for the city's fringes too. You'll find shoreline parks, oceanfront trails and – a little

WHEN TO GO

May to September is ideal for visiting BC, although July and August see peak crowds and the year's highest hotel prices. Late spring and early fall are often great times to visit, but some attractions, especially in remote regions or smaller towns, may not be operating their full summer schedules. Winter is brilliant for skiing, but driving can be challenging.

further out – BC's most celebrated ornamental-garden attraction. History fans will enjoy Victoria for its huge provincial museum, while the city is also a handy hub for whale-watching trips and spectacular floatplane tours.

Kelowna

The Okanagan Valley's unofficial capital, Kelowna is certainly its biggest city. It's also the perfect base for exploring one of Canada's finest and most scenic wine regions. Head straight to the center and you'll find plenty of places to eat, shop and stock up the car for the rest of your regional journey. Save time for the museums and galleries here, and be sure to whip out your camera for a few panoramic lakeside views.

Whistler

Canada's favorite ski resort is worth a long-weekend stay at any time of year. Base yourself in one of the many hotels in the scenic alpine village for some top-notch winter-powder action, or visit in late spring or summer, when countless hiking, biking, white-water rafting and regional scenic drives are endlessly available. The village is filled with great restaurants and is also less than two hours' drive from Vancouver.

TRANSPORT

You can drive into BC from the US state of Washington and also from across Canada (Alberta is the next province over). Vancouver International Airport is the main arrival point for overseas visitors. There are also smaller airports in Victoria, Kelowna and beyond, mostly servicing US, Canadian and other BC routes. Train, ferry and floatplane services also arrive here from the US.

 WHERE TO STAY

Vancouver's hotel prices rise dramatically in summer, reflecting huge demand and scarce properties. Instead, aim for accommodations outside the metropolis in adjoining Richmond. Book far ahead for peak-season rooms in Victoria and Whistler. Outside the major centers, you'll find B&Bs, historic properties and oceanfront resorts (some of them very high end). BC is also blessed with incredibly scenic campsites; book ahead for the hottest spots (bcparks.ca/reservations) or consider less crowded sites with greater tranquility. Looking for something unique? Consider Vancouver's Indigenous-themed **Skwachàys Lodge** (skwachays.com), Victoria's iconic **Empress Hotel** (fairmont.com/empress-victoria) or Vancouver Island's quirky **Free Spirit Spheres** (freespiritspheres.com).

 WHAT'S ON

Bard on the Beach Shakespeare Festival

(bardonthebeach.org) A summer-long Vancouver showcase of plays, performed in huge tents with an ocean-and-mountain backdrop.

Crankworx

(crankworx.com) Whistler's celebration of downhill biking, complete with races, concerts and more.

Okanagan Spring Wine Festival

(thewinefestivals.com) A multiday celebration of the region's wines and wineries.

Rifflandia

(rifflandia.com) Rub shoulders with Victoria's locals as dozens of cool bands take to alfresco city stages.

Resources

Destination British Columbia (hellobc.com) Official website of BC's tourism organization, with regional profiles, maps, stories and other info.

Indigenous Tourism BC (indigenousbc.com) Pointing visitors to Indigenous attractions and experiences across the province.

BC Parks (bcparks.ca) Online guide to the provincial park system, with info on camping, wildlife watching and more.

01

Fort Langley offers family fun for all ages.

Vancouver & the Fraser Valley

DURATION	DISTANCE	GREAT FOR
2 days	186km/116 miles	Culture, Families, Nature

BEST TIME TO GO	June to September for warm days and ripened fruit.

Stanley Park

As you step onto the swinging Capilano Suspension Bridge, get eyed up by a grizzly bear atop Grouse Mountain or watch your children hone their bartering skills over wolverine skins at Fort Langley, you might wonder what happened to the promised pretty valley drive. But don't worry; it's here. With dramatic mountains rising on either side, a tour along the Fraser River is as action-packed as it is scenic.

Link Your Trip

02 Sea to Sky Highway

Head northwest from Vancouver, rather than east, and wind your way up into the mountains.

03 A Straight Hop

Drive onto the ferry at Horseshoe Bay in West Vancouver.

01 STANLEY PARK

Just steps from downtown Vancouver, which is also worth a walk around, but seemingly worlds away, **Stanley Park** (vancouver. ca/parks) is a spectacular urban oasis, covered in a quarter of a million trees that tower up to 80m. Rivaling New York's Central Park, this 405-hectare peninsula is a favorite hangout for locals, who walk, run or cycle around the 9km super-scenic **seawall** that circles the outer edge of the park. The pathway offers shimmering views of Burrard Inlet and passes impressive **totem poles**, squat **Brockton**

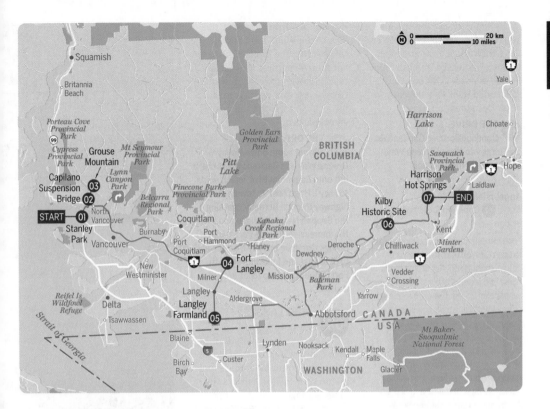

Point Lighthouse and log-strewn **Third Beach**, where you can also take a dip. Watch for the dramatic **Siwash Rock**, standing sentry off the western shoreline. Meaning 'he is standing up,' Siwash was named after a traditional First Nations legend that indicates it is a man transformed into stone; the hole in the rock is where he kept his fishing tackle.

Looking out across tree-fringed English Bay, Second Beach has a heated outdoor **swimming pool** (open May to September) that's wildly popular with families. From here, a long sandy beach stretches south along Beach Ave. Looking for

some kid-friendly action? The park's eastern shoreline is home to a fantastic **water park** that will keep your youngsters happily squealing for hours.

Also in the park is the ever-popular **Vancouver Aquarium** (vanaqua.org). One of the city's biggest attractions, it's home to penguins, otters and a plethora of BC marine critters.

THE DRIVE

Head north on Stanley Park Causeway and cross the beautiful Lions Gate Bridge to North Vancouver. Head east on Marine Dr for a block and turn left onto Capilano Rd, heading north for 2.4km.

02 CAPILANO SUSPENSION BRIDGE

Not for the faint of heart, **Capilano Suspension Bridge Park** (capbridge.com) is home to one of the world's longest (140m) and highest (70m) pedestrian suspension bridges, swaying gently over the roiling waters of Capilano Canyon. As you gingerly cross, try to remember that the steel cables you are gripping are embedded in huge concrete blocks on either side. This is the region's most popular attraction, hence the summertime crowds. The grounds here include rainforest walks, totem poles and some smaller bridges strung between the trees that offer a lovely squirrel's-eye forest walk. You can also test your bravery on the **Cliffwalk**, a glass-and-steel walkway secured with horizontal bars to a granite cliff face and suspended 90m over the canyon floor. Deep breath...

🚗 THE DRIVE
Continue north on Capilano Rd. This turns into Nancy Greene Way, which ends at the next stop.

⛟ DETOUR
Angel Island
Start: **02** Capilano Suspension Bridge

For a free alternative to Capilano, divert to **Lynn Canyon Park** (lynncanyon. ca), a temperate rainforest area that's home to its own lofty but slightly smaller suspension bridge. There are also plenty of excellent hiking trails and some great tree-hugging picnic spots here. Check out the park's **Ecology Centre** (lynn canyonecologycentre.ca) for displays on the region's rich biodiversity. If you're really keen on local flora, drop into a bookstore on your travels and pick-up a copy of the *Vancouver Tree Book* (David Tracey, 2016). It details many of the region's leafy wonders and shows you how to spot them while you're here. To find the park, head east on Hwy 1 from Capilano Rd and turn left on Lynn Valley Rd.

03 GROUSE MOUNTAIN
One of the region's most popular outdoor hangouts, **Grouse Mountain** (grousemountain.com) rises 1231m over North Vancouver's skyline. In summer, Skyride gondola tickets to the top include access to lumberjack shows, bird-of-prey displays and alpine hiking trails plus a **nature reserve** that's home to orphaned grizzly bears and timber wolves. You can also brave the two-hour,

five-line **zip-line course** or the 'Eye of the Wind' tour, which takes you to the top of a 20-story wind turbine tower for spectacular 360-degree views. In winter, Grouse is a very popular magnet for local and visiting skiers and snowboarders.

🚗 THE DRIVE
Return south down Nancy Greene Way and Capilano Rd, taking a left onto Edgemont Blvd, which leads to Hwy 1. Head east, following the highway through Burnaby, crossing the Second Narrows Bridge and then the impressive, 10-lane Port Mann Bridge. Continue on Hwy 1, exiting at 88 Ave East and following signs to Fort Langley. The trip takes around an hour.

04 FORT LANGLEY
Little Fort Langley's tree-lined streets and 19th-century storefronts make it one of the Lower Mainland's most picturesque historic villages. Its main heritage highlight is the evocative **Fort Langley National Historic Site** (parkscanada.gc.ca/ fortlangley), perhaps the region's most important old-school landmark.

A fortified trading post since 1827, this is where James Douglas announced the creation of British Columbia in 1858, giving the site a legitimate claim to being the province's birthplace. Chat with costumed re-enactors knitting, working on beaver pelts or sweeping their pioneer homes. Also open to explore are re-created artisan workshops and a **gold-panning area** that's very popular with kids. And when you need a rest, sample baking and lunchtime meals from the 1800s in the **Lelem' Cafe**.

MARTIN SATYAHADI/SHUTTERSTOCK ©

Grouse Mountain

📷

Photo Opportunity

Wobbling over the Capilano
Suspension Bridge.

Capilano Suspension Bridge (p23)

Be sure to check the fort's website before you arrive: there's a wide array of events that bring the past back to life, including a summertime evening campfire program that will take you right back to the pioneer days of the 1800s.

THE DRIVE
Head south out of the village on Glover Rd, crossing Hwy 1 and then taking a slight left so that you're traveling south on 216th St. The next stop is just past 16th Ave.

05 LANGLEY FARMLAND
The vine-covered grounds of **Chaberton Estate Winery** (chabertonwinery.com) is the setting for the Fraser Valley's oldest winemaking operation, here since 1991. The French-influenced, 22-hectare vineyard specializes in cool-climate whites: its subtle, Riesling-style Bacchus is dangerously easy to drink. There's also a handy bistro here.

Head south and right on 4th St to the charming **Vista D'oro** (vistadoro.com), a working farm and winery where you can load up on fresh pears, plums, apples and stripy heirloom tomatoes. Sample preserves such as piquant mango lime salsa and sweet rhubarb and vanilla jam. Also pick up a bottle of their utterly delicious, port-style walnut wine that's made from nuts grown just outside the shop. It's definitely small batch, so if you see it, buy it.

The Fraser Valley is home to countless farms, producing everything from tulips to cheese. Many accept visitors, give tours and sell their wares in farm shops. If you're keen to visit some more, go to circlefarmtour.com for details.

THE DRIVE
Return north up 216th St and turn right on North Bluff Rd. Continue east for four blocks and turn left onto 248th St, which takes you to the Fraser Hwy. Head east toward Abbotsford, and then north on the Abbotsford Mission Hwy over the Fraser River to Hwy 7. Turn right and follow the road along the river. Approximately 1½ hours.

06 KILBY HISTORIC SITE
To get to **Kilby Historic Site** (kilby.ca), turn right onto School Rd and then right again onto Kilby Rd. The clocks turn back to the 1920s when you enter this site, all that remains of the once-thriving Harrison Mills community. Join a tour led by costumed interpreters as you explore the general store, hotel, post office and working farm, complete with friendly farm animals.

THE DRIVE
Return to Hwy 7 and carry on east, passing through farmland and hazelnut orchards. Turn left on Hwy 9, which takes you to Harrison Hot Springs, for a total drive of 21km.

07 HARRISON HOT SPRINGS
Set on the edge of Harrison Lake and with views to forest-carpeted mountains, **Harrison Hot Springs** (tourismharrison.com) is a resort town that draws both locals and visitors to its sandy beach, warm lagoon and lakeside promenade. While the lake itself is glacier-fed, two hot springs bubble at the southern end of

the lake and the warm water can be enjoyed year-round at the town's upscale resort and the indoor public pool. You should time your Harrison visit with the area's cultural festival. July's multiday **Harrison Festival of the Arts** (harrisonfestival.com) has been running for more than 40 years, bringing live music, gallery shows, workshops and more to the area's beachfront streets.

DETOUR
Start: 07 Harrison Hot Springs

Hope's nickname is the 'Chainsaw Capital' and this rather unusual moniker certainly draws attention. The name was earned by the wooden sculptures peppered throughout the town. **Hope** is a small community at the eastern edge of the Fraser Valley, set beneath the shadow of the Cascade Mountains. The 70-plus chainsaw sculptures are the products of both local and visiting artists. Most depict wildlife, including the Sasquatch who is believed to live in the nearby woods.

02

Sea to Sky Highway

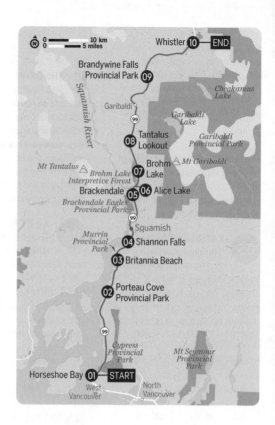

DURATION	DISTANCE	GREAT FOR
1–2 days	132km/82 miles	Culture, Families, Nature

BEST TIME TO GO	November to March has the best snow; June to September offers sunny hiking, plus driving without chains.

Drive out of North Vancouver and straight onto the wild west coast. This short excursion reveals the essence of British Columbia's shoreline with majestic sea and mountain vistas, outdoor activity opportunities, wildlife-watching possibilities and a peek into the regional First Nations culture and pioneer history that's woven into the route. There's even freshly roasted, organic coffee along the way. How much more 'BC' can you get?

Link Your Trip

01 Vancouver & the Fraser Valley

Hwy 99 begins in North Vancouver where you can divert onto this multifarious exploration of Vancouver and its fertile hinterland.

03 A Strait Hop

Strait Hop goes through Horseshoe Bay, also the first stop on this shore-tracking tour of Vancouver Island and the Sunshine Coast.

01 HORSESHOE BAY

As clouds and mist drift in across the snow-capped mountains of Howe Sound, standing at the foot of Horseshoe Bay may well make you feel like you've stepped into middle-earth. Green-forested hills tumble down around the village, which has a small-town vibe that doesn't attest to its proximity to Vancouver. Grab a coffee and some fish and chips from one of the many waterfront cafes and watch the bobbing boats from the seaside park. This first stop is all about slowing down and taking it all in.

BEST FOR

Ski Olympic-style down Whistler Mountain.

NATALIA BRATSLAVSKY/SHUTTERSTOCK ©

Horseshoe Bay

Have a wander through the **Spirit Gallery** (spirit-gallery.com), which is filled with classic and contemporary First Nations art and design from the region. You'll find everything from eye glasses to animal hand-puppets, prints, pewter and carvings.

 THE DRIVE
Head north for 25km on Hwy 99, which curves around the coast and follows Howe Sound. You'll be traveling between steep mountainsides, down which waterfalls plummet, and the often misty ocean where islands are perched like sleeping giants. Watch out for Tunnel Point Lookout on the western side of the highway for a vantage point across the sound.

02 PORTEAU COVE PROVINCIAL PARK
Once popular with regional First Nations communities for sturgeon fishing, Porteau Cove is one of the oldest archaeological sites on the northwest coast. These days it's a haven for divers, with a sunken ship and reefs supporting countless species of marine life, such as octopus and wolf eels. The rocky beach is good for exploring, with plenty of logs to clamber on, and in summer the water is just about warm enough to take a quick dip.

 THE DRIVE
From here, the sound narrows and as you continue 8km north on Hwy 99, the mountains from the opposite shore begin to loom over you.

03 BRITANNIA BEACH
Don a hard hat and hop on a bone-shaking train that trundles you through a floodlit mine tunnel. With hands-on exhibits, gold panning, an engaging film and entry into the dizzying 20-story mill, the **Britannia Mine Museum** (britanniaminemuseum.ca) has plenty to keep you (and any kids in tow) busy. Factor in a couple of hours here.

THE DRIVE
Continue 7km north on Hwy 99, through the lush green Murrin Provincial Park.

04 SHANNON FALLS

Torpedoing 335m over the mountaintop, **Shannon Falls** (bcparks.ca) is the third- largest flume in the province. Historically, the medicine people of the Squamish First Nation trained alongside these falls. A short, picturesque walk through the woods leads to a viewing platform.

You can also hike from here to the peak of the **Stawamus Chief** (two to three hours round-trip) or hop back in your car and continue another minute or two along Hwy 99 to the **Sea to Sky Gondola** (seatoskygondola.com), where a cable car zips you up to a summit lodge at 885m. From here you can walk across a shaky suspension bridge to access a network of above-the-treeline trails.

🚘 THE DRIVE

Continue north on Hwy 99, past the Stawamus Chief and through Squamish, where you can stop for gas or sample from a raft of craft breweries and distilleries. Carry on along the highway, taking a left on Depot Rd and then another left onto Government Rd. The next stop is a few minutes up the road on your right.

05 BRACKENDALE

Brackendale is home to one of the largest populations of wintering bald eagles in North America. Visit between November and February to see an almost overwhelming number of these massive, magnificent birds feasting on salmon in the Squamish River. A path running alongside the riverbank offers a short walk and plenty of easy eagle-spotting opportunities. Across the river are the tall trees of **Brackendale Eagles Provincial Park**, where the beady-eyed birds perch in the night.

⛽ Gas Station

There is nowhere to fill your tank between North Vancouver and Squamish, a distance of around 50km. This is mountain driving so make sure you've got at least half a tank when you set out.

Also in this neighborhood is the historic **West Coast Railway Heritage Park** (wcra.org). This large, mostly outdoor museum is the final resting place of British Columbia's legendary *Royal Hudson* steam engine and has dozens of other historic railcars, including working engines and cabooses, sumptuous sleepers and a cool vintage mail car. Check out the handsome **Roundhouse** building, housing the park's most precious trains and artifacts.

THE DRIVE
Hwy 99 leaves the Squamish River 5km north of Brackendale and heads into the trees. The next stop is on the right.

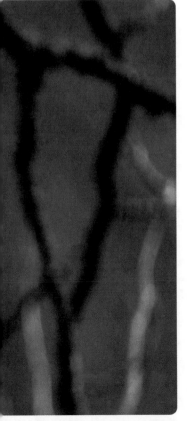

Brackendale Eagles Provincial Park

THE STAWAMUS CHIEF

Towering 700m above the waters of Howe Sound like 'The Wall' in *Game of Thrones*, the Chief is the world's second-largest freestanding granite monolith. The three peaks have long been considered a sacred place to the Squamish people; they once came here seeking spiritual renewal. It's also the nesting grounds of peregrine falcons, who are increasingly returning to the area.

The views from the top are unbelievable. The sheer face of the monolith has become a magnet for rock climbers, while hikers can take a steep trail starting from the base station of the Sea to Sky Gondola to one or all of the three summits.

06 ALICE LAKE
Delve into an old-growth hemlock forest for hiking and biking trails as well as lakeside picnic opportunities. Surrounded by a ring of towering mountains and offering two sandy beaches fringed by relatively warm water in summer, **Alice Lake Provincial Park** (discovercamping.ca) is a popular spot for a dip, a walk and an alfresco lunch.

Next stretch your legs on the 6km **Four Lakes Trail**, an easy hike that does a loop around all four lakes in the park, passing through stands of Douglas fir and western red cedar. Keep your eyes (and your ears) peeled for warblers, Steller's jays and chickadees as well as for the box turtles that sometimes sun themselves on the logs at Stump Lake.

 THE DRIVE
Continue north along Hwy 99 for around 6km to Brohm Lake.

07 BROHM LAKE
Less developed than Alice Lake Provincial Park, **Brohm Lake Interpretive Forest** has 10km of walking trails, many of them easy and flat. The lake is warm enough for summer swimming as the sun filters down onto the tree-studded shoreline.

Archaeological digs from this area have unearthed arrowheads and tools from early First Nations communities that date back 10,000 years. The area was later the scene of a logging mill and today is home to **Tenderfoot Fish Hatchery**, a facility aimed at replenishing depleted chum and chinook salmon stocks, which fell from around 25,000 in the 1960s to around 1500 in the early 1980s. You can visit the hatchery and take a self-guided tour by following a 3km trail from Brohm Lake.

 THE DRIVE
Continue up Hwy 99 just over 3km to the next stop.

08 TANTALUS LOOKOUT
This viewpoint looks out across the **Tantalus Mountain Range**. Tantalus was a character in Greek mythology who gave us the word 'tantalize'; apparently the mountains were named by an explorer who was tempted

to climb the range's snowy peaks, but was stuck on the other side of the turbulent Squamish River. In addition to Mt Tantalus, the Greek hero's entire family is here – his wife Mt Dione, his daughter Mt Niobe, his son Mt Pelops and his grandson Mt Thyestes.

The Squamish people once used this area to train in hunting, and believe that long ago hunters and their dogs were immortalized here, becoming the soaring mountain range. Those stone hunters must be rather tantalized themselves; the forested slopes of the mountains are home to grizzly bears, elk, wolves and cougars.

THE DRIVE
Follow Hwy 99 22km north through the woods, skirting the edge of Daisy Lake before reaching the next stop on your right.

09 BRANDYWINE FALLS PROVINCIAL PARK
Surging powerfully over the edge of a volcanic escarpment, **Brandywine Falls** (bcparks.ca/brandywine-falls-park/) plunge a dramatic 70m – a straight shot into the pool below. Follow the easy 10-minute trail through the woods and step out onto the viewing platform, directly over the falls.

From here you can also see **Mt Garibaldi**, the most easily recognizable mountain in the Coast

Photo Opportunity
Get the ultimate snowy-peak picture from Tantalus Lookout.

Range. Its distinctive jagged top and color has earned it the name Black Tusk. This mountain is of particular significance to local First Nations groups, who believe the great Thunderbird landed here. With its supernatural ways, it shot bolts of lightning from its eyes, creating the color and shape of the mountaintop.

A 7km looped trail leads further through the park's dense forest and ancient lava beds to **Cal-Cheak Suspension Bridge**.

THE DRIVE
Continue north for 17km along Hwy 99, passing Creekside Village and carrying on to the main Whistler village entrance (it's well signposted and obvious once you see it).

10 WHISTLER
Nestled in the shade of the formidable Whistler and Blackcomb Mountains, Whistler has long been BC's golden child. Popular in winter for its world-class ski slopes and

in summer for everything from hiking to one of North America's longest zip lines, it draws fans from around the world. It was named for the furry marmots that fill the area with their loud whistle, but there are also plenty of berry-snuffling black bears about.

The site of many of the outdoor events at the 2010 Winter Olympic and Paralympic Games, Whistler village is well worth a stroll and is filled with an eclectic mix of stores, flash hotels and seemingly countless cafes and restaurants.

Crisscrossed with more than 200 runs, the **Whistler-Blackcomb** (whistlerblackcomb.com) sister mountains are linked by a 4.4km gondola that includes the world's longest unsupported span. Ski season runs from late November to April on Whistler and to June on Blackcomb. **Ziptrek Ecotours** (ziptrek.com) offers year-round zip-line courses that will have you screaming with gut-quivering pleasure.

While you're here, be sure to take in the wood-beamed **Squamish Lil'wat Cultural Centre**, built to resemble a traditional longhouse. It's filled with art, images and displays that illuminate the traditional and contemporary cultures of the Squamish and Lil'wat Nations.

A short stroll away, **Audain Art Museum** (audainartmuseum.com) is home to an array of paintings from BC icons, including Emily Carr and EJ Hughes, plus a collection of historic and contemporary First Nations works. Allow at least an hour here.

THE STORY BEGINS
As you enter the **Squamish Lil'wat Cultural Centre** (slcc.ca) in Whistler, take a look at the carved cedar doors you're passing through. According to the center's guide map, the door on the left shows a grizzly bear – protector of the Lil'wat – with a salmon in its mouth, representing sharing. The carving references a mother bear and cub that walked into the center during construction. The door on the right, depicting a human face and hands up, symbolizes the Squamish welcoming all visitors.

Brandywine Falls

03

Dive into some delightful regional flavors in Cowichan Bay.

A Strait Hop

DURATION	DISTANCE	GREAT FOR
2–3 days	351km/219 miles	Nature

BEST TIME TO GO	June to September offers the most sunshine and least rain.

Goldstream Provincial Park

Perhaps it's the way sunlight reflects across the ever-shifting ocean, or the forest walks and beachcombing that seem an essential part of coastal life. Whatever the reason, the towns and villages snuggled next to the Pacific draw artistic folk from around the world to settle here and create strong communities and beautiful art. Take this leisurely tour for a slice of life on both the mainland and Vancouver Island.

Link Your Trip

02 Sea to Sky Highway

Join this trip at Horseshoe Bay, winding your way up Hwy 99 past the climbing hub of Squamish to the peerless ski-town of Whistler.

05 Vancouver Island's Remote North

From Nanaimo explore the more remote flavor of Vancouver Island by pitching north to Qualicum Beach or west to Tofino.

01 VICTORIA

British Columbia's lovely, walkable and increasingly bike-friendly capital is dripping with colonial architecture and has enough museums, attractions, hotels and restaurants to keep many visitors enthralled for an extra night or two.

Must-see attractions include the excellent **Royal BC Museum** (royalbcmuseum.bc.ca). Come eye to beady eye with a woolly mammoth and look out for cougars and grizzlies peeking from behind the trees. Step aboard Captain Vancouver's ship, enter a First Nations cedar longhouse, and explore a re-created early colonial street complete with shops, a movie house and

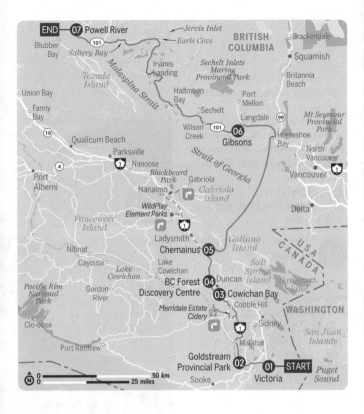

Sunshine Coast Gallery Crawl

Along Hwy 101, near Gibsons (p39), keep your eyes peeled for jaunty purple flags fluttering in the breeze. These indicate that an artist is at work on the adjoining property. If your eyesight isn't up to the task (or you're the designated driver), pick up the handy Sunshine Coast Purple Banner flyer from visitor centers and galleries in the area to find out exactly where these artists are located. Some are open for drop-in visits while others prefer that you call ahead. The region is studded with arts and crafts creators, working with wood, glass, clay and just about everything else. For further information, check coastculture.com.

an evocative replica Chinatown. A few minutes' stroll away, you'll also find the hidden gem **Miniature World** (miniatureworld.com), an immaculate, old-school attraction crammed with 80 diminutive dioramas themed on everything from Arthurian Britain to a futuristic sci-fi realm.

Also worth visiting is the **Art Gallery of Greater Victoria** (aggv.ca), home to one of Canada's best Emily Carr collections. Aside from Carr's swirling nature canvases, you'll find an ever-changing array of temporary exhibitions.

And save time to hop on a not-much-bigger-than-a-bathtub-sized **Victoria Harbour Ferry** (victoriaharbourferry.com). This

colorful armada of tiny tugboats stop at numerous docks along the waterfront, including the Inner Harbour, Songhees Park and Fisherman's Wharf (where alfresco fish and chips is heartily recommended).

THE DRIVE
Follow Hwy 1 (which begins its cross-country journey in Victoria) 19km west onto the sometimes narrow, heavily forested Malahat Dr section, also known as the Malahat Hwy.

02 GOLDSTREAM PROVINCIAL PARK
Alongside the Malahat, the abundantly forested **Goldstream Provincial Park**

(goldstreampark.com) drips with ancient, moss-covered cedar trees and a moist carpet of plant life. The short walk through the woods to the **Freeman King Visitors Centre** is beautiful; once you're there, take in the center's hands-on exhibits about natural history.

The park is known for its chum salmon spawning season (from late October to December), when the water literally bubbles with thousands of struggling fish. Hungry bald eagles also swoop in at this time to feast on the full-grown salmon.

A short 700m trail leads to **Niagara Falls**, which is a lot narrower but only 4m shorter than it's famous Ontario namesake. Hike beyond the falls and you'll reach an impressive railway trestle (which you're not supposed to walk on).

THE DRIVE
From Goldstream, the Malahat climbs north for 8km to its summit with a number of gorgeous viewpoints over Brentwood Bay. Continue on Hwy 1 for another 28km, following signs east off the highway for Cowichan Bay.

DETOUR
Merridale Estate Cidery
Start: 02 Goldstream Provincial Park

After leaving Goldstream, head west off the highway onto Cobble Hill Rd. This weaves through bucolic farmland and wine-growing country. Watch for asparagus farms, beady-eyed llamas, blueberry stalls and verdant vineyards. Stop in at charming **Merridale Estate Cidery** (merridalecider.com), an inviting apple-cider producer offering many varieties, as well as artisan gin and vodka. Cobble Hill Rd crosses over the highway and loops east to Cowichan Bay.

03 COWICHAN BAY
With a colorful string of wooden buildings perched on stilts over a mountain-shadowed ocean inlet, Cowichan Bay – Cow Bay to locals – is well worth a stop. Wander along the pier of the **Maritime Centre** (classicboats.org) to peruse some salty boat-building exhibits and intricate models and get your camera out to shoot the handsome panoramic views of the harbor. Duck into the galleries and studios lining the waterfront or stretch your legs on a five-minute stroll to the **Cowichan Estuary Nature Centre** (cowichanestuary.ca), where area birdlife and marine critters are profiled.

Drop into the **Mud Room** (cowbaymudroom.com) to see potters at work making usable objects like cups and plates. Look for seaside-themed mugs and the popular yellow-glazed dragonfly motif pieces.

The artisans are also at work in Cow Bay's kitchens. This is a great place to gather the makings of a great picnic at **True Grain** (truegrain.ca).

THE DRIVE
Return to Hwy 1 and head north a further 12km.

04 BC FOREST DISCOVERY CENTRE
You won't find Winnie-the-Pooh in this 100-acre wood, but if you want to know more about those giants swaying overhead, stop in at the **BC Forest Discovery Centre** (bcforestdis coverycentre.com). Woodland paths lead you among western yews, Garry oaks and 400-year-old fir trees with nesting bald eagles in their branches. Visit a 1920s sawmill and a 1905 wooden schoolhouse, and climb to the top of a wildfire lookout tower. Hop on a historical train for a ride around the grounds and check out some cool logging trucks from the early 1900s. Visit the indoor exhibits for the lowdown on contemporary forest management.

THE DRIVE
It's a 20km journey to the next stop. Continue north on Hwy 1, turning right onto Henry Rd and then left onto Chemainus Rd.

05 CHEMAINUS
The residents of this tree-ringed settlement – a former resource community that almost became a ghost town – began commissioning **murals**

Cowichan Bay

on its walls in the 1980s, part of a forward-thinking revitalization project. The paintings – there are now almost 50 dotted around the community – soon became visitor attractions, stoking the town's rebirth. Among the best are the 17m-long pioneer-town painting of Chemainus c 1891 on Mill St, the 15m-long depiction of First Nations faces and totems on Chemainus Rd, and the evocative Maple St mural showing the waterfront community as it was in 1948.

Pick up a walking tour map of the murals from the **visitor center** next to Waterwheel Park (where there's also a parking lot). In the same building, the town's small **museum** is well stocked with yesteryear reminders of the old town. Be sure to chat with the

Photo Opportunity

Clouds draped across mountaintops from the deck of a Horseshoe Bay ferry.

friendly volunteers; they'll regale you with real-life stories of the area's colorful past.

The lower part of the town is rather quiet but the southern end of Willow St has many cafes, restaurants and boutique galleries to keep you and your wallet occupied.

The impressive **Chemainus Theatre Festival** (chemainustheatrefestival.ca) is also popular, staging shows for much of the year.

THE DRIVE
Head north on Hwy 1 toward Nanaimo. Follow the signs to Departure Bay and catch a BC Ferries vessel to mainland Horseshoe Bay. From there, hop on a second 40-minute ferry ride to Langdale on the Sunshine Coast (there are many restaurants in Horseshoe Bay if you're waiting between ferries). From Langdale, it's a short drive along Hwy 101 to Gibsons.

DETOUR
WildPlay Element Parks
Start: **05** Chemainus

Fancy zipping, swinging or jumping from a giant tree? It's an easy 21km drive north on Hwy 1 from Chemainus to **WildPlay Element Parks** (wildplay.com) for some woodland thrills involving canopy obstacle courses and a daredevil bungee-jump zone.

MITCH DIAMOND/GETTY IMAGES ©

Willow St, Chemainus

DETOUR

Gabriola Island

Start: **05** Chemainus

If you're tempted by those mysterious little islands peeking at you off the coast of Vancouver Island, take the 20-minute **BC Ferries** (bcferries.com) service from Nanaimo's Inner Harbour to **Gabriola Island** (gabriolaisland.org). Home to dozens of artists plus a healthy smattering of old hippies, there's a tangible air of quietude to this rustic realm. Pack a picnic and spend the afternoon communing with the natural world.

GIBSONS

06 Gibsons *feels* cozy. If you didn't know better, you'd think you were on an island – such is the strong community and almost isolated feel this town exudes. Head straight for the waterfront area – known as **Gibsons Landing** – where you can take in the many brightly painted clapboard buildings that back onto the water's edge, as well as intriguing artisan stores.

A walk along the town's main wooden jetty leads you past a colorful array of houseboats and floating garden plots. You'll also come to the sun-dappled gallery of **Sa Boothroyd** (saboothroyd. com). The artist is typically on hand to illuminate her browse-worthy and often humorous works. Although her bigger canvases are pricey, there are lots of tempting original trivets, coasters and tea cozies.

Need more culture? Head to the charming **Gibsons Public Art Gallery** (gpag.ca), which showcases the work of locals artists and changes its displays every month. Check the website for show openings, always a good time to meet the arty locals.

RULE OF THE ROAD

Bone-shaking automobiles began popping up on the roads of British Columbia in the early years of the 20th century, often the toys of rich playboys with too much time on their hands. But for many years BC had few regulations governing the trundling procession of cars around the region: vehicles could drive on either side of the road in some communities, although the left-hand side (echoing the country's British colonial overlords) gradually became the accepted practice.

Aiming to match driving rules in the US (and in much of the rest of the world) – yet managing to confuse the local issue still further – BC began legislating drivers over to the right-hand side of the road in the early 1920s. One of the last areas to make the switch official was Vancouver Island. During the transition period, some minor accidents were reported around the region as drivers tootled toward each other before veering across at the last minute.

 THE DRIVE

Continue along tree-lined Hwy 101; expect glimpses of sandy coves in the forests on your left. The highway leads through Sechelt (handy for supplies) then on to Earls Cove. Hop on a BC Ferries service across Jervis Inlet to Saltery Bay. This achingly beautiful 50-minute trip threads past islands and forested coastlines. From Saltery Bay, take Hwy 101 to Powell River.

POWELL RIVER

07 Powell River is one of the Sunshine Coast's most vibrant communities. It was founded in the early 1900s when three Minnesota businessmen dammed the river to create a massive hydroelectric power plant. Not long after, a pulp mill was built to take advantage of the surrounding forests and handy deepwater harbor, with the first sheets of paper trundling off its steamy production line in 1912. Within a few years, the mill had become the world's largest producer of newsprint, churning out 275 tonnes daily.

Today there's an active and arty vibe to this waterfront town, including its historic **Townsite** (powellrivertownsite.com) area, which is great for on-foot wandering. Many of Powell River's oldest streets are named after trees and some are still lined with the original mill workers' cottages that kick-started the settlement. The steam-plumed mill is still here, too – although it's shrinking every year and its former grounds are being transformed into parkland. Dip into this history at **Powell River Museum** (powellrivermuseum. ca), which covers the area's First Nations heritage and its tough pioneer days.

If you spend the night in town, catch a film at the quaint **Patricia Theatre** (patriciatheatre. com), Canada's oldest continually operating cinema.

04

Southern Vancouver Island Tour

BEST FOR

Salt Spring Island for cycling and hiking, and kayaking in sun-dappled lakes.

DURATION	DISTANCE	GREAT FOR
4–5 days	290km/182 miles	Wine, Nature

BEST TIME TO GO	June to September for frequent ferries, warm weather and possible whale sightings.

Sidney

Whether you're standing on the deck of a Gulf Islands ferry or on the sandy expanse of China Beach, the untamed ocean is an essential part of life in this part of the world. It seems to foster pods of creativity – small islands where artisans practice crafts from pottery to cheese-making – and it salt-licks the dramatic coastline into shape, with sandy coves fringed by dense, wind-bent woodlands.

Link Your Trip

01 Vancouver & the Fraser Valley

From the Gulf Islands, catch a ferry to Tsawwassen to get a closer look at Vancouver and the farm-dotted Fraser River Valley.

05 Vancouver Island's Remote North

When you reach Hwy 1 after leaving Salt Spring Island, you can carry on north for a taste of off-the-beaten-track Vancouver Island.

01 SIDNEY

A short trip north of Victoria, the sunny seaside town of Sidney is ideal for wandering. Along the main street, an almost unseemly number of bookstores jostle for space with boutique shops and cafes. The best for serious bibliophiles is vaguely Dickensian **Haunted Books**. When you reach the water, you'll find the **Seaside Sculpture Walk** – showcasing a dozen or so locally created artworks – plus a picturesque pier with twinkling island vistas.

While you're at the waterfront, visit the compact but brilliant **Shaw Centre for the Salish Sea** (salishseacentre.org). It opens your eyes to the color

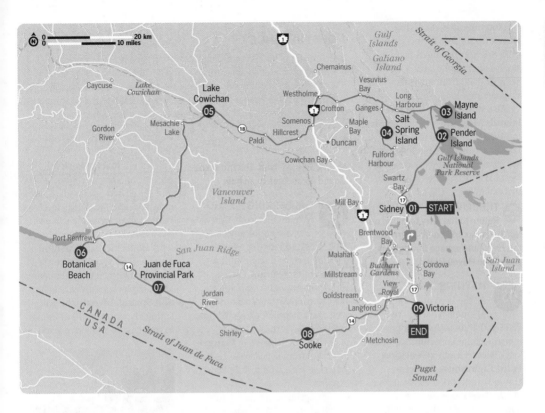

and diversity in the neighboring Salish Sea with aquariums, touch tanks and plenty of hands-on exhibits. The staff are well-versed and the gift shop is a treasure trove.

THE DRIVE
Follow Hwy 17 (Patricia Bay Hwy) north for 6km to its end at the BC Ferries terminal. Board a boat for a beautiful 40-minute crossing to Pender Island.

DETOUR
Butchart Gardens
Start: **01** Sidney

A 16km drive south of Sidney on Hwy 17, turning west on Keating Cross Rd, brings you to Benvenuto Ave and British Columbia's most famous botanical attraction. The century-old **Butchart**

Gardens (butchartgardens.com), which originated from an attempt to beautify an old cement factory site, has been cleverly planned to ensure there's always something in bloom, no matter what the season. In summer, there are Saturday night fireworks displays and in winter the twinkling seasonal lights are magical. Whatever time of year you arrive, give yourself at least a couple of hours to enjoy the spectacle.

02 PENDER ISLAND
Arriving on this small island, you are quickly enveloped in a sense of tangible quietude. Narrow roads wind within deep forests where you'll see countless walking trails, quail crossings and confident deer.

Pender is actually two islands – North and South, joined by a small bridge. **Gowland** and **Tilly Point** on South Pender have beach access; head to Tilly Point for tidal pools and Mt Baker views. Sheltered, sandy **Medicine Beach** on the North Island has lots of clamber-worthy logs. While on the beaches, look out for bald eagles, seals and otters.

Pender is also home to many artists. Pick up a copy of the *Pender Island Artists Guide* on the ferry. A great place to start is **Talisman Books & Gallery** (talismanbooks.ca) in the central Driftwood Centre, where you'll also find great cakes and coffee.

For locally produced wine, head to **Sea Star Vineyards**

(seastarvineyards.ca). Using grapes from its own vine-striped hills, Sea Star produces tasty small-batch tipples plus a wide array of fruit, from kiwis to raspberries.

Also worth a look is **Pender Islands Museum** (penderislands museum.ca), housed in a 1908 farmhouse. Explore the history of the island through its re-created rooms, vintage photos and evocative exhibits.

 THE DRIVE
Return to the ferry terminal on North Pender and board a ferry for the 25-minute voyage through the channel to Mayne Island.

03 MAYNE ISLAND
As the boat pulls into Mayne Island, you're greeted with colorful wooden houses, quaint communities and lots of deer. Head to **Georgina Point Lighthouse** for ocean and mountain-filled views across Active Pass. The water literally bubbles here with the strength of the current. This is a popular spot for eagles to fish and you're also likely to see (and hear) sea lions resting on nearby rocks.

For a quiet retreat, visit the **Japanese Garden**, dedicated to the many Japanese families who settled on the island from 1900 onward. Once constituting a third of the population, they contributed more than half of the island's farming, milling and fish-preservation work. During WWII the government saw them as a national threat and forced their removal. The garden contains traditional Japanese elements within a forest, including shrines and a peace bell.

THE DRIVE
Return to the ferry terminal and board a ferry to Long Harbour

OFF THE FENCE

Going strong for nearly 25 years, Art Off the Fence started as just that – an artist exhibiting her work all over her fence. Each year in mid-July, a dozen or so additional artists hang their work on the fence and in the orchard of a Pender property, creating a weekend-long grassroots outdoor gallery. Look, shop, enjoy the live music and meet the island locals.

on Salt Spring Island. The trip takes around 45 minutes to an hour.

04 SALT SPRING ISLAND
When folks from Vancouver talk about quitting their jobs and making jam for a living, they're likely mulling a move to Salt Spring. Once a hippie haven and later a yuppie retreat, it's now home to anyone who craves a quieter life without sacrificing everyday conveniences. The main town of **Ganges** has it all, from grocery stores to galleries. It's a wonderful place to explore.

Salt Spring is also home to many an artisan, from bakers to carvers and winemakers. Stop in at **Waterfront Gallery** (water frontgallery.ca), which carries the work of many local artists with pottery, glassware, knitwear, candles and even birdhouses prominent. Also stop in at **Salt Spring Mercantile** (saltspring mercantile.com), which sells lots of local products, including Salish Sea Chocolates, jars of fresh chutney and flower-petal-packed soaps.

Save time for **Salt Spring Island Cheese** (saltspringcheese. com) on Weston Creek Farm. Meet the goats and sheep that produce milk for the cheese, see it being made, and be awed by the beautiful finale – taste cheeses adorned with lemon slices, flowers and chilies.

Head to **Ruckle Park** for ragged shorelines, arbutus forests and sun-kissed farmlands. There are trails here for all skill levels as well as ocean views for a picnic. **Mt Maxwell** offers a steep but worthwhile hike and **Cushion Lake** and **St Mary's Lake** are summertime swimming haunts. Fancy exploring sans car? Visit **Salt Spring Adventures** (salt springadventures.com) in Ganges to rent kayaks and join excursions.

LINDA C MACLEAN/SHUTTERSTOCK ©

Lake Cowichan

THE DRIVE

Head 7km north of Ganges to Vesuvius Bay and take a 25-minute ferry ride to Crofton on Vancouver Island. From the east coast, curve inland for 38km along Hwy 18 and the glassy-calm waters of Lake Cowichan.

05 LAKE COWICHAN

Hop out of the car at Lake Cowichan for some deep breaths at the ultra-clear, tree-fringed lakefront. This is a perfect spot for swimming or setting out for a hike along the lakeside trails.

THE DRIVE

From Lake Cowichan, follow South Shore Rd and then Pacific Marine Rd to Port Renfrew and on to Botanical Beach, 66km from Lake Cowichan.

Photo Opportunity

Botanical Beach's crashing waves.

06 BOTANICAL BEACH

Feeling like the edge of the earth, it's worth the effort to get to Botanical Beach. Follow the winding road from Port Renfrew and then the sometimes steep pathway down to the beach. The tidal pools here are rich in colorful marine life, including chitons, anemones, gooseneck barnacles, sea palms and purple sea urchins. Surrounded by windblown coastline

and crashing waves, this is also a favorite springtime haunt of orcas and gray whales, plus a feeding ground for harbor seals.

The rocks here can be slippery and the waves huge; take care and watch the tide.

THE DRIVE

Head southeast on Hwy 14 for around 40km to nearby Juan de Fuca Provincial Park.

07 JUAN DE FUCA PROVINCIAL PARK

Welcome to the dramatic coastal wilderness of **Juan de Fuca Provincial Park** (bcparks. ca/juan-de-fuca-park/). There are good stop-off points along this rugged stretch, providing memorable views of the rocky, ocean-carved seafront where trees cling for dear life and whales slide past

Market Day

If you arrive on Salt Spring Island on a summer weekend, the best way to dive into the community is at the legendary **Saturday Market** (saltspring market.com) where you can tuck into luscious island-grown fruit and piquant cheeses while perusing locally produced arts and crafts.

Saturday Market, Salt Spring Island

just off the coast. Our favorite is **China Beach**, reached along a fairly gentle, well-maintained trail through dense forest. The prize is a long stretch of windswept sand. **French Beach** is also popular with day-trippers and requires less of a leg-stretch.

🚗 THE DRIVE
Continue southeast along Hwy 14, skirting the coastline to Sooke, 74km away.

08 SOOKE
Once considered the middle of nowhere, seaside Sooke is gaining popularity thanks in part to the thriving 55km Galloping Goose trail, a cycling and hiking path linking it with Victoria. For an introduction to the area, stop at **Sooke Region Museum** (sookeregion museum.com), which has intriguing exhibits on the district's pioneer past, including the tiny **Moss Cottage**, one of the island's oldest pioneer homes.

🚗 THE DRIVE
From Sooke, follow Hwy 14 (Sooke Rd) east, all the way to Hwy 1. Join the eastbound traffic, which will lead you to nearby Victoria, 40km from Sooke.

09 VICTORIA
The provincial capital is vibrant, charming and highly walkable. The boat-filled Inner Harbour, magnetic boutique shopping and belly-thrilling cuisine make it understandably popular. Add an outgoing university crowd plus a strong arts community and you get an interesting, diverse population.

05

Watch massive, frothy waves crashing onto Long Beach, especially in winter.

Douglas fir, Cathedral Grove

Vancouver Island's Remote North

DURATION	DISTANCE	GREAT FOR
2–3 days	537km/336 miles	Culture, Families

BEST TIME TO GO	May to September for the most sunshine and the least chance of relentless rain.

Following this trip is like following Alice down the rabbit hole – you'll feel you've entered an enchanted land that's beyond the reach of day-to-day life. Ancient, moss-covered trees will leave you feeling tiny, as bald eagles swoop above and around you like pigeons. You'll see bears munching dandelions and watching you inscrutably. And totem poles, standing like forests, will seem to whisper secrets of the past. Go on. Jump in.

Link Your Trip

03 A Strait Hop

From Qualicum Beach, travel south on Hwy 19 to Nanaimo, where you can hook up with this water-hugging circuit of the Georgia Strait.

04 Southern Vancouver Island Tour

Drive east from Coombs on Hwy 4A, then south on Hwy 1 for a vision of the Island's more cultivated side.

01 **TOFINO**
Packed with activities and blessed with stunning beaches, former fishing town Tofino sits on Clayoquot (clay-kwot) Sound, where forests rise from roiling waves that continually batter the coastline. Visitors come to surf, whale-watch, kayak, hike and hug trees. For the scoop on what to do, hit the **visitor center** (tourismtofino.com).

The area's biggest draw is **Long Beach**, part of Pacific Rim National Park. Accessible by car along the Pacific Rim Hwy, this wide sandy swath has untamed surf, beachcombing nooks and a living museum

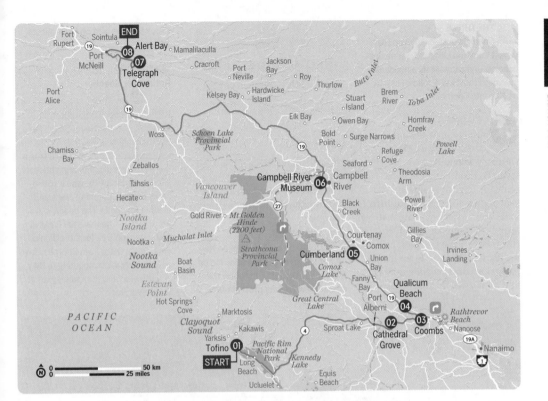

of old-growth trees. There are plenty of walking trails; look for swooping eagles and huge banana slugs. Tread carefully over slippery surfaces and never turn your back on the mischievous surf.

Kwisitis Visitor Centre houses exhibits on the region, including a First Nations canoe and a look at what's in the watery depths.

While you're in Tofino, don't miss **Roy Henry Vickers Gallery** (royhenryvickers.com), housed in an atmospheric traditional longhouse. Vickers is one of Canada's most successful and prolific Indigenous artists.

If you're freshly arrived in Tofino and want to know what makes this place so special, head down First St and join the undulating gravel trail to **Tonquin Beach** (1.2km one-way), where a magical parting of the trees reveals a rock-punctuated swath of sand well-known for its life-affirming sunsets.

🚗 THE DRIVE

Follow Pacific Rim Hwy 4 southeast, and then north as it turns into the Mackenzie Range. Mountains rise up on the right as you weave past the unfathomably deep Kennedy Lake. The road carries on along the racing Kennedy River. Continue to the next stop, just past Port Alberni. This longish 140km leg should take a little over two hours.

02 CATHEDRAL GROVE

To the east of Port Alberni, **Cathedral Grove** (bcparks.ca) is the spiritual home of tree huggers and the mystical highlight of MacMillan Provincial Park. Look up – way, waaaaay up – and the vertigo-inducing views of the swaying treetops will leave you swooning. Extremely popular in summer, its accessible forest trails wind through dense woodland, offering glimpses of some of British Columbia's oldest trees, including centuries-old Douglas firs more than 3m in diameter. Try hugging that.

THE DRIVE
Continue east for 17km on Hwy 4, past Cameron Lake, with swimming beaches and supposedly a resident monster. From Hwy 4, follow Hwy 4A for 2km into Coombs.

03 COOMBS
The mother of all pit stops, Coombs' **Old Country Market** (oldcountrymarket.com) attracts huge numbers of visitors almost year-round. You'll get inquisitive looks from a herd of goats that spends the summer season on the grassy roof, a tradition here for decades. Nip inside for giant ice-cream cones, heaping pizzas and all the deli makings of a

Photo Opportunity

The forest of totem poles watching over the sea at Alert Bay.

great picnic, then spend an hour or two wandering around the attendant stores, which are filled with unique crafts, clothes and antiques.

THE DRIVE
Continue east for 9km on Hwy 4A, crossing Hwy 19 to Parksville on the coast. Turn left and follow the coastline west past pretty French

Creek for 11km and on to Qualicum Beach.

DETOUR
Rathtrevor Beach
Start: **03** Coombs

It's only around 20 minutes from Coombs, but Rathtrevor Beach feels like it's a million miles away. Visit when the tide is out and you'll face a huge expanse of sand. Bring buckets, shovels and the kids, who'll spend hours digging, catching crabs and hunting for shells. The beach is in a provincial park just east of Parksville, and is backed by a forested picnic area. To get there from Coombs, drive east on Hwy 4A, connecting to Hwy 19 northwest and then turning off at Rathtrevor Rd.

ROXANA GONZALEZ/SHUTTERSTOCK ©

Sand dollar, Qualicum Beach

04 QUALICUM BEACH

A small community of classic seafront motels and a giant beachcomber-friendly bay, Qualicum Beach is a favorite family destination. This coastline is thick with shellfish; many of the scallops, oysters and mussels that restaurants serve up come from here. Wander the beach for shells, and look for sand dollars – they're readily found here.

Hungry? Any local will tell you to head straight to **Bistro 694**, where you'll find an intimate, candlelit dining room little bigger than a train carriage and a big-city menu fusing top-notch regional ingredients with knowing international nods. It's worth taking the seafood route, especially if the Balinese prawn curry or highly addictive seafood crepes are available.

🚗 THE DRIVE
While it's slower than Hwy 19, Hwy 19A is a scenic drive, following the coast north past the Fanny Bay Oyster Farm and Denman Island. After 55km turn left just north of Union Bay to connect with Hwy 19. Turn right, continue north for 5km and take the exit for Cumberland.

05 CUMBERLAND

Founded as a coal-mining town in 1888, Cumberland was one of BC's original pioneer settlements, home to workers from Japan, China and the American South. These days, it's officially a 'village' with a main street that's still lined with early-20th-century wood-built stores. But Cumberland has also moved with the times. Instead of blacksmiths and dry-goods shops, you'll find cool boutiques, espresso bars and a local community that's pioneered one of the finest mountain-biking networks in BC in an adjacent forest. You can get kitted out for two-wheeled action at **Dodge City Cycles** (dodgecitycycles.com). If you prefer something more sedentary, take time to peruse the very impressive **Cumberland Museum** (cumberlandmuseum.ca), which explores the area's coal-mining past.

A microbrewery that's mastered the neighborhood-pub vibe, **Cumberland Brewing** (cumberlandbrewing.com) combines a woodsy little tasting room with a larger outdoor seating area striped with communal tables. Dive into a tasting flight of four beers; make sure it includes the Red Tape Pale Ale.

🚗 THE DRIVE
Carry on north on Hwy 19, with mountain and island views. Turn right onto Hamm Rd, heading east across farmland and passing a bison farm. Turn left onto Hwy 19A, which skirts Oyster Bay. The next stop is on your left, on the outskirts of Campbell River. Total distance: 55km.

06 CAMPBELL RIVER MUSEUM

Stretch your legs and your curiosity with a wander through the **Museum at Campbell River** (crmuseum.ca). Hop behind the wheel of an early logging truck, explore a settler's cabin, see First Nations masks and watch footage of the removal of the legendary, ship-destroying Ripple Rock, which was blasted with the largest non-nuclear explosion in history.

TOP TIP:

Vancouver Island North Online

For maps, activities, tide charts and photos to inspire you, visit vancouverislandnorth.ca.

🚗 THE DRIVE
From Campbell River, head northwest on Hwy 19. As you inch into Vancouver Island's north, follow the signs and an increasingly narrow road for 16km to Telegraph Cove. En route, you'll pass Beaver Cove with its flotilla of logs waiting to be hauled away for milling. It's a beautiful drive, but isolated. Fuel up before you head out.

🧭 DETOUR
Strathcona Provincial Park
Start: 06 Campbell River Museum

BC's oldest protected area and also Vancouver Island's largest park, **Strathcona** (bcparks.ca/strathcona-park/) is a 40km drive west on Hwy 28 from Campbell River. Centered on Mt Golden Hinde, the island's highest point (2200m), it's a pristine wilderness crisscrossed with trail systems that deliver you to waterfalls, alpine meadows, glacial lakes and looming crags. On arrival at the main entrance, get your bearings at **Strathcona Park Lodge & Outdoor Education Centre**. It's a one-stop shop for park activities, including kayaking, guided treks and rock climbing for all ages.

BRITISH COLUMBIA 05 VANCOUVER ISLAND'S REMOTE NORTH

TOP TIP:

Pacific Rim Park Pass

First-timers should drop by the **Pacific Rim Visitors Centre** (pacificrimvisitor.ca) for maps and advice on exploring this spectacular region. If you're stopping in the park, you'll need to pay and display a pass, available here.

07 TELEGRAPH COVE

Built on stilts over the water in 1912, Telegraph Cove was originally a station for the northern terminus of the island's telegraph. A salmon saltery and sawmill were later added. Extremely popular with summer day-trippers, the boardwalk and its many houses have been charmingly restored, with plaques illuminating their original residents. During the season, the waters off the cove are also home to orcas. See (and hear) them on a trip with **Prince of Whales** (princeofwhales.com). You might also encounter minke and humpback whales as well as dolphins and porpoises.

THE DRIVE

Return to Hwy 19 and carry on for 26km to Port McNeill, from where you can catch a BC Ferries vessel for the 45-minute journey to Alert Bay on Cormorant Island.

08 ALERT BAY

This spread-out island village has an ancient and mythical appeal underpinned by its strong First Nations culture and community. In some respects, it feels like an open-air museum. On the southern side is an old pioneer fishing settlement and the traditional **Namgis Burial Grounds**, where dozens of gracefully weathering totem poles stand like a forest of ageless art.

Next to the site of the now-demolished St Michael's Residential School is a much more enduring symbol of First Nations community. The must-see **U'mista Cultural Centre** (umista.ca) houses ceremonial masks and other items confiscated by the Canadian government in the 1920s and now repatriated from museums around the world.

Continue over the hill to the Big House, where **traditional dance performances** are held for visitors. One of the world's tallest totem poles is also here. Alert Bay is home to many professional carvers and you'll see their work in galleries around the village.

Head to the **visitor center** (alertbay.ca) for more information.

Totem poles, Namgis Burial Grounds

06

Okanagan Valley Wine Tour

DURATION	DISTANCE	GREAT FOR
2 days	35km/22 miles	Wine

BEST TIME TO GO	July and September bring hot sunny days – perfect for a slow-paced meander.

Quails' Gate Winery

Filling up on sun-ripened fruit at roadside stalls has long been a highlight of traveling through the Okanagan on a hot summer day. Since the 1980s, the region has widened its embrace of the culinary world by striping its hillsides with grapes. More than 180 vineyards take advantage of the Okanagan's cool winters and long summers. Ice wine, made from grapes frozen on the vine, is a unique take-home tipple. And when you're done soaking up the wine, you can soak up the scenery at the countless beaches along the way.

Link Your Trip

01 Vancouver & the Fraser Valley

Follow Hwys 3A and 3 from the southern end of Okanagan Lake to Hope and the pastoral Fraser Valley.

02 Sea to Sky Highway

Head northwest from Okanagan Lake on Hwy 97 through Kamloops to Hwy 99 for this spectacular melding of mountains and sea.

01 MISSION HILL FAMILY ESTATE

Begin your leisurely taste-tripping trawl on the western shore of the 100km-long Okanagan Lake, the region's centerpiece. Following Boucherie Rd north, between the lake and Hwy 97, will bring you to Westbank's **Mission Hill Family Estate** (missionhillwinery.com). The estate is a modernist reinterpretation of mission buildings, reached through imposing gates and dominated by a 26m-high bell tower. Several tours and tastings are available, including some that include lunch. Aside from checking out vineyards and barrel cellars,

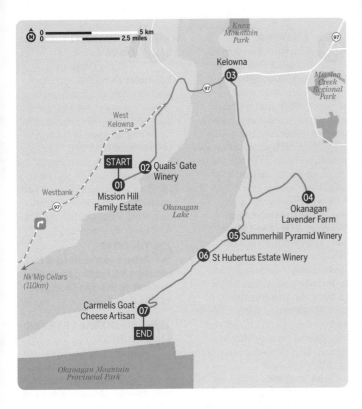

The Ogopogo

For centuries, traditional First Nations legends have told of a 15m-long sea serpent living in Okanagan Lake. Called the N'ha-a-itk, or Lake Demon, it was believed to live in a cave near Rattlesnake Island, just offshore from Peachland. People would only enter the waters around the island with an offering, otherwise they believed the monster would raise a storm and claim lives. Beginning in the mid-1800s, Europeans also began reporting sightings of a creature with a horse-shaped head and serpent-like body. Nicknamed Ogopogo, the serpent has been seen along the length of the 129km lake, but most commonly around Peachland. In 1926, 30 carloads of people all claimed to have seen the monster and film footage from 1968 has been analyzed, concluding that a solid, three-dimensional object was moving through the water.

Cryptozoologist Karl Shuker suggests that the Ogopogo may be a type of primitive whale like the basilosaurus. Keep your eyes peeled, but if you don't have any luck spotting it, you can visit a statue of the Ogopogo at Kelowna's City Park.

you may be lucky enough to see an amazing (and rare) tapestry by French-Russian artist Marc Chagall hanging in one of the rooms.

The winery's **Terrace** restaurant sits atop a glorious terrace overlooking vineyards and a lake. Its spectacular food matches the setting. Nearby, a grassy amphitheater hosts summer concerts (accompanied by wine, of course). You can also visit the shop for souvenir bottles. Try Oculus, the winery's premium Bordeaux blend.

THE DRIVE
Return to Boucherie Rd and continue 2km north, following the lakeshore.

 QUAILS' GATE WINERY
Charming stone and beam architecture reigns at **Quails' Gate Winery** (quails gate.com). Tours run throughout spring and summer and begin in an on-site pioneer home built in 1873. Tastings are held throughout the day – the rhubarby Chenin Blanc and pleasantly peppery reserve Pinot Noir are recommended. The winery's **Old Vines** restaurant is a foodie favorite, with a menu showcasing seasonal BC ingredients and a commitment to sourcing sustainable seafood. Or you could just chill at vine-side picnic benches.

THE DRIVE
Head 9km northeast on Boucherie Rd before merging

with Hwy 97. Cross the lake at the William R Bennett Bridge and head for the 'east coast' town of Kelowna, the Okanagan capital.

WHY I LOVE THIS TRIP

Brendan Sainsbury, writer

Even as a BC resident you still have to sometimes pinch yourself when traveling through the Okanagan to check that you haven't been accidentally teleported over to France or Italy. Not only do the vine-striped hills and glassy water vistas resemble Provence or Lake Garda, the quality and quantity of the wines have also burgeoned to challenge the hegemony of the European stalwarts across the 'pond.'

⚑ DETOUR
Nk'Mip Cellars
Start: 02 **Quails' Gate Winery**

Add a day to your visit and head for this multifarious **cultural center** (nkmip-desert.com) just east of Osoyoos, part of a First Nations empire that includes a desert golf course, the noted winery **Nk'Mip Cellars** (nkmipcellars.com/The-Winery), a resort and more. The architecturally slick cultural center celebrates the Syilx people of the Okanagan nation and the delicate desert ecosystem where they traditionally live. Those with a little reptilian courage can also check out the on-site rattlesnake enclosure.

Save a bit more time to sample one of the region's most distinctive wineries at Nk'Mip Cellars, North America's first Indigenous-owned and -operated winery when it opened in 2003. Tastings of five different wines cost $5. The place is known for its ice wines and is open 10am to 6pm in the summer (to 5pm November to March). The two Nk'Mip sites are located about 112km south of Westbank along Hwy 97.

03 KELOWNA

The wine industry has turned Kelowna into a bit of a boomtown. The population has almost doubled since the early 1990s and property prices have risen accordingly. A wander (especially along Ellis St) will unearth plenty of art galleries and lakeside parks, along with cafes and – delightfully – wine bars.

Continue your wine education at the **Okanagan Wine and Orchard Museum** (kelownamuseums.ca). Housed in the historic Laurel Packinghouse and expanded to include fruit memorabilia in 2016, the museum offers a look at celebrated bottles, labels and equipment, along with an overview of winemaking in the region. There's a separate section on fruit packing.

With vineyards cozied up to Knox Mountain, **Sandhill Wines** (sandhillwines.ca), formerly known as Calona Vineyards, was the Okanagan's first winery, kicking off production in 1932. Its architecturally striking tasting room is an atmospheric spot to try the ever-popular, melon-note Pinot Blanc, along with the port-style dessert wine that makes an ideal cheese buddy. You'll find the winery north of Hwy 97.

🚗 THE DRIVE
Head south of Kelowna on Lakeshore Rd, keeping Okanagan Lake on your right. Take a left onto Dehart Rd and follow it to Bedford Rd. Turn right and then right again so that you're heading south on Takla Rd. The 10km drive should take less than 15 minutes!

04 OKANAGAN LAVENDER FARM
Visiting **Okanagan Lavender Farm** (okanaganlavender.com) is a heady experience. Rows and rows of more than 60 types of lavender waft in the breeze against the backdrop of Okanagan Lake. You can enjoy a guided or self-guided tour of the aromatic acreage and pop into the shop for everything from bath products to lavender lemonade. Your wine-soaked palate will be well and truly cleansed.

🚗 THE DRIVE
Retrace your route back to Lakeshore Rd, heading south and then veering left onto Chute Lake Rd after 6.5km.

05 SUMMERHILL PYRAMID WINERY
In the hills along the lake's eastern shore, you'll soon come to one of the Okanagan's most colorful wineries. **Summerhill Pyramid Winery** (summerhill.bc.ca) combines a traditional tasting room with a huge pyramid where every Summerhill wine ages in barrels, owing to the belief that sacred geometry has a positive effect on liquids. The winery's vegan-friendly **Sunset Organic Bistro** is much loved and the Ehrenfelser ice wine is particularly delightful.

🚗 THE DRIVE
Return to Lakeside Rd and continue south for 2.5km. The next stop is across from Cedar Creek Park.

06 ST HUBERTUS & OAK BAY ESTATE WINERY
Lakeside **St Hubertus & Oak Bay Estate Winery** (sthubertus.bc.ca) is another twist on the winery approach. Visiting

Photo Opportunity

View from the terrace at Mission Hill Family Estate Winery.

is like being at a traditional northern European vineyard, complete with Bavarian architectural flourishes.

Despite its emphasis on Germanic wines, including Riesling, St Hubertus isn't conservative: try its floral, somewhat spicy Casselas and the rich Marechal Foch. While there are no formal tours, you can stroll around the vineyard or head to the complimentary tasting room to try four different wines. There's also a shop selling artisan foods and, of course, wine.

THE DRIVE
Continue south on Lakeside for 4km and then take the left turning onto Rimrock Rd. Follow it for 200m to a T-junction and take a right onto Timberline Rd.

07 CARMELIS GOAT CHEESE ARTISAN

End your tour by treating your driver to something they can sample at **Carmelis Goat Cheese Artisan** (facebook. com/carmelisgoatcheese). Call ahead to book a tour of the dairy, milking station and cellar. Even without the tour, you can sample soft-ripened cheeses with names like Moonlight and Heavenly, or the hard-ripened Smoked Carmel or Goatgonzola. For those who prefer something milder, try the super-soft unripened versions like feta and yogurt cheese. The showstopper is the goat's-milk gelato, which comes in 24 different flavors.

Summerhill Pyramid Winery

NALIDSA/SHUTTERSTOCK ©

Wine Festivals

The Okanagan stages four major multiday seasonal **wine festivals** (thewinefestivals. com) throughout the year. Time your visit right and dip into one of these:

Winter Wine Festival January

Spring Wine Festival May

Summer Wine Festival August

Fall Wine Festival October

07

Haida Gwaii Adventure

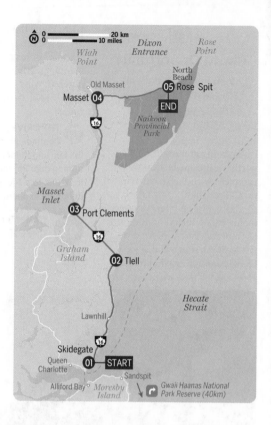

DURATION	DISTANCE	GREAT FOR
2 days	136km/85 miles	Culture, Nature

BEST TIME TO GO	July and August: more likely sunshine and less vicious wind.

You'll be welcomed to what feels like the edge of the earth. Once known as the Queen Charlotte Islands, this rugged northwestern archipelago maintains its independent spirit, evident in its quirky museums, rustic cafes, down-to-earth art and nature-loving locals. You'll feel closer to the natural world than ever before, and some of the Northern Hemisphere's most extraordinary cultural artifacts are found here.

Link Your Trip

05 Vancouver Island's Remote North

After a seven-hour boat ride from Skidegate to Prince Rupert you travel along the inside passage on a 22-hour ferry to Port Hardy. From here drive 40km along Hwy 9 to Port McNeill to pick up this trip.

14 Klondike Highway

Take the ferry from Skidegate to Prince Rupert, then boat north to Skagway, Alaska to reach the iconic Klondike Hwy.

01 SKIDEGATE

If you're not bringing your car, you can rent a car in advance of your **BC Ferries** (bcferries.com) arrival in Skidegate on Graham Island (or air arrival in Sandspit). Spend some time perusing the clapboard houses or fueling up at the home-style pub or cafes in nearby Queen Charlotte. Save an hour or two for the unmissable: **Haida Heritage Centre** (haidaheritagecentre.com), a striking crescent of totem-fronted cedar longhouses that's arguably British Columbia's best First Nations attraction. Check out ancient carvings and artifacts

BEST FOR

Gain insight into the resurgence of Haida culture at Haida Heritage Centre.

Balance Rock, Skidegate

recalling 10,000 years of Haida history and look for the exquisite artworks of the legendary Bill Reid, such as huge canoes and totem poles.

Hitting Hwy 16, head north to explore the distinctive settlements that make latter-day Haida Gwaii tick. You'll wind along stretches of rustic waterfront and through shadowy woodland areas.

THE DRIVE
Follow Hwy 16 north along the shoreline. Take a few minutes to walk down to the beach when you see the pullout and signage for Balance Rock just out of Skidegate. At 35.4km you'll enter the flat, arable land around Tlell River. Turn left at Wiggins Rd when you see signs for Crystal Cabin, then right on Richardson Rd.

DETOUR
Gwaii Haanas National Park Reserve
Start: 01 Skidegate

Famed for its mystical élan, **Gwaii Haanas National Park Reserve** (pc. gc.ca/en/pn-np/bc/gwaiihaanas) covers much of Haida Gwaii's southern section, a rugged region only accessible by boat or floatplane. The reserve is the ancient site of Haida homes, burial caves and the derelict village of Ninstints with its seafront totem poles (now a Unesco World Heritage site). Visitors often remark on the area's magical and spiritual qualities, but you should only consider an extended visit if you are well prepared. It is essential that you contact **Parks Canada** (pc. gc.ca/en/pn-np/bc/gwaiihaanas) in advance, as access to the park is very limited and most visitors will find it best to work with officially sanctioned tour operators.

02 TLELL
Crystal Cabin (crystal cabingallery.com), in Tlell, features the works of 20 Haida artists at the jewelry workshop of April and Sarah Dutheil, second-generation artisans and sisters who were taught by their father, local legend and authority on island geology, Dutes. April has written on Haida Gwaii agate collecting and is happy to explain Dutes' Tlell Stone Circle, which is just outside the cabin. There are many forms of art here, including carvings from argillite, a local rock that can only be carved by Haida artisans.

THE DRIVE

Continue 21.7km northwest along Hwy 16. This incredibly straight route was a walking trail until 1920, when a road was built by placing wooden planks end-to-end along the ground. Watch for deer by the road and shrub-like shore pines along the now-paved route.

03 PORT CLEMENTS

At Port Clements, head around through town on Bayview Ave until it turns south and becomes a gravel road. Follow this for 3.5km to the **Golden Spruce Trail**. This easy 15-minute (one-way) walk through the forest leads to the banks of the Yakoun River and the site of the legendary Golden Spruce. Tragically cut down in 1997 by a deranged environmentalist, the tree – a 46m, 300-year-old genetic aberration with luminous yellow needles – was revered by local Haida as the transformed spirit of a little boy.

Photo Opportunity

Capture the islands' wilderness from Tow Hill's viewpoint.

The tree's death was traumatic for many island residents. You can see a seedling taken from a cutting from the felled tree in Millennium Park in Port Clements. For a gripping read, pick up *The Golden Spruce: A True Story of Myth, Madness and Greed* by John Vaillant (2006).

Head back to the village and nip into **Port Clements Museum** (portclementsmuseum.ca), where you're welcomed by a forest of rusty logging machinery. Learn about early logging practices and check out toys and tools from pioneering days. You'll also encounter a stuffed albino raven, another genetic aberration that was also revered until it electrocuted itself on local power lines.

THE DRIVE

Head north along Hwy 16, which hugs Masset Inlet, to the northern coast. Continue north to Masset and Old Masset, 43.5km from Port Clements. Hwy 16 is officially the Yellowhead Hwy and Mile 0 is at Masset. From here Yellowhead Hwy runs to Winnipeg, Manitoba, although you'll have to take the ferry between Haida Gwaii and Prince Rupert.

04 MASSET

Masset primarily occupies the rather stark, institutional buildings of a disused military base and the adjoining **Old Masset** is a First Nations village where wood-fired homes are fronted by broad, brooding totem poles. There are several stores here where visitors can peruse and buy Haida carvings and paintings.

TOP TIP:

Getting There

From mainland Prince Rupert in northern BC, take the BC Ferries service to Skidegate on Graham Island. The crossing usually takes seven to eight hours.

Golden Spruce Trail

Also in Masset is the **Dixon Entrance Maritime Museum** (massetbc.com/visitors/maritime-museum). Housed in what was once the local hospital, the museum features exhibits on the history of this seafaring community, with displays on shipbuilding, medical pioneers, military history, and nearby clam and crab canneries. Local artists also exhibit their work here.

🚗 **THE DRIVE**
Head east off Hwy 16 along a well-marked road signposted for North Beach and Naikoon Provincial Park. The next stop is 27.4km from Masset.

05 ROSE SPIT
The region's wild northern tip is home to **Naikoon Provincial Park** (env.gov.bc.ca/bcparks). This dense, treed park has more than 96km of white-sand beach and is the area's most popular destination for summertime nature fans.

Continue along the tree-lined dirt road until you reach **Tow Hill**, a steep, dense and easily enjoyed short forest walk (1km each way). Look out for trees where strips of bark have been carefully removed for Haida basket-making over the decades, then catch your breath at the summit while you gaze over the impenetrable coastal forest stretching into the mist.

Finally, head for the park's extreme coastal tip and **North Beach**. Leave the car here and tramp along the sandy expanse, where locals walk in the surf plucking Dungeness crabs for dinner. With the wind watering your eyes, you'll feel closer to nature than you've ever felt before.

RANPLETT/GETTY IMAGES ©

Haida Gwaii totem pole

RETURN OF THE HAIDA

The Haida are one of Canada's First Nations peoples, and had lived here for thousands of years before Europeans turned up in the 18th century. Centered on the islands, these fearsome warriors had no immunity to such diseases as smallpox, measles and tuberculosis that were brought by the newcomers, and their population of tens of thousands was quickly decimated. By the early 20th century, their numbers had fallen to around 600.

Since the 1970s, the Haida population – and its cultural pride – has grown anew, and the Haida now make up about half of the 5000 residents on the islands. In 2009, the Government of British Columbia officially changed the name of the islands from the Queen Charlottes to Haida Gwaii ('Islands of the People') as part of the province's reconciliation process with the Haida.

Historically, the Haida have one of the most vibrant of First Nations cultures, with very strong narratives and oral history. Legends, beliefs, skills and more are passed down from one generation to the next and great importance is placed on the knowledge of past generations. Today the Haida seek to live in harmony with their environment. Traditional laws recognize the stunning nature of the islands and embrace both the past and look to the future.

To learn more about the Haida, visit haidanation.ca.

08

Circling the Rockies

DURATION	DISTANCE	GREAT FOR
3 days	294km/183 miles	Nature, Families

BEST TIME TO GO	July and August when the snow has melted and all of the roads are open.

Bighorn sheep

This route will give you a new perspective on nature. This is where mountains stretch up to the stars and where bears and moose own the woods (and sometimes the road). Waterfalls, canyons and gem-colored lakes lie deep in the forest, waiting to be discovered. It's impossible not to be awed, not to feel small and not to wish you had longer to explore.

Link Your Trip

02 Sea to Sky Highway

Mountain-hop to the Coast Mountains by heading west from Golden on Hwy 1 and then taking Hwy 99 southwest to Whistler.

06 Okanagan Valley Wine Tour

From Golden, a lovely 345km drive along Hwys 1 and 97 will take you to Kelowna in the heart of the Okanagan Valley wine country.

01 ### RADIUM HOT SPRINGS

Set in a valley just inside the southern border of **Kootenay National Park**, the outdoor **Radium Hot Springs** (pc.gc.ca/hotsprings) has a hot pool simmering at 39°C (102°F) and a second pool to cool you off at 29°C (84°F). Originally sacred to Indigenous groups for the water's curative powers, these springs are uniquely odorless and colorless. The large tiled pool can get crowded in summer. You can rent lockers, towels and even swimsuits.

THE DRIVE

From Radium Hot Springs, it's a lovely 83km drive on Hwy 93 through the park to Ochre Ponds and Paint Pots.

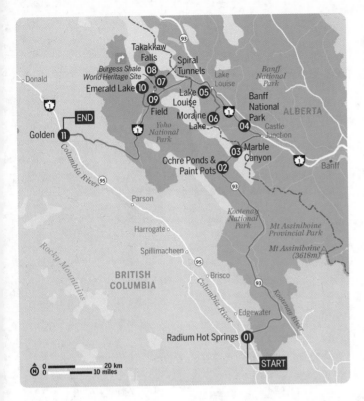

04 BANFF NATIONAL PARK

More of a drive than a stop, the stretch of Hwy 1 running from Castle Junction to Lake Louise is one of the most scenic routes through Banff National Park. The highway runs through the Bow Valley, following the weaving Bow River and the route of the Canadian Pacific Railway. The craggy peaks of the giant Sawback and Massive mountain ranges sweep up on either side of the road. The resulting perspective is much wider than on smaller roads with big open vistas.

There are several viewpoint pull-offs where gob-smacked drivers can stop to absorb their surroundings. Watch for the unmissable **Castle Mountain** looming in its crimson glory to the northwest. The Panorama Ridge then rises in the south, after which the enormous **Mt Temple** comes into view, towering at 3541m. Stop at the **Mt Temple Viewpoint** for a good gander.

THE DRIVE

The turnoff for Lake Louise Village is 24km from Castle Junction.

05 LAKE LOUISE

With stunning emerald-green water and tall, snowy peaks that hoist hefty Victoria Glacier up for all to see, Lake Louise has captured the imaginations of mountaineers, artists and visitors for over a century. You – and the enormous numbers of other visitors – will notice the lake's color appears slightly different from each viewpoint.

Follow the **Lakeshore Trail**, a 4km round trip, or head up the gorgeous (though somewhat more

02 OCHRE PONDS & PAINT POTS

As the road dips down into the woods along Hwy 93, a signpost leads to a short, flat interpretive trail. Follow this to the intriguing red-and-orange **Ochre Ponds**. Drawing Kootenay indigenous groups for centuries – and later European settlers – this iron-rich earth was collected, mixed with oil and turned into paint. Further along the trail are three stunning crystal-blue springs that are known as the **Paint Pots**.

THE DRIVE

Continue north along Hwy 93 for 3km to the next stop.

03 MARBLE CANYON

This jaw-dropping stop is not for the faint-of-heart. An easy 15-minute trail zigzags over Tokumm Creek, giving phenomenal views deeper and deeper into Marble Canyon below. The limestone and dolomite walls have been carved away by the awesome power of the creek, resulting in plunging falls and bizarrely shaped cliff faces. The trail can be slippery. Take sturdy shoes and your camera.

THE DRIVE

Continue north along Hwy 93 and across the provincial border into Alberta to the junction with Hwy 1 (Castle Junction). Head west.

difficult) route to **Lake Agnes** and its sun-dappled teahouse, perched 7km from Lake Louise's shore. For a more relaxed experience, rent a canoe from **Lake Louise Boathouse** (fairmont. com/lake-louise/promotions/ canoeing) and paddle yourself through the icy waters.

Drive back downhill and cross over Hwy 1 to reach the **Lake Louise Gondola** (lakelouisegon dola.com), which lands you at a lofty 2088m for a view of the lake and the surrounding glaciers and peaks. En route you'll sail over wildflowers and possibly even a grizzly bear. At the top is the **Wildlife Interpretation Centre**, which hosts regular theater presentations and guided walks.

THE DRIVE
From Lake Louise Dr, head south along Moraine Lake Rd for 14km.

06 MORAINE LAKE
You'll be dazzled by the scenery before you even reach Moraine Lake, set in the Valley of the Ten Peaks. En route, the narrow, winding road gives off fabulous views of the imposing **Wenkchemna Peaks**. Look familiar? For years this scene was carried on the back of the Canadian $20 bill. In 1894, explorer Samuel Allen named the peaks with numbers from 1 to 10 in the Stoney Indian Language (*wenk-chemna* means 'ten'); all but two of the mountains have since been renamed. You'll quickly notice the **Tower of Babel**, ascending solidly toward the heavens at the northeastern edge of the range.

Many people prefer the more rugged and remote setting of Moraine Lake to Lake Louise. The turquoise waters are surprisingly

Takakkaw Falls

clear for a glacial reservoir. Take a look at the surrounding mountains through telescopes secured to the southern shore (free!) or hire a boat and paddle to the middle for a 360-degree view. There are also some great day hikes from here and, to rest your weary legs, a cafe, dining room and lodge. The road to Moraine Lake and its facilities are open from June to early October.

THE DRIVE
Return to Hwy 1 and continue west, across the provincial border and into Yoho National Park.

07 SPIRAL TUNNELS
Upon completion of the railway in 1885, trains struggled up the challenging **Kicking Horse Pass**, which you'll cross soon after the Alberta–British Columbia provincial border. This is the steepest railway pass in North America, and wrecks and runaways were common. In 1909 the Spiral Tunnels were carved into Mt Cathedral and Mt Ogden and are still in use today. If you time it right, you can see a train exiting from the top of the tunnel while its final cars are still entering at the bottom. Watch from the main viewing area on the north side of the highway.

THE DRIVE
Continue west on Hwy 1 and then turn north onto Yoho Valley Rd (open late June to October). This road climbs a number of tight switchbacks.

08 TAKAKKAW FALLS
Named 'magnificent' in Cree, Takakkaw Falls is one of the highest waterfalls in Canada (245m). An impressive

torrent of water travels from the Daly Glacier, plunges over the edge of the rock face into a small pool and jets out into a tumbling cloud of mist.

En route to the falls you'll pass a second **Spiral Lookout** and the **Meeting of the Rivers**, where the clear Kicking Horse runs into the milky-colored Yoho.

THE DRIVE
Return to Hwy 1 and continue west to Field.

09 FIELD
In the midst of Yoho National Park, on the southern side of the Kicking Horse River, lies the quaint village of Field. This historic but unfussy railroad town has a dramatic overlook of the river. While Field may be short on sights, it's a beautiful place to wander around.

This is also the place to come if you want to organize an activity in the park – from dogsledding in winter to canoeing and white-water rafting in summer.

TOP TIP:

Road Conditions

Weather is very changeable in the mountains. Be sure to carry chains outside of the summer months of June, July and August. Check drivebc.ca in BC for current road conditions; in Alberta check 511.alberta.ca or dial 511.

THE DRIVE
Continue west on Hwy 1 and take the first right. Continue north for 10km.

DETOUR
Burgess Shale World Heritage Site
Start: **09** Field

In 1909, Burgess Shale was unearthed on Mt Field. The fossil beds are home to perfectly preserved fossils of marine creatures, dated at least 500 million years old and recognized as some of the earliest forms of life. The area is now a World Heritage site and accessible only by guided hikes, led by naturalists from the **Yoho Shale Geoscience Foundation** (burgess-shale.bc.ca). Reservations are essential, as is stamina: it's a 19.3km round-trip, ascending 762m.

10 EMERALD LAKE
Gorgeously green Emerald Lake gains its color from light reflecting off fine glacial rock particles that are deposited into the lake by grinding glaciers. It's a highlight of the park, so the lake attracts visitors year-round, either to simply admire its serenity or to fish, skate, hike or horseback ride. In summer, the water warms up just enough for a very quick dip.

En route to the lake, watch for the impressive **natural bridge** stretching across the Kicking Horse River.

THE DRIVE
Return to Hwy 1 and continue to Golden, 54km from the turnoff.

Photo Opportunity
Mt Temple Viewpoint in Banff National Park for postcard-perfect mountain shots.

11 GOLDEN
With six national parks in its backyard, little Golden is a popular base. It's also the center for white-water rafting trips on the turbulent Kicking Horse River. Powerful grade III and IV rapids and breathtaking scenery along the sheer walls of Kicking Horse Valley make this rafting experience one of North America's best. Full-day trips on the river are about $159; half-day trips $99. Operators include **Alpine Rafting** (alpinerafting. com).

More than 60% of the 120 ski runs at **Kicking Horse Mountain Resort** (kickinghorseresort. com) are rated advanced or expert. It's 14km from Golden on Kicking Horse Trail.

The **Northern Lights Wolf Centre** (northernlightswild life.com) is a refuge for this misunderstood animal, which is being hunted to extinction. Meet a resident wolf or two and learn about their routines and survival.

Mt Temple, Banff National Park

09

Biking, hiking, and – best of all – white-water rafting.

Around the Kootenays

DURATION	DISTANCE	GREAT FOR
5–6 days	870km/543 miles	Families, Nature

BEST TIME TO GO	June to September when roads and trails are snow-free and accessible.

Radium Hot Springs

The commanding ranges of the Monashee, Selkirk and Purcell Mountains striate the Kootenays, with the Arrow and Kootenay Lakes adding texture in the middle. This drive allows you to admire their placid alpine meadows and rugged sawtooth ridges while popping into appealing towns such as Revelstoke, Golden, Nelson and Radium Hot Springs in between. Herein lie plenty of launchpads for year-round outdoor adventures.

Link Your Trip

06 Okanagan Valley Wine Tour

After completing the tour at Revelstoke, head three hours southwest to the start of this scenic drive among the rolling, vine-covered hills.

08 Circling the Rockies

At Radium Hot Springs, divert east onto Hwy 93, which will take you into Kootenay National Park on this epic Rockies loop.

01 GOLDEN

Golden sits at the confluence of two rivers, three mountain ranges and five national parks – all of them less than 90 minutes drive away. The town is the center for white-water rafting trips on the turbulent and chilly Kicking Horse River. Along with the powerful grade III and IV rapids, the rugged scenery that guards the sheer walls of the Kicking Horse Valley makes this rafting experience one of North America's best.

Indelibly linked to Golden is the **Kicking Horse Mountain Resort** (kickinghorseresort.com) 6km to the west – a ski resort that opened in 2000 and

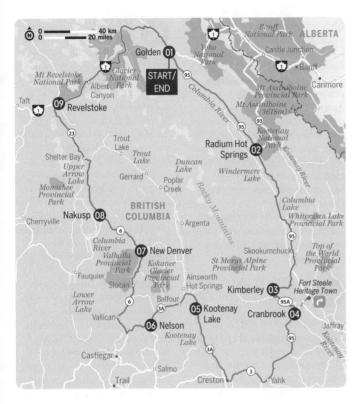

THE DRIVE
Heading south, Hwy 93/95 follows the wide Columbia River valley between the Purcell and Rocky Mountains. It's not especially interesting, unless you're into the area's industry (ski resort construction), agriculture (golf courses) or wild game (condo buyers). South of Skookumchuck on Hwy 93/95, the road forks. Go right on Hwy 95A and within 30 minutes you'll be in Kimberley.

03 KIMBERLEY
Welcome to Kimberley, a town famous for its erstwhile lead mine, contemporary alpine skiing resort and Canada's largest cuckoo clock.

For well over half a century, Kimberley was home to the world's largest lead-zinc mine, the Sullivan mine, which was finally decommissioned in 2001. Since 2015, the local economy has switched track somewhat and now hosts Canada's largest solar farm.

In the 1970s, Kimberley experimented with a Bavarian theme in the hope of attracting more tourists. Remnants of the Teutonic makeover remain. The central pedestrian zone is named the Platzl and you can still bag plenty of tasty schnitzel and sausages in its restaurants, but these days the town is better known for the **Kimberley Alpine Resort** (ski kimberley.com) with 700 hectares of skiable terrain.

For a historical detour, take a 15km ride on **Kimberley's Underground Mining Railway** (kimberleysundergroundmining railway.ca), where a tiny train putters through the steep-walled Mark Creek Valley toward some sweeping mountain vistas.

---

is known for its abundance of expert runs. In the summer, the resort and its gondola are handed over to mountain bikers and, more recently, climbers keen to tackle several newly installed via ferrata routes.

THE DRIVE
Head south on Hwy 95 through the Columbia River Wetlands, a hugely important ecological area that's home to 260 species of bird and numerous animals, including grizzly bears. In just over an hour, you will arrive in Radium Hot Springs.

02 RADIUM HOT SPRINGS
Lying just outside the southwest corner of Kootenay National Park, Radium Hot Springs is a major gateway to the entire Rocky Mountains national park area.

The town itself isn't much more than a gas and coffee pit-stop. The main attraction is the namesake hot springs, 3km north of town at the jaws of Kootenay National Park (you can hike in via the Sinclair Canyon). One of three hot springs in the Rockies region, Radium is the only one that is odorless. Keeping its water between 37°C (98.6°F) and 40°C (104°F), the facility is more public baths than fancy spa, although the exposed rock and overhanging trees make for a nice setting.

THE DRIVE

It's a short 30-minute drive southeast out of Kimberley on Hwy 95A to Cranbrook where you'll merge with Hwy 95 just east of the town.

04 CRANBROOK

The region's main commercial center with a population of just under 20,000, Cranbrook is a modest crossroads. Hwy 3/95 bisects the town, which is a charmless array of strip malls.

The main reason for stopping here is to visit the multifarious **Cranbrook History Centre** (cranbrookhistorycentre.com). Dedicated primarily (though not exclusively) to train and rail travel, the center displays some fine examples of classic Canadian trains, including the luxurious 1929 edition of the Trans-Canada Limited, a legendary train that ran from Montréal to Vancouver. Also on-site is a fabulous model railway, the town museum (with plenty of First Nations and pre-human artifacts), and the elegant Alexandra Hall, part of a grand railway hotel that once stood in Winnipeg but was reconstructed in Cranbrook in 2004.

THE DRIVE

Take Hwy 3 (Crowsnest Hwy) out of Cranbrook. The road is shared with Hwy 95 as far as Yahk, beyond which you pass through the Purcell Mountains to Creston. North of Creston, turn onto Hwy 3A and track alongside the east shore of Kootenay Lake. This leg takes around 2½ hours.

DETOUR

Fort Steele Heritage Town
Start: 04 Cranbrook

Fort Steele is an erstwhile gold rush town that fell into decline in the early 1900s when it was bypassed by the railway, which went to Cranbrook instead. In the early 1960s, local authorities elected to save the place from total oblivion by turning it into a **heritage site** (fortsteele.ca) of pioneering mining culture. Buildings were subsequently rescued or completely rebuilt in vintage 19th-century style to lure in tourists. The site today consists of old shops, stores and a blacksmith, plus opportunities to partake in gold-panning, go on train rides or see a performance in a working theater.

In summer there are all manner of activities and re-creations, which taper off to nothing in winter, although the site stays open.

05 KOOTENAY LAKE

Lodged in the middle of the Kootenays between the Selkirk and Purcell Mountains, Kootenay Lake is one of the largest bodies of freshwater in BC. It's crossed by a year-round toll-free **ferry** (gov.bc.ca/gov/content/transportation/passenger-travel) that runs between the two small communities of Kootenay Bay on the east bank and Balfour on the west. The ferry's a worthwhile side trip if traveling between Creston and Nelson for its long lake vistas of blue mountains rising sharply from the water. Ferries run every 50 minutes throughout the day and the crossing takes 35 minutes. On busy summer weekends, you may have to wait in a long line for a sailing or two before you get passage.

THE DRIVE

From where the ferry disembarks in Balfour on the western shore of Kootenay Lake, take Hwy 3A along the north shore of the West Arm for 32km before crossing the bridge into the town of Nelson.

06 NELSON

Nelson is a great reason to visit the Kootenays and should feature on any itinerary in the region. Tidy brick buildings climb the side of a hill overlooking the west arm of deep-blue Kootenay Lake, and the waterfront is lined with parks and beaches. The thriving cafe, culture and nightlife scene is a bonus. But what really propels Nelson is its personality: a mix of hippies, creative types and rugged individualists (many locals will tell you it's the coolest small town in BC). You can find all these along Baker St, the pedestrian-friendly main drag.

Founded as a mining town in the late 1800s, Nelson embarked on a decades-long heritage-preservation project in 1977. Almost a third of Nelson's historic buildings have been restored to their original architectural splendor. Pick up the superb *Heritage Walking Tour* from the visitor center, which gives details on more than 30 buildings and offers a good lesson in Victorian architecture.

The town is also an excellent base for hiking, skiing, kayaking the nearby lakes, and – in recent years in particular – mountain-biking. Freeriding pedal-heads have plenty of favorite spots in British Columbia and the Rockies, but many particularly enjoy Nelson's unique juxtaposition of top-notch single-track and cool bikey ambience. The surrounding area is striped with great trails, from the epic downhill of **Mountain Station** to the winding **Svoboda Road Trails** in West Arm Provincial Park.

Baker St, Nelson

THE DRIVE

Heading north from Nelson to Revelstoke, Hwy 6 threads west for 16km before turning north at South Slocan. The road eventually runs alongside pretty Slocan Lake for about 30km before reaching New Denver, 97km from Nelson.

07 NEW DENVER

With only around 500 residents, New Denver is an historic little gem that slumbers away peacefully right on the clear waters of Slocan Lake. Chapters in its not-so-sleepy history have included silver mining and a stint as a WWII Japanese internment camp. Details of the former can be found at the **Silvery Slocan**

Photo Opportunity

Summit of Mt Revelstoke.

Museum (newdenver.ca/silvery -slocan-museum), located in an 1897 Bank of Montreal building.

THE DRIVE

It is a relatively straightforward 46km drive from New Denver to Nakusp on Hwy 6 via Summit Lake Provincial Park. Look out for mountain goats on the rocky outcrops.

08 NAKUSP

Situated right on Upper Arrow Lake, Nakusp was forever changed by BC's orgy of dam building in the 1950s and 1960s. The water level here was raised and the town was relocated to its current spot, which is why it has a 1960s-era look. It has some attractive cafes and a tiny museum. If you missed Radium Hot Springs or just can't get enough of the Rocky Mountains' thermal pleasures, divert to **Nakusp Hot Springs** (nakusphotsprings.com), 12km northeast of town, to soak away your cares amid an amphitheater of trees.

MARCELA MIU/SHUTTERSTOCK ©

View of the Columbia River Valley from Mt Revelstoke

THE DRIVE
Head north on Hwy 23 along the east shore of Arrow Lake for 48km. You'll need to cross this lake, too, on a ferry between Galena and Shelter Bay. Hwy 23 continues on the west shore and will take you all the way to Revelstoke, 52km north of Shelter Bay.

09 REVELSTOKE

Gateway to serious mountains, Revelstoke doesn't need to blow its own trumpet – the ceaseless procession of freight trains through the town center makes more than enough noise. Built as an important point on the Canadian Pacific transcontinental railroad that first linked Eastern and Western Canada, Revelstoke echoes not just with whistles but with history. If you haven't yet been satiated with Canadian railway memorabilia, you can sample a bit more at the **Revelstoke Railway Museum** (railwaymuseum.com).

Revelstoke's compact center is lined with heritage buildings, yet it's more than a museum piece. **Grizzly Plaza**, between Mackenzie and Orton Aves, is a pedestrian precinct and the heart of downtown, where free live-music performances take place every evening in July and August.

Notwithstanding, this place is mainly about the adjacent wilderness and its boundless opportunities for hiking, kayaking and, most of all, skiing. North America's first ski jump was built here in 1915. One year before, Mt Revelstoke became Canada's seventh national park. From the 2223m summit of Mt Revelstoke, the views of the mountains and the Columbia River valley are excellent. To ascend, take the 26km

Revelstoke Railway Museum

Meadows in the Sky Parkway, 1.6km east of Revelstoke off the Trans-Canada Hwy. Open after the thaw, from mid-May to mid-October, this paved road winds through lush cedar forests and alpine meadows and ends at Balsam Lake, within 2km of the peak. From here, walk to the top or take the free shuttle.

THE DRIVE
Keep your eyes on the road or, better yet, let someone else drive as you traverse the Trans-Canada Hwy (Hwy 1) for 148km between Revelstoke and Golden. Stunning mountain peaks follow one after another as you go.

TRPHOTOS/SHUTTERSTOCK ©

Bow Lake (p83), Icefields Pkwy

The Prairie Provinces & the North

Explore

The Prairie Provinces & the North

Nature's vast and stately splendor is on full display in this grippingly inviting region, where towering crags jostle for attention with gargantuan forests and where endless grassland 'oceans' lap the highways under wide blue skies. Not surprisingly, wildlife is abundant and a driving tour can deliver a camera-worthy cavalcade of bears, bighorn sheep, plains bison and much more. It's not just about gazing from your car windows, though. From hiking to kayaking, there are countless ways to tackle the great outdoors in this region, alongside a full array of world-class museums, immersive Indigenous sites and distinctive hidden-gem communities.

Calgary

Although Edmonton is the provincial capital, Calgary is the biggest city in Alberta. Its airport also receives more international flights. And while its reputation as a magnet for corporate headquarters is deserved, there's much more to 'cowtown' than the glass towers of downtown's business district. Spend a couple of days exploring here and you'll find excellent museums and cultural attractions; a full menu of highly inviting independent restaurants (especially in Kensington, Inglewood and along downtown's Stephen St); and, depending on the time of year, some iconic festivals.

Jasper

More than its heavily touristed sibling Banff, mountain-shadowed Jasper is the soul of the Canadian Rockies. In this low-rise town in the heart of a national park, elk routinely wander the streets, and long-distance trains rumble up to the gabled railway station as they have done for more than a century. Restaurants abound in the blocks radiating from the station, and there are lots of places to stay if you want to wake up in the Rockies. It's worth doing just that for a few days, to take advantage of the backcountry experiences offered by local operators, from guided hikes to horseback tours and from wildlife walks to white-water rafting.

WHEN TO GO

July and August are crowded in many parts of the Rockies and temperatures can also be uncomfortably high in parts of Saskatchewan. Instead, consider June or September for both areas. September is also a great time to visit the Yukon, especially if you're hoping to see the spectacular aurora borealis. Avoid winter driving in all areas.

Saskatoon

More enticing than provincial capital Regina, this under-the-radar Saskatchewan city is a favorite with visitors, who often feel as though they're the first ones to discover it. Give yourself a couple of days to scratch beneath the surface of this friendly and culturally vibrant place: its concrete-heavy appearance can look a little bland at first glance. You'll be rewarded with some revealing historical attractions, a sparkling arts sector, and a dining and bar scene rich with independent establishments, local craft beers and farm-to-fork restaurants, especially in the downtown and Riversdale areas.

Whitehorse

Visitors to the Yukon shouldn't miss winningly quirky Dawson City, but be sure to check out the larger regional capital of Whitehorse as well, despite its sprawling, transportation-hub feel. Consider uncovering the gritty history of the gold rush

at local museums, tackling the legendary Yukon River on a canoe excursion or hiking some of the scenic trails that fringe the community. Sleepover-wise, there are more places to stay here than in Dawson, and you'll also find some great spots to eat with the locals, especially in the downtown core.

TRANSPORT

Both Calgary and Edmonton have quite large international airports, and there are smaller ones in Saskatoon, Regina and Whitehorse. The Trans-Canada Hwy (aka Hwy 1) links Alberta and Saskatchewan to the rest of Canada. The Yukon can be reached via major highways from both Alaska and British Columbia.

WHAT'S ON

Calgary Stampede

(calgarystampede.com) Gigantic celebration of cowboy culture, with midway rides, calorific food and rodeo contests.

Dawson City Music Festival

(dcmf.com) Unique live-music party in the land of the midnight sun.

Edmonton International Fringe Theatre Festival

(fringetheatreadventures.ca) One of the world's oldest and largest fringes, with hundreds of performances.

Saskatchewan Jazz Festival

(saskjazz.com) Saskatoon's 10-day live music party, with blues, funk and more also part of the fun.

WHERE TO STAY

Calgary and Edmonton have plenty of hotels, but summer accommodations are at a premium (in terms of both price and scarcity) in crowded destinations such as Banff and Jasper. Scarcity is also an issue in remote regions, particularly in the Yukon and in Saskatchewan beyond Regina and Saskatoon. It's certainly worth booking far ahead for a night or two in the Canadian Rockies or in delightful Dawson City. If your budget allows, consider a luxurious log cabin at **Jasper Park Lodge** (fairmont.com/jasper) or check into unique gold-rush digs in Dawson, such as the **Midnight Sun Hotel** (midnightsunhotel.ca).

Resources

Travel Alberta (travelalberta.com) Comprehensive selection of things to see and do in the Canadian Rockies and beyond.

Discover Saskatoon (tourismsaskatoon.com) A one-stop shop of trip-planning resources for Saskatchewan's favorite city.

Travel Yukon (travelyukon.com) Handy website showing you how to plan your up-north adventure.

10

Dinosaurs, Hoodoos & the Wild West

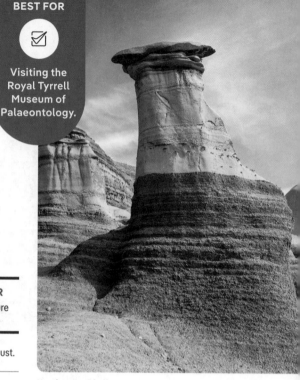

BEST FOR

Visiting the Royal Tyrrell Museum of Palaeontology.

DURATION	DISTANCE	GREAT FOR
2–3 days	1020km/634 miles	Culture, Nature

BEST TIME TO GO	Best driven between June and August.

Hoodoo, Drumheller

This road trip has a lot of driving but the payoff is seeing some of the most stunning historical sites Canada has to offer. However, we'd be remiss if we didn't point out that you also get to climb the wazoo of the world's biggest dinosaur and stare out at the town of Drumheller from between its fearsome, gaping jaws.

Link Your Trip

11 Icefields Parkway

After reaching the Cowboy Trail (stop 10), it's another three hours west northwest to stunning Lake Louise and the beginning of this outdoors-loving road trip.

12 Explore Southern Saskatchewan

From Lethbridge (stop 8), drive three hours east to Maple Creek and the start of this grasslands and forest journey.

01 **HORSESHOE CANYON**
Head east! Leave Calgary behind and almost immediately you'll feel like time's slowing down. It's all flat farmland out here, with rolling hills and big, big sky. The placid monotony is what makes the Badlands so impressive. The multicolored hills descend into beautiful Horseshoe Canyon (Hwy 9), where there are well-maintained hiking trails, restrooms and even a **helicopter viewing option** (mvheli.com). Whether you stretch your legs a bit or jump into the helicopter for a bird's-eye view, it's a nice introduction to the landscape in these parts that will only get better as you continue the drive.

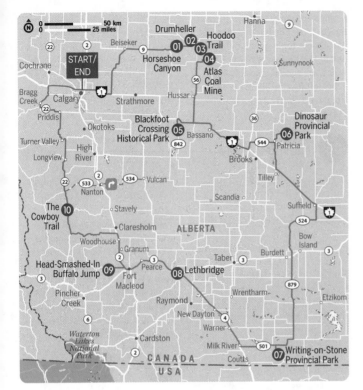

03 HOODOO TRAIL

You'll see instantly why this stretch of road is called the Hoodoo Trail: like something from a Dr Seuss book, hoodoos rise up on either side of the river – majestic, strange shapes created by erosion of the substrate around a flat rock. This gives them the shape of a king oyster mushroom: a wide cap at the top, a narrower, smooth, even delicate neck below, which gradually becomes broader as it joins the riverbed or cliffs.

The **Rosedale Suspension Bridge** is a lovely excuse to get out of the car, bringing you over the river to a hillside (that's often slippery!) with some walking trails and viewpoints.

THE DRIVE

Keep going on Rte 56 for now. In a few kilometers you'll see the town of East Coulee on your left. A little past that, on the right and across the river, is the weird shape of the Atlas Coal Mine's tipple, seeming too rickety to even stand.

04 ATLAS COAL MINE

At the **Atlas Coal Mine** (atlascoalmine. ab.ca), you can tour the mine shaft and tipple, and even ride an above-ground coal train for a bit, learning about the history and the workers here. For adults there's an 'Unmentionables' tour, discussing the more sordid side of Atlas' history. Plan on spending an hour here if you want to do a tour, though you can just peek at the gift shop or marvel at the tipple for free from the parking lot.

If history's your thing, you'll also want to stop at the **East Coulee School Museum** (ecs museum.ca). The museum has

THE DRIVE

Back in the car, drive just 18km more and you'll be in Drumheller. It's essentially a straight shot on Rte 9 all the way; just be sure to turn left (east) when you leave the canyon.

02 DRUMHELLER

This tiny town is big on just one thing: dinosaurs. Head straight to the **Royal Tyrrell Museum of Palaeontology** (tyrrellmuseum.com) and plan on spending at least three hours here, more if you have kids who want to make a fossil cast or participate in other activities. Take your time wandering around this incredible museum, filled with some of the world's best examples of the dinosaur age.

At the **World's Largest Dinosaur**, just a few minutes down the road in the center of town, you can climb in near the tail, ahem, and ascend until you're looking out through the mouth. It's good ole hokey fun at its best.

If you're hungry, swing by **Café Olé** (facebook.com/cafeoledrum) and grab some soup, a sandwich, a smoothie or some coffee for the road, then hit the trail again.

THE DRIVE

The Hoodoo Trail, mainly Rte 56, runs for about 25km along the Red Deer River. Just head south out of Drumheller rather than back the way you came.

fascinating historical details about a real school that's been preserved and the lives of people in the town; there's a good cafe inside (if you didn't eat in Drumheller).

THE DRIVE
Don't cross back over the river, but head up the coulee on Rte 569, saying goodbye to the hoodoos (for now). At the church in Dalum, turn left onto Rte 56 S. Follow it for 52km until you hit Hwy 1. Turn right, then after 16km jog left onto Rte 842. Expect to see prairie dogs and many hawks.

05 BLACKFOOT CROSSING HISTORICAL PARK

Sitting on the top of a lovely hill that extends down into a valley, **Blackfoot Crossing Historical Park** (blackfootcrossing.ca) is worth the $5 per person admission fee to wander around outside, even if you don't see the museum. There are hiking trails and a tipi village, and bear sightings from time to time, but the real gem is the visitor center and museum, built with great care to make it blend into not just the landscape, but also the culture of the Blackfoot people.

Inside, part of it is shaped like a tipi. There's a wall of windows that look over the valley, and you feel almost hawk-like staring outside. The entryway has a shade made from giant feathers – invoking the feathered headdresses that First Nations peoples wore. Inside, the history of what these people had, and what they lost, as settlers actively or passively took away their land and culture, is very poignant, staying with you long after you leave.

THE DRIVE
Head north on Rte 842, turn right onto Hwy 1 E, then zip through prairies and small towns until you hit Rte 36 N. Turn left and drive for 6km before turning right onto Rte 544 E. This merges with Rte 876, which you should follow when it veers left (north). There are signs from there (you're only a few minutes away).

06 DINOSAUR PROVINCIAL PARK

This Badlands area is a jaw-dropping collection of hills and valleys that contain the highest concentration of dinosaur fossils in the world. That's right, in the world. It's so easy to find fossils that you'll likely find some yourself if you take a guided tour. Set this up at the **Dinosaur Visitors Centre** (albertaparks.ca). You can also see videos explaining the area and (if it's been a full day) camp.

The finds and history of this area can't be understated: some of the world's best-preserved, most complete dinosaur skeletons were here. So many, in fact, that scientists decided to stop excavating certain ones, leaving them in the ground undisturbed.

THE DRIVE
Get back on Hwy 1 and continue east to Suffield. Turn right, take Range Rd 93 to Rte 524 W, turn right again, and then go left (south) onto Rte 879. Follow that for almost 100km, at which point you'll see signs as you turn right onto Rte 501. Drive 20km and turn left onto Rte 500 S…and you're there.

07 WRITING-ON-STONE PROVINCIAL PARK

At **Writing-on-Stone Provincial Park** (albertaparks.ca) you'll say hello to hoodoos again. There's a great self-guided hike that brings you past some of the best petroglyphs and the indescribable hoodoos, and along a riverbank. You can take a guided tour to some of the best (and protected) glyphs, and the **visitor center** has lots of information about the area, the people who may have made the glyphs and more.

There's a **campground** (albertaparks.ca) here as well, but nothing to eat, so it's better to push on for another 1½ hours to Lethbridge.

THE DRIVE
Heading in a general northwest direction, you'll go another 128km. Rte 500 takes you back to Rte 501, where you'll turn left and follow it west for 32km until it intersects with Rte 4. Turn right (there's a small jog at Railway Rd) and follow Rte 4 all the way to Lethbridge, about 78km away.

08 LETHBRIDGE

Plan to overnight in Lethbridge, Alberta's third-largest city, which still feels like a tiny rural town. When you're ready, head to **Fort Whoop-Up** (fort.galtmuseum.com) and get a feel for what Wild West living was like. There are wagon rides, exhibits, and a gift store with minerals and raccoon-skin hats and the like. Also stop by the **Helen Schuler Nature Centre & Lethbridge Nature Reserve** (lethbridge.ca/nature), meandering the paved walking trails looking for porcupines, deer and other denizens of the riparian woods.

THE DRIVE
Head west for about half an hour, returning to seemingly endless prairies and canola fields. Hop on Rte 3 for 45km, then get on Rte 2 N at Fort Macleod. After just 2km,

WHY I LOVE THIS TRIP

Ray Bartlett, writer

This trip is what I think of when I say 'I love Alberta.' You simply can't get more classic, wonderful, majestic or amazing than what you'll see on this giant loop, which takes in nearly 1000km of Canada's most impressive natural wonders: dinosaurs, fossils, haunting Indigenous legacies, the iconic Wild West that still exists today as it has for centuries. It's all here.

turn left onto Rte 785 and follow it until you see signs on the right for the Head-Smashed-In Buffalo Jump parking area.

09 **HEAD-SMASHED-IN BUFFALO JUMP WORLD HERITAGE SITE**

The **museum and visitor center** (headsmashedin.ca) here are so well blended into the landscape that you could easily drive past without noticing them, were it not for the large Head-Smashed-In Buffalo Jump signage. Inside, you'll find a stunning depiction of all aspects of Blackfoot culture, including the buffalo jump, which involved – when conditions were just right – herding the bison to stampede over cliffs, fatally injuring themselves by the hundreds or thousands. Start by taking a walk out to the 'kill site,'

Photo Opportunity

The painted, eerie, fossil-strewn hills of the Badlands.

where the buffalo plummeted. Then go back inside, and level by level, you'll see the complete picture of Blackfoot life, culture, religion and the rituals around the sacred buffalo jump.

THE DRIVE
Heading north now, retrace your steps to Rte 2 N, then use any of the rural side roads to get to Rte 22, which parallels Rte 2. Rte 22, aka the Cowboy Trail, was an old wagon route, now known for its tourist sites and scenic beauty.

10 **THE COWBOY TRAIL**
Only an hour's drive from Calgary, the **Bar U Ranch** (parkscanada.gc.ca/baru) is one of the key reasons this stretch of Rte 22 is known as the Cowboy Trail. It's a preserved historic site, one of the only parks that commemorates the vital importance of ranching in Alberta's history.

This spot is a unique combination of part living-history museum, part gallery, part exhibition, and a stop will bring all kinds of Western ranch life and livelihood into clear detail. See cabins and other buildings that have been meticulously preserved.

It's a taste of the West that once was the norm for this area; now, like the dinosaurs, the petroglyphs and the buffalo jumps, it has become a cherished, revered part of the past.

Head-Smashed-In Buffalo Jump

JEFF WHYTE/SHUTTERSTOCK ©

THE DRIVE

Hop in the car, set your sights on Calgary and hit the gas. You're only an hour away. The prettiest way back is also the easiest – stay on Rte 22 all the way to Hwy 1, passing through Turner Valley, Priddis and Bragg Creek. Turn right onto Hwy 1 and you'll be back in Calgary in no time.

DETOUR

Vulcan

Start: 10 The Cowboy Trail

You've been driving back through time this whole trip, so why not detour and head into the future for a bit? The town of Vulcan, a short detour from the Bar U Ranch, will let you do just that. Though the town's name had absolutely nothing to do with *Star Trek* (it was named for the Roman god of fire), that didn't stop the town of fewer than 2000 residents rebranding it the 'Official Star Trek Capital of Canada.'

Now, with a statue of the *Starship Enterprise* for folks to take selfies in front of, a tourism center shaped like a spacecraft, and even the streetlights made to look like the *Enterprise,* it's pretty clear they're in deep on the theme. It's hokey, sure, but it's also a fun diversion, and you can even don costumes and have your photo taken, then have the image digitally placed onto *Star Trek*–themed backgrounds. Ever wanted to sit in Kirk's chair? Voilà! You just did!

And it's become evermore popular with die-hard Trekkies. Leonard Nimoy himself came here in 2010. In addition to the ship, there's a bust of Spock, and the town hosts a Vul-Con convention each year. Vul-Con... get it?

From Rte 2 take Rte 533 and Rte 534. Vulcan is about a 30-minute drive.

WIRESTOCK CREATORS/SHUTTERSTOCK ©

Horned lark

COMMON ANIMALS OF THE PRAIRIES

You won't be able to miss the **prairie dogs**, and we may mean that literally – some of them seem hell bent on diving underneath your vehicle. Slow down though, and it's not just prairie dogs you'll see. There's a host of other cool animals to look for as well.

Ducks, **grebes**, **herons** and **avocets** line the edges of nearly every pasture pond.

Horned larks, a common bird in the area, so named for the two prominent 'horns' (feather tufts, really) that stick up on either side of their ears.

Hawks, **vultures** and even **eagles** soar overhead – look for the characteristic 'v' of a vulture's wings to tell it from its raptor cousins.

Coyotes and **foxes** are shy but not uncommon. Look for them slinking around near fences or across fields, especially at dawn or dusk.

Pronghorn antelope, the fastest land animal in North America, which can run faster than 97 km/h. Spy them in the middle of fields. At a distance they have a much pinker color than deer or elk.

Another ungulate, the **moose**, is unmistakable – the dark chocolate coat, the large rack on males and the beard are all distinctive.

11

Icefields Parkway

BEST FOR

BEST FOR

Walking on the ice at Athabasca Glacier.

Peyto Lake

DURATION	DISTANCE	GREAT FOR
2 days	230km/143 miles	Families, Nature

BEST TIME TO GO	June through September for best weather and road conditions.

No North American road trip compares to the Icefields Pkwy. Smack along the Continental Divide, this 230km odyssey leads you through one of the least-developed stretches of Canada's magnificent Rocky Mountain wilderness. Along the way you'll pass jewel-hued glacial lakes, roaring waterfalls, unbroken virgin forest and a relentless succession of shapely mountain crags, culminating in the awe-inspiring Columbia Icefield. At every turn, spontaneous wildlife sightings are a distinct possibility.

Link Your Trip

08 Circling the Rockies

Continue exploring Canada's national parks on this scenic ramble through Banff, Kootenay and Yoho. Join the route in Lake Louise.

09 Around the Kootenays

Get off-the-beaten-track amid the small towns and lakes of British Columbia's Monashee, Selkirk and Purcell Mountains. Start in Golden, 84km west of Lake Louise.

01 **LAKE LOUISE**

Considered by many the crown jewel of Banff National Park, Lake Louise is nearly impossible to describe without resorting to shameless clichés. This serene, implausibly turquoise lake spreads out elegantly below a stately amphitheater of finely sculpted mountains, with Victoria Glacier gleaming high above it all on the opposite shore. You could easily spend an entire morning gazing at the lake, but anyone with a penchant for hiking should head off to explore the surrounding trails. The most famous leads 4km uphill to the historic **Lake Agnes teahouse** (lakeagnesteahouse.com),

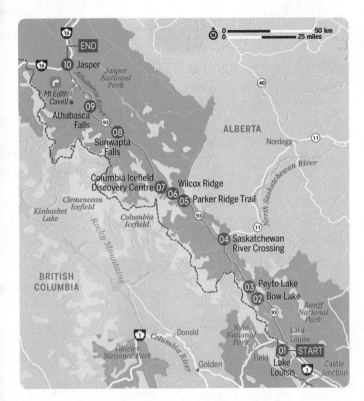

Map scale: 0 — 50 km / 0 — 25 miles. N

END — Jasper 16, 10 Jasper — Jasper National Park

Mt Edith Cavell • — 09

Athabasca Falls — 93 — 08 Sunwapta Falls

Columbia Icefield Discovery Centre — 07 06 — Wilcox Ridge — 05 Parker Ridge Trail

Clemenceau Icefield — Kinbasket Lake — Columbia Icefield — 93

ALBERTA — Nordegg ○ 11 — 40

North Saskatchewan River

11 — 04 Saskatchewan River Crossing

BRITISH COLUMBIA — Rocky Mountains

03 Peyto Lake — 02 Bow Lake — 93 — Banff National Park

Donald — Columbia River — Yoho National Park — Lake Louise

Glacier National Park — Golden — Field — Lake Louise — 01 START — Castle Junction — 1

complete with stone fireplace and majestic views. At the time of research, the hotel and restaurant had just reopened after renovations. Usually, non-hotel guests can stop in here for breakfast or return at night to dine on elk burgers or crispy steelhead trout beneath the watchful eye of moose, wolverines and other hunting trophies. Guests get seating priority; reserve ahead.

THE DRIVE
Your next stop is just a short 7km up the hill. Get back on the Icefields Pkwy and climb north to Bow Summit. Here, follow the signs on the left for Peyto Lake and park in the first (lower) parking lot.

03 PEYTO LAKE
You'll have already seen the indescribably vibrant blue color of Peyto Lake in a thousand publicity shots, but there's nothing like gazing at the real thing – especially since the viewing point for this lake is from a lofty vantage point high above the water. The lake gets its extraordinary color from sunlight hitting fine particles of glacial sediment suspended in the water. The lake is best visited in the early morning, between the time the sun first illuminates the water and the first tour bus arrives.

From the bottom of the lake parking lot, follow a paved trail for 15 minutes up a steady gradual incline to the wooden platform overlooking the lake. From here you can return to the parking lot or continue uphill for more fine views from the Bow Summit Lookout trail.

THE DRIVE
Head north on the Icefields Pkwy and enter the Mistaya Valley watershed. After 16km, pass

where you can rejuvenate with scones and hot tea before continuing up to the top of the Big Beehive for spellbinding views back down over blue-green Lake Louise.

THE DRIVE
Lake Louise sits a stone's throw from the southern entrance to the Icefields Pkwy. Follow the Trans-Canada Hwy a mere 2km west, then take the first exit, purchase (or display) your park entrance pass at the Icefields Pkwy entrance booth, and begin your northward journey into the majestic Rockies, turning left after 37km at the parking lot for Num-Ti-Jah Lodge.

02 BOW LAKE
Ringed by massive peaks and tucked beneath the imposing **Crowfoot Glacier**, Bow Lake is one of the prettiest sights in the Canadian Rockies. Early Banff entrepreneur and wilderness outfitter Jimmy Simpson built his pioneering Num-Ti-Jah Lodge here in 1923 – 12 years before the Icefields Pkwy itself – and it still stands today, its carved-wood interior full to the brim with backcountry nostalgia, animal heads and photos from the golden age.

The hotel's rustic yet elegant **Elkhorn Dining Room** (num-ti-jah.com) lets you step back in time to Simpson's world,

Waterfowl Lakes on your left, a good place to stretch your legs and soak up more views. Another 19km north, just before Saskatchewan River Crossing, pause on the bridge over the North Saskatchewan River for dramatic views of the river meandering out toward the prairies.

04 SASKATCHEWAN RIVER CROSSING

This junction of Hwy 93 (the Icefields Pkwy) and Hwy 11 (the David Thompson Hwy) marks the site where 19th-century fur trappers crossed the North Saskatchewan River on their way through the Rockies to British Columbia. Today, just west of the junction, you'll find interpretive historical displays, along with a **motel** (thecrossingresort. com), restaurant and gas station – the only facilities between Lake Louise and the Columbia Icefield.

THE DRIVE
Follow the parkway north along the North Saskatchewan River valley towards an imposing mountain wall. Near the 30km mark, a huge hairpin bend signals the beginning of the ascent to Sunwapta Pass. Stop at the Bridal Veil Falls parking area for fine views back down the valley you're leaving behind. After 38km you'll reach Parker Ridge parking area.

05 PARKER RIDGE TRAIL

If you only do one hike along the Icefields Pkwy, make it the Parker Ridge Trail. It's short enough to crack in an afternoon, but leads to one of the most impressive lookouts of any of Banff's day hikes, with a grandstand view of Mt Saskatchewan, Mt Athabasca and the gargantuan Saskatchewan Glacier. From the parking lot the trail runs through

a narrow wood before emerging on the hillside and entering a long series of switchbacks. Crest the ridge at the 2km mark, to be greeted by a blast of arctic wind and an explosive panorama of peaks and glaciers.

To the west loom Mts Athabasca and Andromeda, and just to their south is the gleaming bulk of the Saskatchewan Glacier, which lurks at the end of a deep valley. At almost 13km long, the glacier is one of the longest in the Rockies, but it's actually just a spur from the massive 230-sq-km Columbia Icefield that lies to the north. For the best views, follow the trail southeast along the edge of the ridge.

THE DRIVE
A short drive northwest on the Icefields Pkwy brings you to your next stop. Shortly after crossing Sunwapta Pass and passing from Banff National Park into Jasper National Park, look for signs for Wilcox Campground on your right and park at the Wilcox Ridge trailhead.

TOP TIP:
Spotting Wildlife

To increase your odds of seeing wildlife, travel the Icefields Pkwy in the early morning or late afternoon. Top areas for wildlife-spotting include Tangle Falls (137km north of Lake Louise) and the Goats & Glaciers Viewpoint (195km north of Lake Louise).

06 WILCOX RIDGE

One of Jasper's most accessible high country walks is this 9km out-and-back jaunt to Wilcox Ridge. From the trailhead, the path climbs rapidly above the treeline, reaching a pair of red chairs after 30 minutes, where you can sit and enjoy fine Athabasca Glacier views.

If you've had enough climbing, you can simply return from here to the parking lot. Otherwise continue ascending, gazing down over a river canyon on your left as you traverse wide-open meadows to reach Wilcox Pass (2370m) at the 3.2km mark. Here you'll turn left, following the undulating trail another 1.3km to reach the Wilcox Ridge viewpoint. Up top, dramatic, near-aerial views of the Athabasca Glacier unfold across the valley. To return to the parking lot, simply retrace your steps downhill.

THE DRIVE
Drive 2.5km west along the Icefields Pkwy to the Columbia Icefield Discovery Centre.

07 COLUMBIA ICEFIELD DISCOVERY CENTRE

The massive green-roofed **Columbia Icefield Discovery Centre** marks your arrival at the Icefield Pkwy's star attraction, the **Athabasca Glacier**.

The glacier has retreated about 2km since 1844, when it reached the rock moraine on the north side of the road. To reach its toe (bottom edge), walk from the Icefield Centre along the 1.8km Forefield Trail, then join the 1km Toe of the Glacier Trail. You can also park at the start of the latter trail. Visitors are

Parker Ridge Trail

allowed to stand on a small roped section of the ice, and you should not attempt to cross the warning tape – the glacier is riddled with crevasses.

To walk safely on the Columbia Icefield, you'll need to enlist the help of **Athabasca Glacier Icewalks** (icewalks.com), which supplies all the gear you'll need and a guide to show you the ropes. Its basic tour is three hours; there's a six-hour option for those wanting to venture further out onto the glacier.

The other, far easier (and more popular) way to get on the glacier is via the **Columbia Icefield Adventure** (banffjaspercollection.com/attractions/columbia-icefield) tour. A giant all-terrain vehicle known as the Ice Explorer grinds a track onto the ice, where it stops to allow

Photo Opportunity

The glacial blue-green surface of Peyto Lake.

you to go for a 25-minute wander on the glacier. Dress warmly, wear good shoes and bring a water bottle so you can try some freshly melted glacial water. Tickets can be bought at the Icefield Centre or online; tours depart every 15 to 30 minutes.

Snacks and meals are available at the **Columbia Icefield Discovery Centre dining room** (banffjaspercollection.com), a rather humdrum mall-like affair catering to bus tourists.

THE DRIVE
Begin your long descent down the Athabasca River valley, following the parkway north. Soon after leaving the Columbia Icefield Discovery Centre, watch for Tangle Falls on your right. Bighorn sheep are commonly sighted here. At the 49km mark, follow signs left off the main highway to the Sunwapta Falls parking lot.

08 SUNWAPTA FALLS
Meaning 'turbulent water' in the language of the Stoney First Nations, the 18m Sunwapta Falls formed when the glacial meltwaters of the Sunwapta River began falling from a hanging valley into the deeper U-shaped Athabasca Valley. The falls are a magnificent sight as they tumble into a deep narrow gorge; stand on the bridge above for the best views. Afterwards you

Maligne Canyon Wilderness Kitchen, Jasper

can stop in for a snack, a meal or an overnight stay at the **Sunwapta Falls Rocky Mountain Lodge** (sunwapta.com/restaurant).

🚗 THE DRIVE
Return to the main highway and drive 24km north. Turn left onto Hwy 93A, following signs for the Athabasca Falls parking area.

09 ATHABASCA FALLS
Despite being only 23m high, Athabasca Falls is Jasper's most dramatic and voluminous waterfall, a deafening combination of sound, spray and water. The thunderous Athabasca River has cut deeply into the soft limestone rock, carving potholes, canyons and water channels. Interpretive signs explain the basics of the local geology. Visitors crowd the large parking lot and short access trail. It's at its most ferocious during summer.

🚗 THE DRIVE
You're on the home stretch. A mere 30km jaunt north takes you to Jasper townsite. About 6km before town, you'll cross the Athabasca River and bid farewell to the Icefields Pkwy.

🏳 DETOUR
Mt Edith Cavell
Start: 09 Athabasca Falls

Rising like a snowy sentinel west of the Icefields Pkwy, Mt Edith Cavell (3363m) is one of Jasper National Park's most distinctive and physically arresting peaks. What it lacks in height it makes up for in stark, ethereal beauty. The mountain is famous for its flowery meadows and wing-shaped Angel Glacier.

It was named in honor of a humanitarian British nurse, who was executed by a German firing squad during WWI after helping to smuggle more than 200 wounded Allied soldiers into neutral Holland.

Sunwapta Falls

To get here, leave the Icefields Pkwy at the Athabasca Falls turnoff and follow Hwy 93A north 18km, then turn left onto sinuous Edith Cavell Rd, following it until it dead ends at a parking lot. To return to the main route, retrace your steps north on Edith Cavell Rd, then turn left onto Hwy 93A for 5km to its junction with the Icefields Pkwy.

10 JASPER
With a long and fascinating history that has included fur trappers, explorers, railway workers and some of the Canadian Rockies' earliest tourists, Jasper is the hub town for Jasper National Park. Less than 5000 residents live here year-round, but it feels like a major metropolis after the long journey through the Canadian wilderness. Celebrate with dinner at one of Jasper's diverse selection of eateries: lamb shank or coconut seafood at **Raven Bistro** (theravenbistro.com), Greek food at **Something Else** (something elserestaurant.com), a vegan 'dragon bowl' at **Olive Bistro** (olivebistro.ca), a slow-cooked barbecue at **Maligne Canyon Wilderness Kitchen** (banffjaspercollection.com) or burgers and microbrews at **Jasper Brewing Co** (jasperbrewingco.ca). Afterwards, settle in for the night at one of the many local cabins or bungalows.

12

Explore Southern Saskatchewan

DURATION	DISTANCE	GREAT FOR
3–4 days	688km/428 miles	Culture, Families

BEST TIME TO GO	June to August when things are up and running.

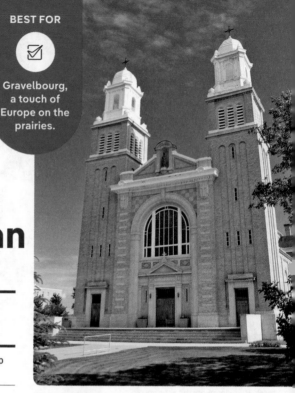

Our Lady of the Assumption Co-Cathedral, Gravelbourg (p92)

The province's south is often regarded as boring flat prairies to be raced through as fast as possible, but the backroads to Regina offer up some spirited little communities with surprisingly interesting things going on. Give yourself a few days from the Alberta border and go on a voyage of discovery through the small towns, parks and historic sites on your way to the provincial capital.

Link Your Trip

10 Dinosaurs, Hoodoo & the Wild West

Drive the Southern Saskatchewan itinerary in reverse, then continue from Maple Creek west to Lethbridge (stop 08) for the last part of this fossil and Wild West road trip.

13 North from Saskatoon

Head north after exploring the south by driving from Regina to Saskatoon.

01 **MAPLE CREEK**
If you've come from Calgary or points west on the Trans-Canada Hwy (Hwy 1), about 30km east of the Alberta border, head 8km south on Hwy 21 to find the town of Maple Creek. Founded in 1883, this small town is on the railroad main line and makes a good stop. Jasper St, the town's main shopping street, is a nice stroll. Maple Creek is a gateway to Cypress Hills Interprovincial Park, south of town. The park has two large blocks of land separated by about 20km. The Western Block, half of which is in neighboring Alberta, is hard to

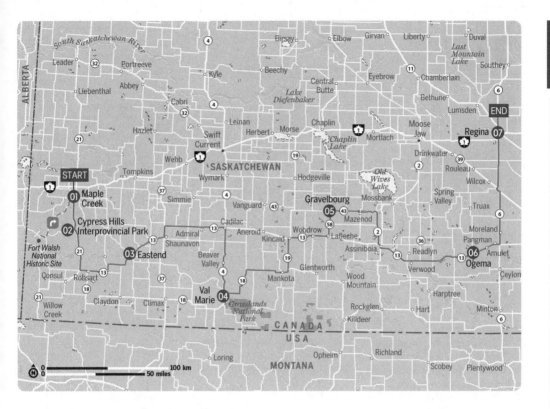

access, with few facilities apart from Fort Walsh, while the Central Block has year-round access and plenty of human-made fun. Eat in town at the **Rockin' Horse Cookhouse & Bar** (the horse.ca) and if you're looking for a good coffee, head to **Shop Bakery & Deli** (facebook.com/theshopmc).

THE DRIVE

Drive south on Hwy 21 for about 20 minutes (40km), trying to avoid countless gophers on the sealed road, to get to the Cypress Hills Interprovincial Park Central Block turnoff. It's 5km from there on Hwy 221 to the park entrance.

DETOUR

Fort Walsh National Historic Site
Start: 01 **Maple Creek**

Established in 1875 and operational for eight years, the **Fort Walsh outpost** (parkscanada.ca/fortwalsh) had a small yet significant role in the history of the west. It was originally built to curb the illegal whiskey trade, protect Canada's nearby border with the United States, and aid with indigenous policy. It was built after the Cypress Hills Massacre of 1873 in which 21 people were killed in a battle among American bison hunters, wolf hunters, whiskey traders and Assiniboine people – that brought about the establishment of the North-West Mounted Police (NWMP). Then, after the Battle of the Little Big

Horn, also known as Custer's Last Stand, Chief Sitting Bull and 5000 of his followers arrived in the area. The local mounties maintained peaceful relations with the Sioux while they remained in Canada. Though the fort was closed and dismantled in 1883, it was reconstructed in the 1940s to breed horses for the Royal Canadian Mounted Police.

Located 55km southwest of Maple Creek on sealed Hwy 271, Fort Walsh sits amid rolling prairies across two sections: the Western and the Central Block. Gap Rd, an unpaved, frequently boggy track links the two, but if you make the effort to go to Fort Walsh, you'd be best to return to Maple Creek before driving south on Hwy 21 to go to the Central Block.

02 CYPRESS HILLS INTERPROVINCIAL PARK

The Central Block of the inter-provincial park is fully developed with year-round facilities. It's much easier to access than the Western Block and perfect for families, with lots of things to do. There are places to stay like **Resort at Cypress Hills** and at **campgrounds** (cypress hills.com), plus a plethora of activities such as a swimming pool, zip line, golf, Segway, canoeing and paddleboats. There's a park visitor center next to Loch Leven, a general store, restaurants and one of the largest Dark Sky Preserves in the world for star-watching.

THE DRIVE
Back out on Hwy 21, head south until you hit Hwy 13 at a T-junction. The flat prairie road may seem endless, but eventually you'll reach the junction. Turn left and follow Hwy 13 east to Eastend. All up, the distance is 186km on good sealed roads.

03 EASTEND

Isolated in southwest Saskatchewan, Eastend would be tumbleweed quiet if not for the discovery of Scotty, the biggest T. rex ever to be found. Scotty was stumbled upon nearby in 1991 and the Royal Saskatchewan Museum's glitzy working lab **T-rex Discovery Centre** (royalsaskmuseum.ca/trex) has put Eastend on the tourist map. The Discovery Centre, carved into a hillside above town, has Scotty's massive skeleton, a variety of tours, a documentary film on Scotty's dig, plenty of other dinosaur discovery info and a gift shop. You can even see what the on-site paleontologists are up to.

Down in town, the **Eastend Historical Museum** (eastend historicalmuseum.com) has interesting fossils and bones, while its Machine Shed has all sorts of old transportation.

THE DRIVE
From Eastend, carry on driving on Hwy 13 to Shaunavon township, where the road turns north, then east to Cadillac. It's all Hwy 13 to here. At Cadillac, turn south on Hwy 4 to Val Marie. All up it's 128km of good, sealed roads from Eastend to Val Marie.

04 VAL MARIE

You've come to the tiny town of Val Marie, originally populated by French settlers, to visit Grasslands National Park. This is a unique opportunity to try to spot plains bison, reintroduced to the park after a 120-year absence, and to see black-footed prairie dogs in the wild. Make the most of your visit and follow the Ecotour Scenic Drive through the park. Be sure to visit the **Grassland National Park Visitors Centre** (pc.gc.ca/en/pn-np/sk/grasslands) in Val Marie before heading out.

Val Marie is also home to **Convent Inn** (convent.ca), offering a holier than thou sleeping experience with beds amid classic brickwork and beautiful hardwood floors in a convent built in 1939. In what was the brick Val Marie school-house (1927–85), the Friends of Grasslands, known as **Prairie Wind & Silver Sage** (pwss.org), have set up a museum, gallery, bookstore, gift shop and cafe. It's beautifully done, with free wi-fi, brewed coffees and daily homemade treats.

THE DRIVE
From Val Marie, take Hwy 18 to past Mankota, then turn north on Hwy 19 to Kincaid. At Kincaid, turn east on Hwy 13 to Lafleche, then north again on Hwy 58 to Gravelbourg. All up, it's 155km to Gravelbourg.

THE DISCOVERY OF 'SCOTTY'

Scotty (pictured right) is the biggest, most complete *Tyrannosaurus rex* skeleton ever found. The 67-million-year-old specimen, estimated to have weighed 8800kg, was found in August 1991 by Robert Gebhardt, a local high school principal. Gebhardt was with paleontologists Tim Tokaryk and John Storer on an exploratory expedition in the Frenchman River Valley when he stumbled across a T. rex tail vertebra on a cattle trail. The group later found a piece of dinosaur jaw, with teeth still attached, sticking out of the side of a hill. Scotty was duly named after the celebratory bottle of scotch used to toast the discovery.

T-Rex Discovery Centre, Eastend

Photo Opportunity

Scotty the T. rex at the T-rex Discovery Centre.

GRAVELBOURG

05 Delightful Gravelbourg is one of the last places you'd expect to find a taste of France, adrift on a vast sea of prairie. Lavish buildings designed to lure French settlers date to the early 1900s. Palatial buildings and houses are scattered along 1st Ave. The undisputed centerpiece of this *très jolie* little town is the disproportionately large and beautiful **Our Lady of the Assumption Co-Cathedral** (La Co-Cathédrale Notre Dame de l'Assomption; gravelbourg

cocathedral.com), built in 1919 in a Romanesque and Italianate style. It was designated a National Historic Site in 1995. Next door, the handsome yellow-brick former **Bishop's Residence** has been turned into a unique B&B with nine rooms. Take a look at individual rooms online before you book them. On the main street, pop in to see the friendly folk at the **Café de Paris** (facebook. com/CafeParisGravelbourg) for a light lunch and a delicious milkshake. It's right downtown; vintage details include a pressed-tin ceiling.

THE DRIVE

Head east out of Gravelbourg on Hwy 43, before turning south when you hit Hwy 2. At Assiniboia, turn east on Hwy 13 and follow it all the way to Ogema. All up, it's 150km on sealed roads.

OGEMA

06 You've come to tiny Ogema to ride the historic **Southern Prairie Railway** (southernprairierailway.com), which has been turning heads since its maiden voyage for the town's centenary in 2012. The informative 1½- to three-hour tours chug across the prairie

Southern Prairie Railway, Ogema

to explore an abandoned grain elevator and some even get robbed by train bandits. Special tours are held throughout the year, including the occasional stargazing expedition. To make the most of your explorations in southern Saskatchewan, get your dates sorted out to be in Ogema on a day when the Southern Prairie Railway is operating. In general, this is on Fridays, Saturdays and Sundays, as well as the special events.

Also in Ogema, the **Deep South Pioneer Museum** (ogema.ca) is an astounding collection of more than 30 preserved buildings, along with farming equipment, scores of vehicles and a huge volume of historic artifacts.

🚘 THE DRIVE

From Ogema, continue east on Hwy 13, then turn north when you hit Hwy 6. Head straight up this major highway to the provincial capital, Regina. All up, it's 116km to Regina.

07 REGINA

With a population of 230,000, Regina is definitely the 'big smoke' of southern Saskatchewan. It's the province's capital and boasts a bustling central city, heritage buildings, a beautiful park and lake area, and a plentiful choice of restaurants and pubs. Head to Tourism Regina at the Wascana Centre in **Wascana Park** for recommendations and walking tours.

STEPHAN OLIVIER/SHUTTERSTOCK ©

Bison, Grasslands National Park

SCENIC DRIVE: GRASSLANDS NATIONAL PARK

A top way to see Grasslands National Park is to do the well-organized self-guided Ecotour Scenic Drive. An explanation brochure, a map and good advice are all available at the Grassland National Park Visitors Centre (p90) in Val Marie, so be sure to go there first. From Val Marie, head east on Hwy 18 for 15km, then drive 5km south on a gravel road to reach the entrance to the park.

There are seven points of interest and two short walks on the ecotour. All the points of interest have full explanation boards. Do the full 80km drive through the park and back to Val Marie as a big loop in a couple of hours, or drive into Frenchman Valley campground and back (34km return from the park entrance).

A highlight is **Top Dogtown** (stop two), where prairie dogs line the side of the gravel road and yap at visitors. This is the only place in Canada where colonies of black-tailed prairie dogs still exist in their native habitat. There is also the possibility of spotting bison, with the herd now numbering more than 400 after plains bison were reintroduced to the park in 2005, after a 120-year absence. While there were more than 60 million bison roaming the Great Plains of North America before European contact, there were only a few hundred left by 1880. The bison live in a large territory, so count yourself lucky if you see one. This is also rattlesnake country, so keep your wits about you and watch where you step!

13

North from Saskatoon

DURATION	DISTANCE	GREAT FOR
3–4 days	448km/ 278 miles	Culture, Families, Nature
BEST TIME TO GO	June to August when the days are long and warm.	

This trip is for explorers, those who are willing to get off the beaten track and see what rural Saskatchewan and the north of the province has to offer. This is the land of the immigrants, and the further north you go, the more you'll feel like you are 'out there.' Prairies and flat farmland give way to the vast boreal forest, lakes and wilderness of the north.

Link Your Trip

10 Dinosaurs, Hoodoos & the Wild West

From Saskatoon, drive five hours southwest to Horseshoe Canyon where you can pick up this road trip replete with history and raw natural beauty.

12 Explore Southern Saskatchewan

Head to the province's south after exploring the north by driving to Maple Creek, near the Alberta border in southern Saskatchewan.

01 SASKATOON

Saskatoon, Saskatchewan's biggest city, with 270,000 people, is full of hidden treasures. Head into the downtown core and inner neighborhoods to get a sense of this vibrant city. The majestic South Saskatchewan River winds through downtown, offering beautiful, natural diversions. Leafy parks and rambling riverside walks help you make the most out of long, sunny summer days, and there are plenty of great spots to stop for a refreshing drink and a chat with locals.

JASON YODER/SHUTTERSTOCK ©

BEST FOR

☑

Keep your eyes open in Prince Albert National Park.

South Saskatchewan River, Saskatoon

Saskatoon knows how to heat up cold winter days and short summer nights, with a proud heritage of local rock and country music and a vibrant live-music scene. Local girl Joni Mitchell made good and there are plenty hoping to follow.

🎧 THE DRIVE
Head north out of Saskatoon on Hwy 11 until it splits with Hwy 12. Take Hwy 12 directly north past Martensville. About 30km north of Saskatoon, you'll find signage for Sunnyside Creamery on the right side of Hwy 12.

🧭 DETOUR
Manitou Beach
Start: 01 Saskatoon

Near the town of Watrous, Manitou Lake is a hidden gem. The lake is one of only three places in the world with Dead Sea–like waters full of minerals and salt, meaning that you can't sink! The others are Karlovy Vary in the Czech Republic and the Dead Sea itself. If the cool waters of the lake don't appeal, there's an indoor heated pool option in town too.

Right on the water, the village feels like a throwback to a simpler time. In the 1920s and '30s it was extremely popular, with thousands coming to enjoy the mineral waters and beach during summer. There were three large dance halls, two indoor bathhouses, restaurants, cafes and apparently bootleggers and a brothel too. Things went downhill during the Great Depression, but now there's a new energy in Manitou Beach to return to the glory days.

Today, you can browse the artwork of over 100 Saskatchewan artists at the **Little Manitou Art Gallery** (littlemanitouartgallery.com). You can stop in for a meal at the waterfront **Oda Coffee & Wine Bar**, and join the dance crowd at **Danceland** (danceland.ca). You can also overnight (or soak in the famed waters) at the **Manitou Springs Resort & Mineral Spa** (manitousprings.ca).

Manitou Beach is 120km southeast of Saskatoon, via Hwys 16 and 2.

02 SUNNYSIDE CREAMERY
This is a great opportunity to check out a Saskatchewan dairy farm and try fresh milk. Bas and Martha Froese-Kooijenga run 30 cows, individually named, on the farm that Martha's parents raised 12

Prince Albert Historical Museum (p99), Prince Albert

children. At **Sunnyside Cream-ery** (sunnysidedairyfarm.com), as well as selling dairy products the Farmyard Market has pierogies (filled dumplings) and pies, eggs and veggies. Pierogies are extremely popular throughout Saskatchewan. Try the freshest of milk for $2.50 per liter and chat with Martha and locals who buy produce here. The market also sells produce sourced from local farmers.

THE DRIVE
Head north on Hwy 12 from Sunnyside Creamery, turning on to Rte 312 after about 19km. Continue through tiny Waldheim, then turn left on Rte 312 to Rosthern.

03 ROSTHERN
Tiny Rosthern (pop 1700) is a good place to get a feel for rural north-ern Saskatchewan. Be sure to visit the **Mennonite Heritage Museum** (historicplaces.ca).

The first Mennonite settlers arrived in Rosthern in 1891 and this lovingly cared for little museum tells the story of the Mennonite community's com-mitment to the preservation of its identity. The building was the German-English Academy until 1963, established to provide in-struction in English, to preserve the German language, and to maintain the Mennonite religion and way of life.

On the main street, stop at the old train station. Here, at the **Station Arts Centre & Tea Room** (stationarts.com), is a beautiful gallery showing the works of local artists, plus a tea room offering lunch and baked snacks. There is also a 160-seat theater with a strong line-up of events, and a small museum in a train caboose (donated by Ca-nadian National Railway) on the tracks side of the station.

THE DRIVE
It's 19km direct from Rosthern to Duck Lake on Hwy 11.

04 DUCK LAKE INTERPRETIVE CENTER
This excellent **museum** (ducklakemuseum.com), just off Hwy 11, focuses on the preserva-tion of the Willow Cree First Na-tion, Métis and Pioneer cultures through stories and artifacts. A circular path around the gallery looks at the various groups, their religion, their education, the political period of upheaval around the rebellion of 1885 and the development of economic life. A stairway to the top of the museum's distinctive 24m tower reveals sweeping views.

THE DRIVE
From Duck Lake, Hwy 11 north will connect with Hwy 2 just short of Prince Albert. Hwy 2 then runs straight through Prince Albert. All up it's 44km to PA.

05 PRINCE ALBERT
Prince Albert (PA), Saskatchewan's third-biggest city, has a dilapidated yet evocative old brick downtown in a pretty location beside the North Saskatchewan River. Es-tablished in 1776 as a fur-trading post, PA was later named after Queen Victoria's husband, Prince Albert of Saxe-Coburg-Gotha, who died in 1861. Prince Albert became the capital of the District of Saskatchewan, a regional administrative division of what then constituted the Northwest Territories, and there were hopes for a great future. This ended in 1905 when Saskatchewan be-came a full province and Regina was chosen as the new provincial capital. PA's plans for greatness

Photo Opportunity

Reflections on a Prince
Albert National
Park lake.

were based on the hope that the Transcontinental Railway would pass through the city, but the Canadian Pacific Railway chose a more southerly route.

Make sure to visit the **Prince Albert Historical Museum** (historypa.com). This packed little museum is in what was the Central Firehall from 1912 until 1975, right on the banks of the North Saskatchewan River. It takes in many aspects of the town's long history.

A great place to stay here is **Keyhole Castle B&B** (keyhole castle.com). This is an opportunity to stay in an extraordinary 'castle,' built during Prince Albert's boom times of the early 1900s. In the East Hill neighborhood, it's a designated National Historic Site.

THE DRIVE
From Prince Albert, cross the river on the bridge (the only bridge for kilometers in each direction) and head directly north on Hwy 2 for 60km to Rte 264, the turnoff for Waskesiu in Prince Albert National Park. The park entry is about 5km off Hwy 2 and it's another 5km to Waskesiu Lake and township.

06 PRINCE ALBERT NATIONAL PARK
Prince Albert National Park is a jewel in the wild. Just when you thought the vast prairie would never end, the trees begin, signaling the start of the vast boreal forest. This national park is one of those special places that will give you the feeling

that you are truly on the edge of the known world. A forested sanctuary of lakes, untouched land and wildlife, the park puts the 'wild' back into 'wilderness.' Outdoor activities such as canoeing, hiking and camping are at their shining best here. There is a multitude of potential adventures to be had, whether it be the unforgettable 20km trek to Grey Owl's Cabin, a canoe trip or even just chilling out on a beach.

The quaint resort village of **Waskesiu Lake** is your base for exploration within the park. Make sure you drop in at the **Prince Albert National Park Visitor Center** (pc.gc.ca) for everything you need to know. There are campgrounds, and in Waskesiu, **Hawood Inn** (hawood.com) is a top place to stay. This family-run lodge right on the waterfront is a good spot to relax. There's a decent dining room and lounge, rooftop hot tubs, and nearby shops, restaurants and activities

For pizzas, burgers and beers, stop by **Pete's Terrace Restaurant and Bar** (facebook.com/ petesterrace), overlooking the lake waterfront in Waskesiu. Time it right for live music in summer – check out the Facebook page for concert information.

THE DRIVE
Back out on Hwy 2, you've got 180km of driving virtually straight north to what feels like the end of the line at La Ronge.

07 LA RONGE
La Ronge is the southern hub of the far north – your last chance for supplies before heading off the grid. It's a rough, basic town, popular with anglers, hunters and folks on the run. **Lac La Ronge Provincial Park** (tourismsaskatchewan. com) surrounds huge, island-filled Lac La Ronge and feels all-encompassing. It's great for fishing, canoeing and hikes among stubby pines. There are at least a hundred more lakes and more than a thousand islands. The park has five year-round campgrounds and endless backcountry camping. Before you head out, the legendary **Robertson's Trading Post** is the place to go if you're in the market for a bear trap, wolf hide or case of baked beans. If you need a place to stay, **Waterbase Inn** (water baseinn.ca) is a decent option. If it's quality home-style food served with a side of quirkiness that you're looking for, **Cravings Late Night Food** (facebook. com/airronge) will make sure you won't go hungry.

It's hard to believe that almost half of Saskatchewan still lies further north of here. This is frontier territory, the end of the paved road. If you're not skittish about extreme isolation and you're outfitted appropriately, then this is it! Self-sufficiency here is key: make sure you maintain your vehicle, have plenty of fuel, gear and supplies, and keep your head together.

Lac La Ronge Provincial Park

14

Klondike Highway

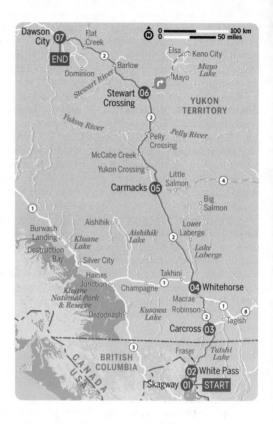

DURATION	DISTANCE	GREAT FOR
4–5 days	714km/443 miles	Culture, Families, Nature

BEST TIME TO GO	June to August when the days are long and warm.

Virtually the whole trip on the Klondike Hwy from Skagway, Alaska, through 56km of British Columbia, then through the Yukon Territory to Dawson City, is wonderful wilderness. These days it's an easy drive, but you'll still need to be prepared and to keep your eyes open and your wits about you – you never know what might pop out of the forest to cross the road.

Link Your Trip

07 Haida Gwaii Adventure

Ferry from Skagway, Alaska to Prince Rupert, BC, by the Alaska Marine Hwy system, then by BC Ferries to Skidegate on Haida Gwaii.

15 Dempster Highway

The start of the Dempster Hwy is 40km southeast of Dawson City.

01 SKAGWAY

At first sight, Skagway appears to be solely an amusement park for cruise-ship day-trippers, a million of whom disgorge onto its sunny boardwalks every summer. But, haunted by Klondike ghosts and beautified by a tight grid of handsome false-fronted buildings, this is no northern Vegas. Skagway's history is very real.

During the gold rush of 1898, some 40,000 stampeders passed through; they were a sometimes-unsavory cast of characters who lived against a backdrop of brothels, gunfights and debauched

BEST FOR

Camping along the way.

Historic train, Carcross

entertainment wilder than the Wild West. Today, the main actors are seasonal workers, waitstaff posing in period costume and storytelling national park rangers. Most of the town's important buildings are managed by the National Park Service and this, along with Skagway's location on the cusp of a burly wilderness with trails (including the legendary Chilkoot) leading off in all directions, has saved it from overt Disneyfication.

THE DRIVE
The first 23km of the drive is a steady climb on what is Hwy 98 on the Alaska side of the border. You're climbing from sea level in Skagway to 1003m at the pass. At the 11km mark you'll pass the US Customs Station, where all travelers entering the US must stop. You're heading out of the US and into Canada, so just drive on through.

02 WHITE PASS
The White Pass mountain summit and Summit Lake area more resembles a moonscape than any earthly landscape, with twisted trees, small lakes and barren foliage that create truly unique scenery. Take your time and stop at one of the many pullouts off the road to savor the surrounds. The US–Canada border is just past the pass – spot the signage and small obelisk flanked by US and Canadian flags. At the border you are passing into a different time zone – Canada Pacific time is one hour ahead of Alaska time – so don't forget to change your watch. And you're not in Yukon Territory yet – 56km of the Klondike Hwy is in British Columbia.

THE DRIVE
Continuing on what is now Canadian Hwy 2, the Canadian Customs Station is at Fraser, British Columbia; it's open 24 hours and all vehicles must stop for inspection. Bring your passport. You'll be in BC for a further 44km, with gorgeous views of Tutshi Lake. At 105km from Skagway, you'll arrive in Carcross.

03 CARCROSS
Long a forgotten gold-rush town, cute little Carcross (the name was shortened from

Caribou Crossing in 1902) is an evocative stop. There's a growing artisan community, old buildings are being restored and the site on Lake Bennett is superb – although Klondike prospectors who had to build boats here to cross the lake and head on to Dawson City didn't think so. The old train station has good displays on local history.

Just north of town, on the highway, is the **Carcross Desert**, proudly claimed as the world's smallest desert, covering less than 260 hectares. It's actually the remains of the sandy bottom of a glacial lake left after the last ice age. A dry climate and strong winds created the sand dunes and allow little vegetation to grow.

THE DRIVE
At 12km north of Carcross, pull off for a view of lovely Emerald Lake. At 53km from Carcross, the Klondike Hwy runs into the Alaska Hwy and joins it for 34km. You're about to hit the 'big smoke' of the Yukon – Whitehorse is 176km from Skagway and 71km from Carcross.

04 WHITEHORSE
The capital city of the Yukon Territory since 1953, to the continuing regret of much smaller and isolated Dawson City, Whitehorse is a hub for transportation. It was a terminus for the White Pass & Yukon Route railway from Skagway in the early 1900s, and during WWII a major center for work on the Alaska Hwy.

Whitehorse rewards the curious. It has a well-funded arts community, good restaurants and a range of accommodations. Take time out to visit **MacBride Museum of Yukon History** (macbride museum.com), which covers the gold rush, First Nations people, intrepid Mounties and more. Well

📷 Photo Opportunity
SS Klondike National Historic Site in Whitehorse

worth your time is the **SS Klondike National Historic Site** (pc. gc.ca). Carefully restored, this was one of the largest stern-wheelers used on the Yukon River. Built in 1937, it made its final run to Dawson City in 1955 and is now a National Historic Site.

THE DRIVE
Around 12km north of Whitehorse, the Klondike Hwy (Hwy 2) splits from the Alaska Hwy (Hwy 1) and heads more or less due north. About 7km from the junction, a well-signposted side road heads west to Takhini Hot Springs. Consider taking time for a dip here. Back on the Klondike Hwy, 166km from the junction, you'll reach Carmacks.

05 CARMACKS
This small village sits right on the Yukon River and is named for one of the discoverers of gold in 1896, George Washington Carmack. A rogue seaman wandering the Yukon, it was almost by luck that Carmack (with Robert Henderson, Tagish Charlie and Keish – aka Skookum Jim Mason) made their claim on Bonanza Creek. Considering the life of debauchery that followed, it's fitting that Carmack be honored by this uninspired collection of gas stations, stores and places to stay. Like elsewhere in the territory, residents here are keenly attuned to the land, which supplies them with game and fish throughout the year.

THE DRIVE
Continue north through constant wilderness on the Klondike Hwy for a further 180km.

06 STEWART CROSSING
Stewart Crossing is on the Stewart River, a tributary of the Yukon River, but there's not much to get excited about. Little more than a gas station and store, the village is also at the junction of the Klondike Hwy and the Silver Trail, which makes a 224km round-trip northeast to the village of Mayo and the mining town of Keno City.

THE DRIVE
Continue northwest for 180km to Dawson City. Around 24km from Stewart Crossing is Moose Creek Lodge, a top place to stay with comfy little cabins set back from the highway in the forest. About 40km short of Dawson City, you'll run into the Dempster Hwy, one to consider for your next adventure.

DETOUR
The Silver Trail
Start: 06 Stewart Crossing

As prospectors found it harder and harder to become rich and stake gold claims around Bonanza Creek near Dawson City after 1898, others searched further afield and by 1920, silver had been found at Keno Hill, 200km to the east, and 600 claims staked. A town built up, named after the gambling game Keno, popular in mining camps at that time.

Transporting the heavy ore was a problem though and horse-drawn sleighs were used to haul it to the Stewart River, where it was picked up by specially designed stern-wheeler paddle-steamers and shipped out, initially downriver to Dawson City, then all the way down the Yukon River and out to the Bering Sea, then to a

SS Klondike National Historic Site

EDB3_16/GETTY IMAGES ©

Klondike Hwy, Yukon

DO THE LOOP

The Klondike Hwy is an amazing drive, but most people end up going to Dawson City and then driving back down the same road to Whitehorse. For the adventurous, an exciting loop awaits to take you back to Yukon Territory's capital via Alaska (you'll need your passport).

From Dawson City, the George Black free car ferry crosses the Yukon River from the end of Front St to the scenic **Top of the World Highway** (Hwy 9). Only open in summer, the mostly gravel 107km-long road to the US border has superb vistas across the region.

You'll continue to feel on top of the world as you cross at the most northerly US–Canada border crossing at **Poker Creek**. On the US side, the first 19km connection to the intersection with the **Taylor Highway** (Hwy 5) is newly sealed and gives the impression that the easy roads may last forever.

It's time to go back to the gravel though! Some further 48km south from the intersection with the Taylor Hwy, over unsealed roads, you encounter **Chicken**. The little place was going to be called Ptarmigan, but locals didn't trust their spelling and pronunciation skills so went for Chicken instead.

Another 119km south, now on sealed roading, you reach the Alaska Hwy at **Tetlin Junction**, where a turn east takes you back to the Yukon. Just a tick west, **Tok** has services and motels. The only place between Dawson City and the Alaska Hwy to get fuel or food is in Chicken, so prepare well.

If you're heading east, back to Whitehorse, there are motels and eating places in **Beaver Creek**, just over the Alaska–Canada border and 156km away on the Alaska Hwy. From Beaver Creek, it's 292km to **Haines Junction** and 445km to **Whitehorse**.

smelter in San Francisco. The small town of Mayo built up as a transportation center on the Stewart River, where supplies were dropped off and the silver ore was picked up.

To see these mining communities, take the dead end Silver Trail (Hwy 11) northeast from Stewart Crossing. **Mayo** (population 450; villageofmayo. ca), formerly known as Mayo Landing, is 51km up paved Hwy 11 and is getting a new lease on life. It is the largest community in the region and has become a staging point for backcountry wilderness trips, canoeing, hiking, big-game hunting, fly-in fishing and more.

A further 61km up the now gravel Hwy 11 you'll find **Keno City**, site of the silver mine camp, the **Keno City Mining Museum** (yukonmuseums.ca), which houses a collection of artifacts, memorabilia and photographs that provide a snapshot of Keno's colorful past, and these days, about 20 people. The only way out is back down the road you came on.

07 DAWSON CITY

If you didn't know its history, Dawson City would be an atmospheric place in which to pause for a while, with a seductive vibe. That it's one of the most historic and evocative towns in Canada is like gold dust on a cake: unnecessary but damn nice.

Set on a narrow shelf at the confluence of the Yukon and Klondike Rivers, Dawson was the destination for Klondike Gold Rush prospectors. Today, you can wander the dirt streets of town, passing old buildings with dubious permafrost foundations, and discover Dawson's cultural life. While you're there, be sure to visit the **Bonanza Creek Discovery Site** (Bonanza Creek Rd). Who knows what you may stumble over?

15

Dempster Highway

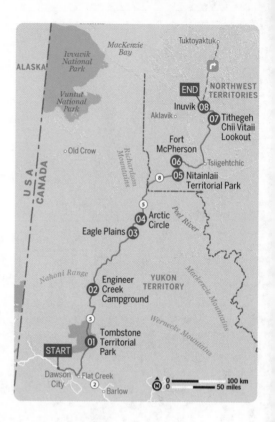

DURATION	DISTANCE	GREAT FOR
6–7 days	773km/480 miles	Nature

BEST TIME TO GO	June to September, when the road conditions are best.

Pristine Arctic scenery accompanies you on your journey to Inuvik, the largest northernmost settlement in the Northwest Territories. The only public highway to cross the Arctic Circle, the Dempster starts some 40km east of Dawson City, Yukon. Its name is uttered with awe by drivers in the know; this trip requires preplanning and is not to be taken lightly. One-way rental car drop-off fees are extortionate; prepare for a round trip.

Link Your Trip

07 Haida Gwaii Adventure

From Dawson City, drive eight hours southeast to Skagway, Alaska, and take the ferry to Prince Rupert, BC, via the Alaska Marine Hwy system. Then take a BC Ferry to Skidegate on Haida Gwaii.

14 Klondike Highway

Combining your road trip with a drive through the Yukon's gold rush country is easy; the Dempster meets the Klondike Hwy near Dawson City and continues south to the Yukon's capital, Whitehorse.

01 TOMBSTONE TERRITORIAL PARK

Some 130km from the start of the journey in Dawson City and accessed via an eponymous campground at Km 72, this 2200-sq-km park consists of a wilderness of rugged peaks, boreal forest and abundant wildlife, including grizzly bears, caribou and wolverines. You need to be wilderness-savvy and self-sufficient, and if you're looking to do full-day hikes here, you need to be prepared for the rough terrain and changeable weather.

At the campground there's an interpretive center that offers free guided walks from May to September,

BEST FOR

☑

Admiring the varied northern landscape of boreal forest, glacial rivers, rugged peaks and endless tundra.

Grizzly Lake, Tombstone Territorial Park

a wheelchair-accessible interpretive trail, a short loop trail and another one that skirts the North Klondike River. The full-service campsite is a good place to stay if you've set off late in the day from Dawson City, and it's worth lingering a day or two. There are also three basic backcountry campsites in the park, reachable on foot only and requiring advance reservations from late June to mid-September. In winter, the park is a popular day-trip destination from Dawson City for snowshoeing, skiing, snowmobiling and wildlife-spotting.

🚗 **THE DRIVE**
From Tombstone, it's 122km of gently winding road to Engineer Creek

Campground. At Km 82, you cross the North Fork Pass (1289m), the highest point of elevation on the Dempster Hwy and the first crossing of the Continental Divide. Spot the plaque at Km 117 that commemorates WJB Dempster, a sergeant of the Royal Mounted Police whose name the highway bears.

02 ENGINEER CREEK CAMPGROUND
Sitting below Sapper Hill – a collection of dolomite cliffs – this small serviced campground is open from May to September and is a popular day stop for those wanting to explore the rock 'forests' of the eroded ridge on foot and with bird-watchers keen to spot the

peregrine falcons and golden eagles that nest on the cliffs.

The Gwich'in name for Sapper Hill is Chü Akan (Beaver House Mountain). It's a reference to millennia past, when giant beavers roamed the land. 'Sapper' is the nickname for army engineers, and the hill is named for the Third Royal Canadian Army Engineers who constructed the Ogilvie Bridge.

🚗 **THE DRIVE**
The 175km drive from Engineer Creek winds its way through boreal forest, followed by rolling plains. It's worth stopping at the Ogilvie Ridge at Km 259 for far-reaching views of the Peel River, meandering tundra and bare, rocky hills in the distance.

Eagle Plains Hotel, Eagle Plains

03 EAGLE PLAINS

Congratulations: you've reached the halfway point! Like a beacon of light, Eagle Plains beckons weary travelers. Literally in the middle of nowhere, it consists of a motel-style hotel, open year-round, as well as a full-service garage with a mechanic and RV park and campground. Odds are that you'll have already suffered a puncture along the Dempster due to its mix of shale and gravel, so get your tires patched up here and fill up on gas – there isn't another gas station for almost 200km. **Eagle Plains Hotel** is a good place to unwind, chow down on poutine, burgers and other Canadian classics at the cafeteria-style restaurant, and admire the Gwich'in crafts on display in the common areas. There's usually a lively gaggle of other travelers here, their RVs parked outside, so go ahead and trade travel tips, as it's the most people you'll see for most of your drive up.

THE DRIVE

From Eagle Plains, the road winds its way for 36km to the Arctic Circle sign through a landscape of boreal forest. If it has been raining, be very careful just north of Eagle Plains, where a stretch of mostly dirt road turns into a mud slide, and if you're not careful, you can slide right off the steep side of the road.

04 ARCTIC CIRCLE

A prominent sign off the side of the highway, and display boards on local flora, fauna and the northern lights, announce your arrival at the Arctic Circle. Beyond this point, the sun doesn't set at summer solstice (June 21) and it doesn't rise on winter solstice (December 21). By this point, the endless boreal forest of northern Yukon has given way to low-growing dwarf trees and scrubland-covered hills. Between the Arctic Circle and Nitainlaii Territorial Park, your next stop, you'll cross the boundary between the Yukon and the Northwest Territories at Km 465. The time zone changes here; set your watch to one hour ahead.

THE DRIVE

From the Arctic Circle, the road winds its way for 141km through snow-topped hills and tundra. At Km 447, Rock River Campground sits in a steep gorge of the Richardson Mountains. Wright Pass Summit at Km 464 marks the Dempster's northernmost high point, while Midway Lake at Km 209 hosts an August music festival. At Km 539, board the free Peel River Ferry (9am to 12:30am) to cross the river and make the final 2km drive to Nitainlaii Territorial Park.

05 NITAINLAII TERRITORIAL PARK

Surrounded by white birch and spruce trees and perched on a bluff overlooking the slow-flowing waters of the Peel River, Nitainlaii Territorial Park is a good place to break your journey. To get here, you will have passed through some of the Dempster's most dramatic scenery of scrubland-covered, craggy hills and a myriad small lakes dotting the tundra.

For an engaging glimpse of the life of the Gwich'in Dene people, stop by the visitor center and peruse the displays on history, language and culture. There are 23 non-powered campsites here, plus washrooms, drinking water, a kitchen shelter and picnic area, and helpful staff.

THE DRIVE

It's a very short drive of just 9km through stunted boreal forest from Nitainlaii Territorial Park to Fort McPherson, the only settlement of any size before you finally reach Inuvik at the end of the Dempster.

Dempster Highway, near Eagle Plains

TOP TIP:
Self-Sufficiency

There is no cell phone reception for most of the drive, and few passing motorists, so be sure to take a satellite phone. The Dempster is also known as 'Puncture Central,' so take at least two spare tires and know how to change them. Food, water and a sleeping bag are essential supplies.

06 FORT MCPHERSON

This Tetl'it Gwich'in settlement, which was originally founded in 1849 as a fur trading post by a Hudson's Bay Company exporter, is a chilled-out place to spend an hour or two. It's worth stopping by **St Mathew's Anglican Church**, just off the main street, and the graveyard where you'll find the graves of the Lost Patrol, the four Mounties who set off for Dawson City in the winter of 1911 but never made it. Visit also the **Chii Tsal Dik Gwizheh Tourist & Heritage Centre** that introduces visitors to Gwich'in culture by organizing traditional dance demonstrations, walking tours, fish-cutting demos and more. Inside, you can peruse the Gwich'in-English dictionary and Gwich'in storybooks.

Fill up on gas here, as it's cheaper than in Inuvik or Eagle Plains.

Photo Opportunity

Standing next to the Arctic Circle sign at Km 403.

Sometimes the water levels of the Peel or Mackenzie Rivers are too high for the car ferries, in which case you have to overnight at the Peel River Inn.

THE DRIVE

From Fort McPherson, a 58km stretch of road winds its way through the tundra to the banks of the mighty Mackenzie River, where you have to take a free car ferry (9am to 12:30am June to mid-October). Alternatively, you can detour by ferry to the hunting, fishing and trapping Gwich'in settlement of Tsiigehtchic, across the river tributary from the highway, before crossing the Mackenzie. Continue for 103km to reach Tithegeh Chii Vitaii Lookout.

07 TITHEGEH CHII VITAII LOOKOUT

Part of Gwich'in Territorial Park that encompasses 880 sq km of the Mackenzie Delta – comprising rare Arctic ecosystems, limestone cliffs and a reversing river delta, this lookout sits at the edge of the cliffs overlooking **Campbell Lake**, an important bird and wood-frog habitat.

THE DRIVE

The last 33km stretch of your journey passes through a stretch of stunted dwarf boreal forest – dwarf birch and arctic willow. You'll drive by the Gwich'in Territorial Campground (Km 705), the Ehjuu Njik Wayside Park (Km 714), popular for Arctic grayling fishing, and the Jak Park Campsite (Km 731) – a favorite berrying spot for Inuvik residents.

08 INUVIK

A veritable metropolis by comparison to the one or two Gwich'in settlements you've passed through to get here,

Igloo church, Inuvik

Inuvik welcomes visitors with its northern charm, its igloo church and a grand choice of places to stay, from the homey **Andre's Place** and **Arctic Chalet** to the business-like **Nova Inn**. And since you're probably hankering after a hot meal, it's worth heading to **Alestine's** for some hearty home cooking or, if you're lucky enough to be staying at Andre's, you'll be treated to a gourmet, French-inspired meal. Inuvik is also the place to organize any manner of outdoor adventures, from husky sledding to boating on the Mackenzie Delta, to visiting remote northern national parks or driving the winter ice road to a remote Inuit community.

🅟 DETOUR
Tuktoyaktuk
Start: 08 Inuvik

The Inuvik–Tuktoyaktuk Hwy was first planned in the 1960s, and was finally completed and opened to the public in 2017. Since then there's been a steady stream of adventurers continuing the journey from the end of the Dempster Hwy at Inuvik all the way to the Arctic Ocean, some 144km north. Before the highway was completed, the Inuvialuit community of Tuk was relatively isolated, accessible either by flights over the tundra or an ice road in winter. Now, it's far easier for visitors to experience relatively traditional Inuit life through **Arctic Ocean Tuk Tours** (eileenjacob son@hotmail.com) and **Ookpik Tours and Adventures** (ookpiktours.ca), staying overnight in one of several B&Bs and checking out traditional sod houses and the icehouse where local hunters keep their catch. The drive out there is wonderful, too, passing through tundra covered in stunted tree growth and myriad small lakes, and skirting an impressive pingo (earth-covered ice hill) near the entrance to Tuk.

VERSHININ89/SHUTTERSTOCK ©

Jack and spare tire, essential for driving the Dempster

HOW TO DRIVE THE DEMPSTER

When to Go

From summer to early fall, driving conditions are easiest – though wildfires can be an issue in July and August, and September brings cooler weather. In the fall, you're likely to spot herds of migrating caribou. Avoid the spring thaw (late April to mid-June), since the route includes two car ferries, and winter freeze-up (mid-October to mid-December), when the highway is closed.

What to Bring

Two spare tires, jack and other tools Parts of the Dempster are covered in shale that's hard on your wheels.

Sleeping bag

Tent For taking advantage of the numerous, beautifully situated campgrounds.

Plenty of food and water Enough for at least three days.

Warm clothing For traveling any time of year.

Bug repellent and head net A must in summer.

Satellite phone

Dos and Don'ts

Do allow yourself at least six days for a round-trip drive up the Dempster. You can get from Dawson City to Inuvik in one day, but it's more relaxing and rewarding to camp and go hiking in various protected areas en route. For current road conditions, see dot.gov.nt.ca.

Don't abandon your vehicle if you break down.

Do be mindful of wildlife, such as grizzlies, and keep a safe distance. Stay in the car if you see one.

Do take all your trash with you, particularly if you camp.

KHAIRIL AZHAR JUNOS/SHUTTERSTOCK ©

Boldt Castle, Gananoque (p147)

Ontario

Explore

Ontario

A leaf-peeping diorama of endless woodlands where the foliage seems to have been painted every imaginable hue, Ontario is a profoundly immersive destination for nature-lovers. A few kilometers from big-city Toronto or national capital Ottawa, you'll soon find yourself sighing deeply in the backcountry, snapping panoramic forest selfies, gazing at mirror-calm lakes, and watching for a chittering surfeit of birdlife as well as larger locals, including the iconic moose. It's not all about nature here, though. You'll also discover fascinating small communities, welcoming artisanal food and wine pit stops, and diverse cultures that exemplify the heart of contemporary Canada.

Toronto

Canada's largest city (and home to its busiest airport), this glass-towered metropolis is packed with experiences for visitors keen to take the pulse of modern-day Canada. Add several days before or after your Ontario driving odyssey to hit famous museums and landmark attractions while also exploring cool neighborhoods such as Kensington Market, Yorkville and Queen West. Dining-wise, there's a full menu of top-notch restaurants and also a sparkling array of under-the-radar indie eateries, many reflecting Toronto's rich ethnic diversity – look for highly authentic dishes from Ethiopia, Argentina, South Korea and beyond. There's also a huge array of accommodations options here, but keep in mind that summer typically combines peak rates with low availability. Also consider timing your Toronto visit for a festival: there's a massive menu of big-ticket events and smaller neighborhood happenings to discover, especially from May to September.

Ottawa

While it might seem as though bigger and brasher Toronto must be Canada's capital, that accolade actually belongs to Ottawa, a four-hour highway drive away. And it's well worth adding a few days to your trip to explore this attractive, historic city. There's an excellent collection of national museums to encounter as well as photo-worthy landmarks including the nation's multi-turreted Parliament buildings. If you're in the country for the July 1 Canada

WHEN TO GO

Ontario's peak season is July–August, which is also the hottest time of year and the priciest period for accommodations. Savvy travelers prefer May, June or September. Fall-foliage viewing is also recommended from late September into October. Winter is not recommended for driving excursions, although visits to Ottawa or Toronto have their own cold-season charms.

Day celebrations, this is the best place to be to channel some Canadian pride (temporary face tattoos of maple-leaf flags are highly recommended). Summer is hot but inviting here, with neighborhoods such as Chinatown, Little Italy and Wellington West to explore and the iconic Rideau Canal providing a cooling presence. Book far ahead for July and August accommodations, and check out the dining scene around the city's ByWard Market.

Niagara-on-the-Lake

A photogenic small town studded with attractively preserved 19th-century buildings, this Southern Ontario community is a magnet for visitors. That means it's often jam-packed in summer, so plan an off-peak visit or book your high-demand accommodations far ahead of time. Aside from its pretty gingerbread architecture, the town offers a smattering of museums and restaurants, and it's a great staging point for exploring Niagara Falls as well as the dozens of nearby vineyards that make up one of Canada's biggest and best wine regions. Theater fan? The town also hosts the almost-yearlong Shaw Festival, Canada's largest and most famous celebration of live theatrical productions.

TRANSPORT

Toronto's huge Pearson International Airport is the arrival point for many visitors. Ottawa also has a smaller international airport. Bus and train services (cross-Canada and from the US) arrive in Toronto. Many visitors drive to Ontario via highways from adjoining Québec or Manitoba. You can also drive from the US state of Michigan; there are four land border crossings.

 WHAT'S ON

Canada Day
The nation's biggest July 1 party is in Ottawa, with concerts, cultural performances and a fireworks finale.

Canadian National Exhibition
(theex.com) Toronto's multiday summer extravaganza of concerts, fairground rides, deep-fried dishes and other drawcards.

Festival of Birds
(festivalofbirds.ca) Point Pelee National Park's famous birding celebration includes talks, guided walks and much more.

Shaw Festival
(shawfest.com) Canada's biggest theatrical celebration, with more than a dozen top-notch productions.

Resources

Destination Ontario
(destinationontario.com) Planning tools for trips around the region.

Destination Toronto
(destinationtoronto.com) Resources for visiting Canada's biggest city.

Ottawa Tourism (ottawatourism.ca) Tips for your visit to Canada's capital.

Toronto Food Blog (torontofoodblog.com) Plan some great meals in the nation's biggest city.

 WHERE TO STAY

Toronto is fully stocked with accommodations options, while smaller Ottawa has a commensurably reduced capacity (which can be an issue in peak summer months). Prices in both cities rise dramatically in July and August. Since you're driving, consider staying in better-value suburban areas where you will still be close to regional highways. Ontario also has a well-developed vacation cottage scene; check on locations and availability via cottagesincanada.com. Keen to stay in a public park? **Ontario Parks** (ontarioparks.com/reservations) offers cabins, campgrounds and more at scenic sites around the region. Alternatively, book a swish stay at Toronto's iconic **Drake Hotel** (thedrake.ca).

16

BEST FOR

☑

Canoeing in Killarney Provincial Park.

Lake Superior Coastline

DURATION	DISTANCE	GREAT FOR
7 days	1691km/1051 miles	Nature

BEST TIME TO GO	June to September for sunny weather and lack of snow on the roads.

Big Nickel, Sudbury

There will be times on this route when you won't see another car for hours. And that's part of the appeal – enjoy the solitude while cruising alongside Lake Superior, keeping an eye out for moose.

Link Your Trip

19 The Kawarthas

Extend your return journey south by picking up this lakes region trip at Algonquin Provincial Park, a 250km drive east of Sudbury along Hwy 11/17.

20 Southern Ontario Nature Loop

From Sudbury, drive 3½ hours south to the start of this scenic nature ramble that takes in mountains, beaches, islands and lush nature reserves.

SUDBURY

01 While Sudbury is not the most idyllic town in northwestern Ontario, it is an important stop to understand what makes this part of the province tick: mining. Most towns in the region started as mining towns and Sudbury's **Dynamic Earth** (dynamicearth.ca) museum is a great intro to nickel mining and the area's history. Be sure to get your picture in front of the **Big Nickel**, a 9m-high stainless steel replica of a 1951 Canadian nickel ($0.05).

If geology is not your thing, Sudbury has a burgeoning food scene. It's easy to while away the rest

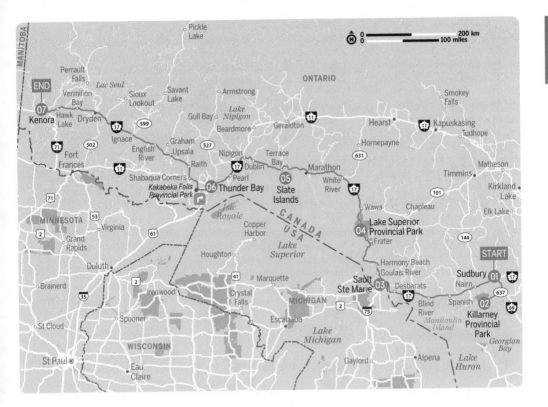

of the day at **46 North Brewing Corp** (46north.ca) followed by dinner at the **Respect is Burning** (ribsupperclub.com) supper club.

 **THE DRIVE**
Be on the lookout for moose and other wildlife on the 100km drive to Killarney Provincial Park, particularly after turning onto Hwy 637 from the Trans-Canada Hwy. The road is quite simple to follow; just keep driving until you reach the park gate.

02 KILLARNEY PROVINCIAL PARK
Killarney Provincial Park (ontarioparks.com/park/killarney) is an outdoor lovers' dream with 645 sq km of nature.

There is a variety of hikes, from the 80km La Cloche Silhouette Trail for experienced hikers to a short 2km loop on the Granite Ridge Trail. This trail also offers great views of the La Cloche mountains and climbs to a lookout point on a ridge overlooking the park.

Those looking to really get away from it all can rent a canoe from **Killarney Kanoes** (killarneykanoes.com) and explore the many lakes in the park. Most people canoe around Bell Lake, but you can also rent canoes at George Lake, Carlyle Lake and Johnny Lake access points. Spend the night at **Killarney Mountain Lodge** (killarney.com), unwinding

in the sauna after your day in nature.

THE DRIVE
It's next to impossible to get lost driving in northwestern Ontario as there's only one main route. To get to Sault Ste Marie, follow Hwy 637 for 65km until you reach the Trans-Canada Hwy, turn right and follow Hwy 17 for around 350km to reach 'the Soo.'

03 SAULT STE MARIE
A stopover in Sault Ste Marie is like a rite of passage for northern Ontario road-trippers. It's not the prettiest city, but it is a friendly place with loads of character. Stay over at the **Water Tower Inn** where the kids can play in the pools

and the parents can head to the pub. There isn't much nightlife here, but that's a good thing because you'll need to get up early the following day if you're keen to make a day trip through the Lake Superior forest on the **Agawa Canyon Tour Train** (agawatrain.com). It departs at 8am and returns at 6pm and is a must-do in autumn as the foliage turns to magnificent shades of red and orange.

THE DRIVE
The 120km drive to Lake Superior Provincial Park is where you really start to get a feel for the region. Follow Hwy 17 as it hugs the coast, offering fleeting glimpses of the sparkling lake through the forest. Stop in at Harmony Beach if the sun is shining to stretch your legs.

04 LAKE SUPERIOR PROVINCIAL PARK
The fjord-like passages, thick evergreen forest and sandy beaches of **Lake Superior Provincial Park** (ontarioparks.com/park/lakesuperior) are straight out of a postcard. The highway runs right through the park, but it's well worth stopping to check out the hiking routes. The **Twilight Resort** is situated just before the park and is a great base for exploration.

If you can drag yourself away from the resort and its idyllic views of Lake Superior, enter the park and head to the **Agawa Bay Visitors Centre**, which is 9km from the southern boundary. The friendly staff can advise you on hiking and take you out to the **Agawa Rock Pictographs**. The ochre-red drawings are a spiritual site for the Ojibwe and are reported to be between 150 and 400 years old.

The restaurant at **Voyageurs' Lodge** (voyageurslodge.com) serves Lake Superior trout or whitefish with chips, mammoth homemade burgers and the best tastin' gravy for miles. The folksy wood-clad dining room, replete with snowshoes, paddles, hockey shirts and canoe bill holders, makes a pleasant pit stop.ochre-red drawings are a spiritual site for the Ojibwe and are reported to be between 150 and 400 years old.

THE DRIVE
One of the most picturesque drives in Ontario, the 360km drive to Terrace Bay cuts through Lake Superior Provincial Park. The road forks after the park – keep left to stay on Hwy 17 instead of heading into Wawa on Hwy 101. You'll head into the Ontario countryside before veering west again to the next stop of this trip, the Slate Islands.

05 SLATE ISLANDS
Formed by an ancient meteorite, inhabited by herds of woodland caribou and featuring pristine paddling opportunities... Need we say more? The **Slate Islands** (ontarioparks.com/park/slateislands), located 13km south of Terrace Bay, are one of the top places in the region for a unique experience. Either grab a ferry, or sign up for a paddling tour with **Naturally Superior Adventures** (naturallysuperior.com). Don't forget your camera as caribou sightings are virtually guaranteed, and you'll no doubt want a selfie in front of the 100-year-old lighthouse. Geology buffs will also love the 'shatter cones,' conical shapes in the rocks formed by the impact of a meteorite 400 to 800 million years ago.

THE DRIVE
You can get to the Slate Islands from Terrace Bay either by ferry or your own paddling steam. Once back from the islands, the trip to the next stop is fairly straightforward – follow Hwy 17 for 220km until you reach Thunder Bay.

06 THUNDER BAY
For a long time, Thunder Bay was referred to by road-trippers as 'a wonderful place to drive through.' Until recently, there were few reasons to stop in the city other than to sleep. But a food culture has emerged in this isolated city. **Tomlin** (tomlinrestaurant.com) serves some of the best food this side of Toronto, and the **Sleeping Giant Brewing Co** (sleepinggiantbrewing.ca) makes great ales and lagers, which you'll find all around town. On top of being an ideal base for exploring the vast forests and lakes in northern Ontario, Thunder Bay also offers local hiking up **Mt McKay** (fwfn.com). You can also learn more about the region's history at **Fort William Historical Park** (fwhp.ca).

THE DRIVE
Take Hwy 17 out of Thunder Bay, which is called Hwy 11/17 for close to 500km until you reach Kenora. There will be one major split in the road, where Hwy 11 veers off toward Atikokan – stay right.

DETOUR
Kakabeka Falls Provincial Park
Start: 06 Thunder Bay

Kakabeka Falls Provincial Park (ontarioparks.com/park/kakabeka falls) is a very short, but worthwhile detour on your trip from Thunder Bay to Kenora. The 40m-high waterfall is one of Ontario's highest and is quite

TOP TIP:
Gas Stations

Hwy 17 is fairly well serviced, but it's still a long route. Be sure to fill up whenever you fall below the half-way point to make sure you don't get stuck. Gas is also much cheaper on Indigenous reserves, of which there are many in northern Ontario.

stunning to view in early spring during the thaw, but also amazing to observe in winter when the falls are encrusted in thick ice. There are also hiking trails in the park, including parts of the 1.3km hike that were historically used by the first Europeans in Canada to portage around the falls.

The falls are also important in Ojibwe folklore. Legend has it that Green Mantle, an Ojibwe princess, pretended to be lost in the region to fool the rival Sioux, which was preparing for an attack, and then led them to their deaths over the falls to prevent the massacre. It's said that you can see Princess Green Mantle when looking into the mist of the falls.

From Thunder Bay, drive along Hwy 11/17 on the way to Kenora for 29km un-

Photo Opportunity

In front of the lighthouse on the Slate Islands.

til you see a turnoff to the left towards the falls. To rejoin the main trip, just exit the park and turn left – you'll be back on the main highway and heading towards Kenora.

07 **KENORA**

Our final stop brings you to the end of northern Ontario before you either head back or on to Winnipeg, Manito-

ba. It's a quaint little town known for its cottages, lakes and hunting. On the drive, be sure to stop at **Busters Barbeque** (busters bbq.com) in Vermilion Bay for a good ol' Canadian BBQ lunch (about 100km before Kenora) and then adjourn for the day by the lake or at **Lake of the Woods Brewing Company** (lowbrewco. com) for some beers and more BBQ (you won't go hungry in this part of Ontario). If you don't feel like paddling yourself around the many small lakes and inlets, take a sunset dinner cruise on the **MS Kenora** (mskenora.com) to explore a fraction of the 14,500 islands that dot the Lake of the Woods.

Left: MS Kenora. Above: Agawa Rock Pictographs, Lake Superior Provincial Park (p118)

17

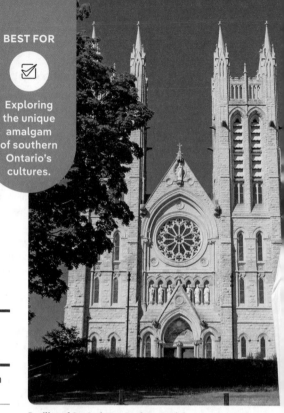

Exploring the unique amalgam of southern Ontario's cultures.

People & Culture Loop

DURATION	DISTANCE	GREAT FOR
4–5 days	450km/280 miles	Culture

BEST TIME TO GO	June to August for gardens in bloom and festivals of all kinds.

Basilica of Our Lady Immaculate, Guelph

Ontario's small communities fit the classic farm-town mold, with country roads lined with corn fields and dairy farms. They also bubble with ethnic histories and cultural traditions. You'll see the signs: horse-drawn buggies, festivals alive with the sound of bagpipes and deerskin drums, and swans floating past theater-bound locals. Stop and explore these unexpected treasures, each a little different, all imbued with Canada's famous charm.

Link Your Trip

18 The Niagara Peninsula

From Brantford, it's just 24km to Hamilton, where the Queen Elizabeth Way (QEW) whisks you through wine country and the area around Niagara Falls.

20 Southern Ontario Nature Loop

Join this spectacular route encompassing craggy cliffs and turquoise waters, birding and beach time from Hwy 6 in Guelph or Hwy 401 in London.

01 GUELPH

A walkabout through the vibrant university town of Guelph, just one hour west of Toronto, is worth every step. Start at the **Art Gallery of Guelph** (artgalleryofguelph.ca), a stark, Edwardian-era building housing a remarkable collection of Canadian art, especially Inuit artists. Outside, meander through its **Sculpture Garden**, Canada's largest, with 39 works of contemporary art dotting its manicured grounds. Stroll north on Gordon St, passing the Speed River and a lovely wooden pedestrian bridge, kayakers paddling underneath. At MacDonnell St, look west to the **Basilica of Our**

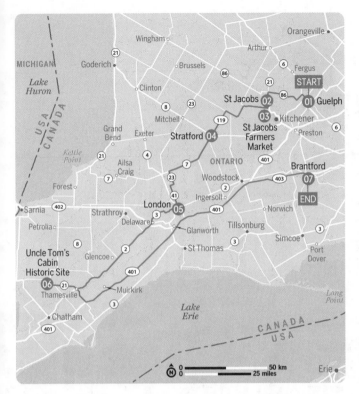

Mennonite Story (stjacobs.com), an interpretive center, to dive deep into the Mennonite history, religion and culture, including the reasons behind their simple dress and resistance to modern-day conveniences like motorized vehicles and radios. Afterwards, walk a couple of blocks to the **Maple Syrup Museum** (stjacobs. com), located in a repurposed mill. A dated but fascinating museum, it has exhibits about the process of making this sweet treat, from pre-colonial times to the present, including antique buckets, taps and tanks.

THE DRIVE
Head 3.5km south on King St, passing expansive farms using horse-pulled machinery. Look out for slower-moving carriages driven by men in straw hats and dark coats, often carrying entire Mennonite families.

03 ST JACOBS FARMERS MARKET
The largest year-round market in Canada, **St Jacobs Farmers Market** (stjacobs market.com) is open every Thursday and Saturday (plus Tuesday in the summer). Head to the biggest barn-like building, which houses two floors of vendors – mostly Mennonite women in long, simple dresses and bonnets. Nosh your way through the ground floor, where farm-fresh produce, homemade jams and maple syrup, all sorts of cheeses, smoked meats and freshly baked breads are sold. Upstairs, hand-crafted items like wooden toys, quilts, soaps and baby clothes are available – perfect for mementos. In the warmer months, the market spills outside, buggies parked behind each stall. Two additional

Lady Immaculate (churchofour lady.com), a Gothic-Revival–style church, whose twin spires have towered over the city since 1888. Turn right and stop for a pint at the **Brothers Brewing Co**, one of five local breweries serving up delicious craft brews; in the summertime, jump on the free **Guelph Beer Bus** (guelph.beer) to visit the others. Walk north on Wyndham St, Guelph's bustling main drag, to **Bookshelf** (book shelf.ca), a bookstore and cultural hub hosting indie films, poetry slams, live music and more.

THE DRIVE
Take Hwy 6 north from downtown Guelph into farm country for 6.2km. At Regional Rd 30, turn west,

doglegging onto Waterloo Regional Rd 86 west, where horse-drawn buggies begin sharing the road. In Elmira, turn left onto Regional Rd 21. At the roundabout 6.6km later, take the first exit onto Regional Rd 17, eventually turning left on King St.

02 ST JACOBS
The heart of Mennonite country since the 1830s, the quaint village of St Jacobs provides a window on this tight-knit community. Just a few blocks long, it's lined with shops, boutiques and the **Stone Crock Bakery** (stonecrock.ca) – one of the most visited bakeries in the region, known for its homestyle pies, tarts and breads. Stop by **The**

TOP TIP:
Toronto Toll Road

Though Hwys 401, 403 and the QEW lead directly into Toronto, they are often overloaded with vehicles. Consider taking Hwy 407 – a toll road that cuts around the congestion. It can be expensive ($8 to $10, depending on the day and time), but can be worth the time and aggravation saved.

buildings on-site house a modern flea market and quick-eats food stalls serving up international dishes and sweet treats – an intersection of cultures.

THE DRIVE
Take Lobsinger Line Rd west toward St Clements village, continuing until it ends in Regional Rd 5, about 16km away. Turn left, passing corn fields and Mennonite homes with signs advertising homemade goods such as jams and quilts. Continue for 15.5km as the road becomes Regional Rd 7. Turn left on Perth Country Rd 119, straight to Stratford 17km away.

04 STRATFORD

A country town turned cultural star, Stratford is internationally acclaimed for its **Stratford Festival** (stratfordfestival.ca), a theater extravaganza of plays and musicals, including Shakespeare's works, on four distinct stages. Shows often sell out so buy tickets early if you can. If not, head straight to the main box office at the Festival Theatre for a chance at rush tickets.

Afterwards, take a leisurely stroll west along the verdant banks of the **Avon River**, as swans float past. Along the way, peruse the works of local artists and craftspeople at **Art in the Park** (artintheparkstratford.ca), a juried showcase during the summer. Continue west along the river to the **Shakespearean Gardens**, a brilliant display of parterre gardens, flowering trees and stone bridges. From here, head east along bustling Ontario St to Downie St and the historic **Stratford Market Square** with its high-end boutiques and restaurants. Pop into the **Stratford Tourism Alliance** (visitstratford.

ca) for a 'Bieber-iffic' map, a self-guided tour of hometown pop star Justin Bieber's old haunts.

THE DRIVE
Take Hwy 7 west for 35km, through the countryside, past corn fields and dairy farms. Take a left on Country Rd 23 near the town of Granton, zigzagging onto Country Rd 41 until arriving in London, 26km away.

05 LONDON

A pleasant city with leafy parks and a river running through it, London has a burgeoning arts and music scene. Start at **Victoria Park**, which has manicured gardens and crisscrossing paths, and is the site of summer festivals and outdoor concerts. The most renowned is **Sunfest** (sunfest.on.ca), a world music and jazz fest attracting performers from around the world and more than 225,000 festival-goers from across Canada. Afterwards, cut west on Kent St to Harris Park, a riverside expanse where **Rock the Park** (rockthepark.ca), a thumping rock and rap fest, brings major headliners to town. Walk south along the verdant banks of the river to **Museum London** (museumlondon.ca), a sleek museum showcasing the intersection between art and history with its collection of more than 20,000 artworks and artifacts. From here, head east on Dundas St, which is lined with Victorian-era buildings, to see what's on at the **TAP Centre for Creativity** (tapcreativity.org), a vibrant arts center focused on emerging players in the visual- and performing arts.

FIRST NATIONS POET

Emily Pauline Johnson, also known by her Indigenous name Tekahionwake, was born in 1861 on the **Six Nations of the Grand River** reservation near Brantford, to a revered Mohawk chief and a British mother. Steeped in both cultures, Johnson was a poet, fiction writer and performer, whose work often examined her mixed-race heritage. She toured for 17 years all over Canada, the US and England, giving dramatic readings of her poems and stories. Her live shows became wildly popular; she often wore indigenous clothing for the first half and a Western gown for the second. Johnson's first book, *The White Wampum,* was published during the height of her fame; she published two more volumes of poetry and a book of First Nations stories before her death, and another two collections of short stories were published posthumously. After her death, as sensibilities changed, Johnson's work was criticized as racially insensitive. But recently, there's growing recognition that Johnson's poems, despite their flaws, contain sophisticated and heartfelt renderings of her experience as a First Nations woman, and of the plight of impoverished Indigenous families. Part of her poem, 'Autumn's Orchestra,' was read during the opening of the Vancouver Olympic winter games in 2010, evoking the sublime magic of an autumn forest.

Johnson's birthplace, now the **Chiefswood National Historic Site** (chiefswoodnhs.ca), offers an insight into this First Nations poet. Open for tours, the grounds are also used for powwows and other community events.

St Jacobs Farmers Market (p123)

THE DRIVE
Head west on Riverside Dr as it winds through suburbia for 8.5km. Turn left on Oxford St, feeding onto Country Rd 3, cutting through cornfields for 11.5km. In Delaware, take Country Rd 2 west for 62km, driving through dairy country. At Thamesville, take Country Rd 21 north to Country Rd 15, which leads to the turnoff, 19km west.

06 **UNCLE TOM'S CABIN HISTORIC SITE**

Sitting on a quiet country road outside of Dresden, the fascinating **Uncle Tom's Cabin Historic Site** (uncletomscabin.org) honors Father Josiah Henson, the inspiration behind the title character in Harriet Beecher Stowe's famous novel. An escapee

Photo Opportunity

Standing in St Jacobs Farmers Market, a sea of colors and cultures meeting all around.

enslaved person, Henson found freedom here with his wife and four children in 1830. Visit their modest clapboard house and learn about the family's day-to-day life as well as Henson's work on the Underground Railroad, leading 118 people to freedom through a network of secret routes and safe houses. As you explore the site, you'll also come across a historic sawmill, smokehouse and church,

all belonging to the Dawn Settlement, a black Canadian community that Henson founded in 1841. End your visit at the **Josiah Henson Interpretive Centre**, which has loads of multimedia exhibits and artifacts related to Henson, the history of enslaved people in the US and their search for freedom in Canada.

THE DRIVE
Head east on Country Rd 17 for 29km, passing through farmlands and the small town of Thamesville. Take the three-lane Hwy 401 east for 125km, a quick ride, cutting through the center of southwestern Ontario. After Woodstock, merge onto Hwy 403. Take Exit 33, heading south on Brant Ave for 7km through Brantford; it eventually becomes Mohawk Ave.

Uncle Tom's Cabin Historic Site

07 BRANTFORD

In southern Brantford, near the **Six Nations of the Grand River** (sixnations.ca) reservation, **Woodland Cultural Centre** (woodlandculturalcentre. ca) is a remarkable nonprofit dedicated to protecting and promoting the voice of First Nations people. Explore the main building, which houses a gallery with rotating exhibits of contemporary Indigenous art; an excellent museum examining the history of the Iroquois and Algonquian peoples; and a stage for performance art, concerts and talks. Next door, peek into the looming **Mohawk Institute Residential School**, once a government-sanctioned boarding school used to force assimilation upon First Nations children from 1828 to 1970. Afterwards, head 650m west to **Her Majesty's Chapel of the Mohawks** (mohawkchapel.ca), the oldest Protestant church in Ontario (established in 1785), gifted to the Mohawk people by the British crown for their assistance during the American Revolution. It's a simple, white, clapboard church – don't miss the eight stained-glass windows depicting historical events from the Iroquois people's past.

🚗 THE DRIVE

Follow Mohawk Ave east around the forested edges of town for 2.5km. Turn right onto Colborne St E and left onto Garden Ave, a quiet residential street 1.2km away. Continue for about 3km as it becomes a larger thoroughfare, passing farms and factories. This leads straight to the three-lane Hwy 403 and directly to Toronto, 95km away.

VADIM RODDNEV/SHUTTERSTOCK ©

Fergus Scottish Festival & Highland Games

REGIONAL FESTIVALS

Towns that travelers might otherwise overlook often have terrific local festivals dedicated to a particular feature of that area.

Kazoo! Fest (kazookazoo.ca) A wonderfully irreverent romp through independent music, and a source of great local pride for this university town. Over 40 acts play at locations around town in April, ranging from Indigenous hip-hop duos to coffee-house electronica. Organizers all but promise you'll leave with a new band-crush.

Fergus Scottish Festival & Highland Games (fergusscottishfestival. com) Many Canadians can trace their roots to Scottish immigrants. August's Scottish Festival and Highlands Games are Fergus' celebration of that culture, with all its idiosyncrasies, plus a dose of serious competition. Crowd favorites include flipping a log end over end, 'pipe band' showdowns and something called 'sheaf tossing': hucking a bag of hay over a high bar using a pitchfork.

Oktoberfest (oktoberfest.ca) It's all about the beer. So it's no surprise there's a ceremonial keg-tapping to kick off this long-running event, and that organizers got into trouble, back in 1970, for a poster depicting stein-toting women – it was frowned upon for 'promoting drinking.' The festival features outstanding German brews, fun events and competitions.

Elmira Maple Syrup Festival (elmiramaplesyrup.com) Hundreds of thousands of pancakes, a Guinness world record ('Largest Single-Day Maple Syrup Festival'), even odes to the joys of turning sap into syrup. Early April is indeed Maple Syrup Festival time in the town of Elmira; just be sure to come hungry.

18

The Niagara Peninsula

DURATION	DISTANCE	GREAT FOR
3 days	62km/39 miles	Wine, Culture, Nature

BEST TIME TO GO	June to September for warm days and the grape-harvest season.

Horseshoe Falls, Niagara Falls

The Niagara Peninsula is a feast for the senses. The thunder of water as it cascades over a towering cliff; the delicate brush of mist during a catamaran trip along the falls; the sight of a colonial-era soldier prepping a musket for battle; the cheers and applause at Ontario's most celebrated stages; and the sweet, viscous flavors of ice wine, grown in vineyards stretching as far as the eye can see.

Link Your Trip

17 People & Culture Loop

Add on a country drive through Ontario, exploring its charming towns and fascinating cultures; pick up this tour at Brantford, just 55km west of the QEW.

20 Southern Ontario Nature Loop

After making the final stop at Tawse winery, drive 2½ hours north to the start of this serene loop around the stunning Bruce Peninsula.

NIAGARA FALLS

01 **Horseshoe Falls** is the shining star of the town of Niagara Falls – a 670m-wide, U-shaped waterfall, North America's highest-volume cascade, moving 8500 bathtubs worth of water per second over its ridges to the frothing Maid of the Mist Pool below. Enjoy the magnificent views and the falls' cooling mist from **Table Rock** viewpoint. Afterwards, walk north for 1km along the curving Niagara Pkwy, taking in the views of the smaller but still impressive **American Falls** and **Bridal Veil Falls**, to the **Hornblower Niagara Cruise**

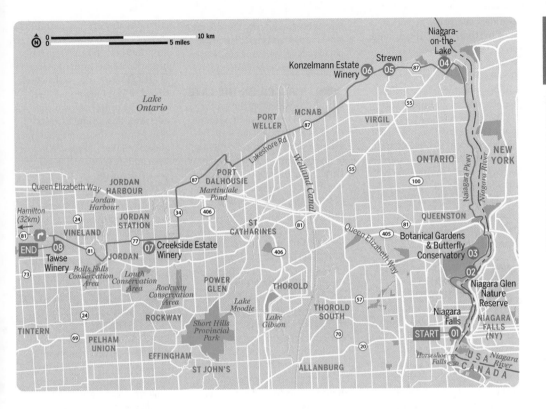

(niagaracruises.com) port. Here, a 20-minute catamaran ride gets you up-close-and-personal with all three of Niagara Falls' cascades; prepare to don a poncho and somehow still get drenched. After this, dry off as you walk up the hill to the 158m **Skylon Tower** (skylon.com), with its jaw-dropping views of the falls and, on a clear day, Toronto. For some grown-up fun, try your luck at **Niagara Fallsview Casino** (fallsviewcasinoresort. com) across the street. Jackpots won, head to the **Niagara Falls History Museum** (niagarafalls museums.ca), 1.5km northwest on Ferry St. A well-curated museum, it has excellent multimedia

exhibits on the transformation of the area from an Indigenous settlement to a modern-day tourist zone; stories of daredevils and coverage of the War of 1812 are especially engaging. End your visit in famously kitschy **Clifton Hill**, 1.5km east, a street filled with wax museums, creepy fun houses and arcades.

🚗 **THE DRIVE**
Follow Niagara Pkwy north for 8km, winding along the verdant road that Winston Churchill once described as 'the prettiest Sunday afternoon drive in the world.' On one side, you'll see souvenir shops eventually give way to Victorian-era homes; on the other, the grassy cliffs above the Niagara River and the

Niagara River Recreation Trail that runs alongside it.

 NIAGARA GLEN NATURE RESERVE
The **Niagara Glen Nature Reserve** (niagaraparks. com) is a local hikers' fave with 4km of trails leading through the Carolinian forest, down the gorge to the fast-moving Niagara River. Start at the **Nature Center**, to get a trail map and to learn about the terrain, flora and fauna. Then take the 17m-high steel staircase to the start of the trail system. At the bottom, turn north (left) on the limestone-lined **Cliffside Trail** to **Terrace Trail**, a short but steep hike with massive

boulders and stone steps that lead to **River Trail**. Head south (right) along the relatively flat trail to take in the beech and tulip trees, the white-capped river, and the towering gorge walls. Finally, dogleg on **Eddy Trail** to take the challenging **Whirlpool Trail** (expect boulders and uneven terrain) to the fast and furious, cyclone-like whirlpool in the river – look for the gondola over it – or just loop back to the Cliffside Trail, to head back.

THE DRIVE
Continue 650m north along Niagara Pkwy.

03 BOTANICAL GARDENS & BUTTERFLY CONSERVATORY

Forty hectares of beautifully landscaped gardens filled with thousands of perennials, sculpted shrubs and towering trees make the **Botanical Gardens** (niagaraparks.com) a visually inspiring and soothing stop. Meander along the leafy paths, passing the parterre garden and the must-see Victorian rose garden with more than 2400 roses – a popular photo op. In the central part of the gardens sits the **Butterfly Conservatory**, a high-glass-domed building with a rainforest-like setting – plants, waterfalls, heat and all – with more than 2000 delicate butterflies flitting about, often landing on visitors. Of the 45 species of butterflies living here, 60% are from Costa Rica, El Salvador and the Philippines; the rest are raised in an on-site greenhouse.

THE DRIVE
Continue 15km north on the leisurely Niagara Pkwy, passing the Floral Clock, a popular pit stop for photos. As you travel north, the

houses become grander, the parkway less crowded and vineyards begin to dot the landscape. Eventually, Niagara Pkwy becomes Queen's Pde.

04 NIAGARA-ON-THE-LAKE

As you enter the pretty colonial town of Niagara-on-the-Lake, the spiked walls of **Fort George** (pc.gc.ca/fortgeorge) appear on your right. Dating to 1797, it was the site of several bloody battles during the War of 1812. Wander among well-restored buildings, watch musket demonstrations and learn about the daily life here from chipper staff in historic dress. Just north on Queen's Pde sits the main theater of the **Shaw Festival** (shawfest.com). A highly respected and popular theater company, it's named after the playwright George Bernard Shaw, whose plays were showcased during the company's first season in 1962. Today, the festival stages plays and musicals from the Victorian

---

☑️

TOP TIP:

Horseshoe Falls Photo Op

A little-known but great spot to take a photo of Horseshoe Falls is inside the **Table Rock Visitor Centre**. Head to the 2nd floor and you'll find a bank of floor-to-ceiling windows high enough to overlook the falls and the crowds in front of it. It's a magazine-worthy vista!

---

era to the modern day in three theaters around town. Splurge on tickets, if you can. From here, head two blocks north on Queen's St (aka Queen's Pde) to the **clock tower**, a WWI memorial. This marks the center of town, an area with flower-lined streets, 19th-century-storefront boutiques and colonial-era homes. Window shop and explore!

THE DRIVE
Head northwest on Mary St, a road that runs parallel to Queen St, five blocks away. Stay on the small road – which becomes Lakeshore Dr – for 5km, as it winds through verdant countryside, passing modest homes and vineyards.

05 NIAGARA-ON-THE-LAKE WINE COUNTRY: STREWN

Tucked into the west side of Lakeshore Dr is **Strewn** (strewnwinery.com). The building itself isn't particularly charming – a modernized and expanded canning facility – but the wines are award-winning and the staff welcoming. Pop in for a wine tasting – its oaky Terroir Chardonnay and sweet Gewurztraminer are the ones you can't miss. In the summer, consider booking a class at the winery's modern **Wine Country Cooking School** (winecountrycooking.com) to hone your cooking skills or to learn new dishes that pair well with wines.

THE DRIVE
Continue northwest on Lakeshore Dr for 1km.

06 NIAGARA-ON-THE-LAKE WINE COUNTRY: KONZELMANN ESTATE WINERY

On the east side of Lakeshore Dr sits **Konzelmann Estate**

Postman butterfly, Butterfly Conservatory

☑

TOP TIP:
Parking in Niagara Falls

Parking is limited and expensive in Niagara Falls. Before handing over a bucket of cash at a random lot, swing by the **Niagara IMAX Theatre** (imaxniagara.com). It has an open-air lot next to the Skylon, and its parking rates are typically a steal – around $10 per day – and the location is tops.

Photo Opportunity

On the thundering edge of Horseshoe Falls, from Table Rock viewpoint.

Winery (konzelmann.ca), one of the oldest vineyards in the region (established 1984) and the only one set on Lake Ontario. The views over its vineyards to Toronto's skyline are spectacular. Tours of the facilities, including tastings in its elegant, château-like building, are a treat. The late-harvest vidal and ice wines are the ticket here.

THE DRIVE
Continue on Lakeshore Dr for 17km, passing over the Welland Canal and through the town of Port Dalhousie until it meets Rte 34. Turn left and continue for 3.4km, passing over the QEW, vineyards and orchards of Twenty Valley Wine Country dotting the landscape. At Rte 77, a quiet country road, turn right and drive for 2km.

07 TWENTY VALLEY WINE COUNTRY: CREEKSIDE ESTATE WINERY

A modest entrance belies the spunky and entrepreneurial spirit of **Creekside Estate Winery** (creeksidewine.com). Come here for a down-and-dirty tour of the cellars and vineyards (really, bring boots) or an afternoon on the patio with live music and a glass of wine in hand. It can also provide picnic lunches to enjoy in the vineyards, including a blanket and wine. Try the Sauvignon Blanc and Syrah, the focus of Creekside's experimental wine portfolio.

THE DRIVE
Turn left on Rte 77, continuing until 19th St. Turn left, passing through the charming village of Jordan; immediately after Jordan House, turn right on King St. Stay on King St for about 4.5km as it curves through farmland and over creeks, eventually passing the outskirts of Vineland. Turn left on Cherry Ave, staying on it for just 0.6km.

Sir Adam Beck Station (left) and Robert Moses Hydro Electric Plant (right)

NIAGARA FALLS & HYDROELECTRIC POWER

Though nowhere near the tallest waterfalls in the world (that honor goes to 979m Angel Falls in Venezuela), Niagara Falls is one of the world's most voluminous, with more than 168,000 cubic meters of water going over its crest lines every minute. At least, that is, from 8am to 10pm during the peak tourist season, April to September.

In fact, the water making it over the falls – Horseshoe, American and Bridal Veil – only accounts for 25% to 50% of their capacity. The rest is diverted into hydroelectric plants on both sides of the border, depending on the time of day and year: Sir Adam Beck Station Stations #1 and #2 in Ontario and Robert Moses Hydro Electric Plant in New York. Built across from each other, the hydroelectric plants divert water from the Niagara River using a system of gates located 2.6km before the falls. The water is run through hydro tunnels on both sides of the border to turbines that generate electricity; the water is eventually returned to the Niagara River, just above Lake Ontario. The entire process is governed under the 1950 Niagara Treaty, an international agreement that assures water levels and a fair division of electricity (Ontario actually gets a little more). Power generated from the Niagara River accounts for 25% of all electricity used in Ontario and New York State – a remarkable figure, especially considering Toronto and New York City are included.

For visitors to Niagara Falls this means that, depending on the time of day and year, the falls may appear more or less voluminous. The highest volume any time of year is from April 1 to October 31, during daylight hours. The rest of the year, or at night, the falls look remarkably smaller but the street lights, somehow, seem to shine a little brighter.

Table Rock viewpoint, Horseshoe Falls (p128)

08 ### TWENTY VALLEY WINE COUNTRY: TAWSE WINERY

A four-time Canada Winery of the Year winner, **Tawse Winery** (tawsewinery.ca) is a must-stop. Sitting on a rise, its elegant tasting room opens to fields of grapes. Known for its organic wines – the Chardonnay is over-the-top delicious – Tawse uses a biodynamic approach to farming, utilizing the land's natural cycles and animals like sheep and chickens that feed on leaves and bugs to keep its soil and vines healthy. A tour of the facilities, including tastings, is interesting and worthwhile.

Niagara Icewine Festival

WINE FESTIVALS

Niagara Peninsula is home to several wine-related festivals (niagara winefestival.com and twentyvalley.ca) throughout the year. Time your visit to attend one of these locals' faves in the wine country of Niagara-on-the-Lake and its neighbor Twenty Valley:

Niagara Homegrown Wine Festival (June) Kicks off Niagara's summer wine-tasting season with two weekends of wine-and-food-pairing events; typically more than 30 wineries participate.

Niagara Grape and Wine Festival (September) Celebrates the harvest season with two weeks of wine tastings and concerts around the region as well as two parades in St Catherines.

Niagara Icewine Festival (January) Showcases Ontario's stickiest, sweetest ice wines during a 16-day winter festival, including winery tours, street festivals and a gala party at the Niagara Fallsview Casino (p129).

Twenty Valley Winter WineFest (January) Celebrates Twenty Valley wines in Jordan Village during one weekend of tastings, live music and outdoor events like ice wine puck shoot-outs and barrel-rolling competitions.

 DETOUR

Hamilton Art Scene
Start: 08 Twenty Valley Wine Country: Tawse Winery

Once a gritty steel-industry hub, downtown Hamilton today has a welcoming air and a burgeoning arts scene. James St N is a good place to explore, with its independent galleries, quirky boutiques and hipster eateries. On the second Friday of each month, James St hosts **Hamilton Art Crawl** (tourismhamilton.com), a veritable party zone when crowds of locals and visitors meander among galleries and shops that are open late, art studios have open doors and street performers do their thing. If quiet art appreciation is more your style, pop into the **Art Gallery of Hamilton** (artgalleryofhamilton.com) instead. A sleek affair in the heart of downtown, the collection focuses on modern and 19th-century Canadian art. The gallery offers free tours, led by knowledgeable docents, covering the highlights and hidden gems of the collection; offered at 1pm on Wednesdays and on weekends, the tours are highly recommended if you can swing it. Afterwards, stop for lunch at the nearby **Hamilton Farmers Market** (hamilton farmersmarket.ca). You'll find vendors selling fresh and local produce, meat and bread of all sorts at this 180-year-old market; head to the ground level for a remarkable variety of international fast-food eateries, a snapshot of the diversity of this town.

A stop in Hamilton is best done at the beginning or end of your Niagara Peninsula tour. Located just off the QEW, it's a quick jaunt to Tawse, just 43km away.

Clock tower, Niagara-on-the-Lake (p130)

WHY I LOVE THIS TRIP

Liza Prado, writer

This trip takes you to one of Canada's most iconic sites: Niagara Falls, a thundering, awe-inspiring set of cascades. Few people realize you can experience them on land, water and even from high above. But the Niagara Peninsula offers more than the falls – including an exploration of leafy trails and botanical gardens, a beautiful colonial town and a landscape of vineyards.

19

The Kawarthas

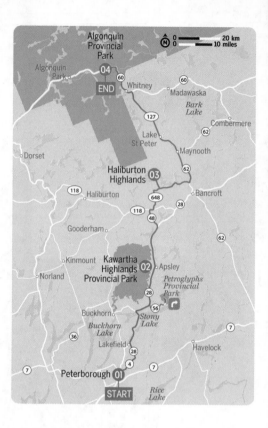

DURATION	DISTANCE	GREAT FOR
5 days	208km/129 miles	Families, Nature

BEST TIME TO GO	In September/October as the leaves begin to change color or May/June when the weather is warmer but the summer crowds are less.

This is a trip for outdoor and nature lovers who may be short on time. It's a short drive from either Toronto or Ottawa and could work for a long-weekend road trip. While the hiking and activities en route are top-notch, the real star here is the drive – a laid-back jaunt through the Kawartha's dense forests, shimmering lakes and small-town vibes.

Link Your Trip

16 Lake Superior Coastline

Take your trip further into Ontario's nature up to Kenora. Follow Hwy 11/17 through North Bay and to Sudbury.

21 Thousand Island Parkway

If coming from Ottawa, join up with this trip by driving north before turning left onto Hwy 7 to hit Peterborough 180km away.

01 PETERBOROUGH

Peterborough has been described as the heart of the Kawarthas, but don't let the fact that it is the biggest city in the area put you off – this is also cabin country and the best accommodations, like Lake Edge Cottages, are on the water's edge. The **Trent-Severn Waterway** (pc.gc.ca/en/lhn-nhs/on/trentsevern), which connects the Kawarthas with Lake Ontario, runs right through Peterborough and offers great canoeing opportunities. Canoeing is so important to the area that the **Canadian Canoe Museum** (canoemuseum.ca) is situated here and is undergoing a massive refurbishment in order to better

BEST FOR

Hiking in the Algonquin Provincial Park.

Trent-Severn Waterway

explain to people how important canoeing is to the area's history.

 THE DRIVE
Exit Peterborough on Parkhill Rd and drive for 11km until County Rd 28. Follow this road north for 50km, over several small bridges including Young's Point and Burleigh Falls, until you see the turnoff (left) for the Kawartha Highlands Provincial Park. The road, Anstruther Park Rd, forks after 2km – turn right for the access road to Loon Call Lake.

DETOUR
Petroglyphs Provincial Park
Start: **01** Peterborough

If you leave Peterborough in the early morning, you have more than enough time to take the one-hour round-trip

detour to **Petroglyphs Provincial Park** (ontarioparks.com/park/petroglyphs), not including time at the park, to view the largest-known concentration of Indigenous rock carvings in Canada.

The sacred site, which features carvings of birds, humans and turtles, is known as 'The Teaching Rocks' and you can learn more about the Ojibwe carvings and history at the super educational **Learning Place Visitor Centre**.

The carvings date back to around CE 900–1100 and were not discovered by non-Indigenous people until 1954. Today, it is a National Historic Site of Canada and an important link to Canada's precolonial history.

From Peterborough, on your way to the Kawartha Highlands Provincial Park, exit Hwy 28 after 40km onto

Regional Rd 56/Northeys Bay Rd. Follow Regional Rd 56 for roughly 11km until you see a sign to turn left into the Petroglyphs Provincial Park. After viewing the paintings, retrace your path back to Hwy 28 and turn right; there is only another 10km until you reach Kawartha Highlands Provincial Park.

 02 **KAWARTHA HIGHLANDS PROVINCIAL PARK**
The **Kawartha Highlands Provincial Park** (ontarioparks. com/park/kawarthahighlands) is the second largest in southern Ontario, after Algonquin, but is much more rustic, with fewer facilities. Don't expect expensive lodges here, though campsites usually

have a toilet and picnic tables, unless you are backcountry camping. You'll also need your own canoe to access many of the campsites, so it's best to come in for the day, swim in nearby **Loon Call Lake** and have a bite to eat before heading for your next destination.

If you have more time to kill, consider venturing further into the park to **Anstruther Lake**, the largest lake in the park, where you can rent boats, jet-skis and other marine craft from **Anstruther Marina**. Accommodations options are limited, so make sure you've packed a tent if you plan on staying overnight.

🚗 **THE DRIVE**
Backtrack down Anstruther Park Rd until you reach Hwy 28 and turn left. Travel 21km then turn left onto Country Rd 48. Turn right at the T-Junction and then onto Loop Rd after 2km. Look for a right turn onto S Baptiste Lake Rd after 10km, after which it is a 3km drive to Clarke Rd into the forest.

Photo Opportunity
Swimming or jet-skiing in one of the many lakes.

Anstruther Lake

03 HALIBURTON HIGHLANDS

Geologically, the Haliburton Highlands are a southern extension of the Algonquin Provincial Park, with 300 sq km of dense forests and shimmering lakes. Legally, they are not because much of the area is privately owned, including **Haliburton Forest** (haliburtonforest. com), where you can hike and mountain bike in the summer and snowmobile and dogsled in the winter. There is also a canopy tour for the adventure-inclined or a canoe lake-crossing tour, which includes entry to the **Haliburton Wolf Center** on the other side of the lakes. Accommodations are available as well as serviced campsites, so there is an option for different budgets.

🚗 **THE DRIVE**
Retrace your drive until you reach the T-junction and head east for 15km until Hwy 62, where you turn north for Algonquin Provincial Park. After 16km you'll reach a junction – keep straight onto Hwy 127, which is signposted for Bancroft. Drive for roughly 38km, and take a left onto Hwy 60, which brings you to the East Gate 9km away.

04 ALGONQUIN PROVINCIAL PARK

The **Algonquin Provincial Park** (algonquinpark.on.ca) is the second-largest and oldest park in Ontario, comprising 7600 sq km of forests, streams, cliffs and lakes. Animal lovers are practically guaranteed moose sightings in the spring along the highway as the moose come to lick leftover salt from the winter de-icing. There is also a wide variety of birds as well as deer, beavers and otters to spot. Paddlers, whether beginner or experienced, are also well-catered for. Beginners should start on the aptly named Canoe Lake in the middle of the park off Hwy 60 and can rent equipment from **Algonquin Outfitters** (algonquinoutfitters. com). Finally, hikers are the most catered for – grab a map from one of the information centers and choose from hikes covering 140km of trail. Once you've exhausted yourself with adventure, splurge a bit and stay at the idyllic **Killarney Lodge** (killarneylodge.com) – you've earned it.

Algonquin Provincial Park

20

Southern Ontario Nature Loop

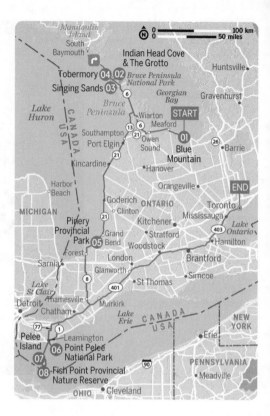

DURATION	DISTANCE	GREAT FOR
5–7 days	1075km/668 miles	Families, Nature

BEST TIME TO GO	March to July for skiing in the earlier months plus good hiking and kayaking conditions for the entire period.

You're standing at the edge of a 'sea' cave. The aquamarine tide surging beneath, the towering cliffs above, the massive expanse of water stretching into the distance – the whole scene screams seashore, yet the sea is a thousand kilometers away. This is Bruce Peninsula, a huge tract of spectacular scenery and rugged pine-clad terrain jutting into Lake Huron, and just one of many jaw-dropping, mind-bending natural treasures in Southern Ontario.

Link Your Trip

17 People & Culture Loop

From Pinery Provincial Park it's just 70km to London, a good place to pick up this tour of Ontario's diverse cultures and rich history.

18 Niagara Peninsula

Tagging on a visit to iconic Niagara Falls is easy. Near Hamilton, take Hwy 403 to the QEW, which leads straight there.

BLUE MOUNTAIN

01 Ontario's biggest ski resort, **Blue Mountain** (bluemountain.ca) sits just two hours north of Toronto. Spread across 147 hectares of Niagara Escarpment, it has breathtaking views over Georgian Bay. In the winter and spring, it boasts **43 ski trails**, ranging from beginner to double black diamond, many of them open at night. The best of the lot are the blue runs, most of them cruisers, some with steeper pitches; the longest, **Butternut** (1.6km), runs alongside the **Badlands Terrain Park**, with expert-level jumps and rails. At the top of the hill,

BEST FOR

Exploring the Bruce Peninsula's national parks, in land and water.

Blue Mountain

don't miss the scenic **Woodview Mountaintop Skating Trail**, a 1.1km trail of ice, looping through a forest thick with trees. At night, tiki torches light the way, and a fire pit and hot cocoa await you at the start. In summer and fall, the highlights here are leafy **trails**, open to hikers and mountain bikers and accessible by **gondola**, though the more ambitious take steep paths from the base to the trailheads.

While you're here, make the trek to **Grandma Lambe's** (grandmalambes.com), west on Hwy 26 just outside of Meaford. The store is a delicious jumble of maple syrup vintages, butter tarts, bushels of vegetables, and tables piled high with pies, buns and jellies.

 THE DRIVE
Take Grey County Rd 19 north to Rte 26, 4km away. Turn left on Rte 26 W, the road running parallel to Georgian Bay, its blue waters occasionally peeking out between the fir trees, which eventually give way to farm country. After 52km, in Owen Sound, pick up Hwy 6, headed north to Bruce Peninsula National Park, 102km away.

02 **BRUCE PENINSULA NATIONAL PARK: INDIAN HEAD COVE & THE GROTTO**

A spectacular 156-sq-km park, **Bruce Peninsula National Park** (pc.gc.ca/brucepeninsula) is filled with ancient cedar trees, craggy limestone cliffs, rare orchids and stunning turquoise waters. Though there are various entrances, start at **Cypress Lake**. After winding your way through the dense forest to the trailhead, set out on foot along the **Georgian Bay Trail** (1.6km). A wide, flat trail, it leads through the forest, over a creek and past Horse Lake to the shoreline. Once there, the waters seem to glow from between the trees. Eventually, you'll hit **Indian Head Cove**, a small, white-boulder beach with huge, flat limestone rocks, and cliffs all around. To the left, high above, is a **natural stone arch**. Continue north along the trail where, steps away, you'll look down and see the **Grotto**, a sea cave surrounded by cliffs, aquamarine water flowing in and an underwater tunnel leading out to Georgian Bay. A rocky tunnel along the cliff allows visitors to corkscrew down – use caution! After exploring, continue north until hitting the **Marr Lake Trail**. This is a more challenging trail – the terrain is uneven and has little signage. If in doubt, look for the impressive **Boulder Beach**, with its seemingly endless number of perfectly round, small white rocks, and turn toward the north side of small Lake Marr, a favorite for water birds. The trail eventually joins the Georgian Bay Trail, which you can follow back to the start.

THE DRIVE
From the Cypress Lake entrance, dogleg on Hwy 6 to Dorcas Bay Rd. Turn left and continue for 1.2km on the small country road.

03 BRUCE PENINSULA NATIONAL PARK: SINGING SANDS

On the Lake Huron side of Bruce Peninsula National Park, **Singing Sands** is another world: a wide sandy beach, with a limestone and alvar shoreline, dunes, marshlands and forests. The unique meeting of ecosystems makes it a botanist's, or simply a flower lover's, paradise. Here, you'll see a variety of orchids in bloom – 44 types exist in the park – as well as rare plants like the scarlet paintbrush and insect-eating pitcher plant. A 3km **forest trail** loops through the unique environs. There's also a 200m **boardwalk** overlooking the beach.

THE DRIVE
Head back to Hwy 6 and turn left for Tobermory, 10km north along the wooded country highway.

04 TOBERMORY

The charming village of Tobermory is the jumping-off point for **Fathom Five National Marine Park** (pc. gc.ca/fathomfive), home to **Flowerpot Island**. A small island with two trails, it's surrounded by crystal-clear turquoise waters and has dramatic limestone formations (aka the Flowerpots), created from hundreds of years of waves hitting its shores. Book a glass-bottom-boat tour with **Bruce Anchor Cruises** (bruceanchor. com) to access the island; on the way, you'll float over two or three shipwrecks – there are **22 shipwrecks** in Fathom Five – before heading to the island and being dropped off for DIY exploring. After disembarking, head east along the **Loop Trail**, a 2.6km flat, leafy path that follows the shoreline, passing the Flowerpots, and ends at the lighthouse before turning back through the hilly, forested center. Back on the mainland, book a snorkeling or diving trip with **Diver's Den** (diversden.ca) to explore more shipwrecks, many in shallow waters. The oldest, a schooner called the *Cascaden,* dates to 1871.

Tiki meets maritime at colorful, quirky **Shipwreck Lee's Pirate Bistro** (shipwrecklees.com), filled with murals, pirate mannequins, and picnic tables (indoors and out). All-you-can-eat fish and chips is the way to go: baskets of melt-in-your-mouth whitefish with piles of fresh fries, all topped with a cocktail umbrella.

THE DRIVE
Take Hwy 6 south 64km to Red Bay Rd (look for the Top Valu gas station). Take a right, staying on Red Bay for 6km until it hits Hwy 13. Turn left, heading to Southampton, where it merges with Hwy 21. Stay on Hwy 21 for 150km, passing several lakeside villages and towns, the last of which is Grand Bend.

DETOUR
Manitoulin Island
Start: 04 Tobermory

A two-hour ferry ride from Tobermory takes you to another world: Manitoulin Island. A 2766-sq-km landmass, it's the world's largest freshwater island. A landscape of farmlands and forests, Manitoulin is dotted with villages and small towns, many of them First Nations communities. Start at the **Ojibwe Cultural Foundation** (ojibweculture.ca), in M'Chigeeng, to learn about the culture and heritage of the Ojibwe, Odawa and Pottawatomi peoples, the original inhabitants of the island. Down the street, book a tour with **Great Spirit Circle Trail** (circletrail.com), a consortium of eight First Nations communities offering cultural tours and outdoors excursions such as paddling on ancient canoe routes. Afterwards, head east to the **Cup & Saucer Trail** for a 9km hike along the Niagara Escarpment, with its 70m cliffs and granite outcrops leading to spectacular views of the North Channel. Try to catch a show at the **Debajehmujig Creation Centre** (debaj.ca) in Manitowaning, home of Canada's most prestigious Indigenous theater company. And if you're on the island in early August, head to Wiikwemkoong, the proudly unceded First Nations reserve – its people never relinquished their land rights to the Canadian government. Here, Manitoulin celebrates its largest **powwow** (wikwemikongheritage.org)

Grotto (p141), Bruce Peninsula National Park

Photo Opportunity

On the cliff's edge, overlooking the Grotto and its impossibly turquoise waters.

with lively dance competitions, drumming and traditional games. Everyone is welcome. The **Chi-Cheemaun ferry** (ontarioferries.com) carries passengers and vehicles from Tobermory to South Baymouth two to four times daily. A swing bridge in Little Current on the north end of the island also connects it to the mainland.

05 PINERY PROVINCIAL PARK

Opening onto gorgeous Lake Huron, **Pinery Provincial Park** (ontarioparks.com) has one of the best **beaches** in Ontario – 10km of wide, sandy beach, emerald waters and picturesque dunes on either side. It's perfect for a day of

beachcombing or just chilling out on the sand. Inland, explore the Pinery's 2549 hectares of protected forest – the largest in southwestern Ontario. On the south side of the park, take the **Nippissing Trail**, a tough 2km loop that winds its way up and down spectacularly tall dunes covered in rare oak savanna, an ecosystem of oak trees, prairie grasses and wildflowers. Stairs are built into the steepest sections of the hike; a platform on the far end reveals a view of the forest's expanse and Lake Huron beyond. Afterwards, rent a kayak and paddle along the **Old Ausable Channel**, a lush wetlands area that cuts through

the park's core and is home to many of the 325 species of birds spotted here.

 THE DRIVE
Take Hwy 21 west for 100km as it cuts south through farmlands, becoming Country Rd 8. Continue south, along country roads until Hwy 401. Head west on Hwy 401 for 50km, exiting on Queen's Line Rd to County Rd 1 south. It eventually hits Country Rd 34 west and Country Rd 33 south to Point Pelee National Park, 37km later.

06 POINT PELEE NATIONAL PARK

Opening onto Lake Erie, **Point Pelee National Park** (pc. gc.ca) is one of the world's best birding sites. It is set on two

Point Pelee National Park

migratory paths, and more than 390 bird species have been spotted here – May and September see the highest concentration of birds, especially songbirds and raptors. It also serves as a resting spot for thousands of migrating monarch butterflies – a fluttering vision in the fall. Grab your binoculars, and head out on the **West Beach Footpath**, a 2km narrow trail running through restored savannahs, with views of Lake Erie shimmering through the trees. The path feeds into the beachfront **Tip Trail**, a 1km path to the very tip of the park, mainland Canada's southernmost point, like a pencil nib jutting out into the lake. Take a pic! Afterwards, head to the spectacular **Marsh**, with its boardwalk floating in a sea of cattails, beavers swimming by and painted turtles sunning themselves. Climb the observation tower for a bird's-eye view, then rent a kayak to explore the waterways.

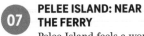

THE DRIVE
Take the quiet lakefront road – Point Pelee Dr, which becomes Robson Rd after the docks – to the town of Leamington, 7km away. Turn left on its main drag, Erie St. It leads straight to the ferry docks of Pelee Island Transportation. A modern, multistoried ferry crosses Lake Erie's blue expanse to Pelee Island here from April to December.

07 PELEE ISLAND: NEAR THE FERRY
Pelee Island feels a world apart from mainland Canada. With about 200 residents,

---

TOP TIP:

Parking at the Grotto

Parking permits are required to visit the Grotto in the Bruce Peninsula National Park (p141). Good for four hours, permits have pre-scheduled start/end times. Don't overstay your visit – ticketing and towing are enforced! Permits can be purchased online or by phone; call well in advance for summer visits.

everything moves just a little slower, with most folks getting around on bikes, small homes dotting the forested island and beachfront trails here and there. Across from the ferry dock, pop into the **Pelee Island Heritage Centre** (peleeislandmuseum. ca). Inside, you'll get a good lay of the land with an excellent natural history collection and well-curated displays explaining Pelee's history, from its early Indigenous inhabitants to the present day. Don't miss the fascinating exhibit on the shipwrecks surrounding the island. Afterwards, walk 950m south along the lakefront to **Pelee Island**

Winery (peleeisland.com), one of Canada's oldest vineyards.

THE DRIVE
Head south on West Shore Rd, which turns into McCormick Rd after Pelee Island Winery. Continue for 3.6km, with Lake Erie to your right and the forest and farmlands to your left.

08 PELEE ISLAND: FISH POINT PROVINCIAL NATURE RESERVE
The **Fish Point Provincial Nature Reserve** (ontarioparks. com/park/fishpoint) is a popular birding spot and home to one of the best swimming beaches on the island. A flat 3.2km trail leads through the dense forest, past Fox Lagoon and eventually near to the shoreline. Rare plants, such as the prickly pear cactus and hop tree, can be seen throughout, with black-crowned night herons and other migrating shorebirds showing their feathers. At the end, the beach finishes in a long, curving point forming a thin peninsula, the calm waters of Lake Erie on either side. This is the southernmost spot of inhabited Canada!

THE DRIVE
Make your way to the ferry, looping around the small island. Back on the mainland, head north on Erie St through farmland until it becomes Hwy 77. After 27km, take Hwy 401 east. Cutting through the middle of southwestern Ontario, it will merge with Hwy 403 outside Woodstock, 185km away. Continue on Hwy 403 east for 135km to Toronto.

21

Being transported to the 1860s at Upper Canada Village in Morrisburg.

Thousand Island Parkway

DURATION	DISTANCE	GREAT FOR
7 days	250km/155 miles	Wine, Culture, Families

BEST TIME TO GO	May to June when the weather is not too hot and crowds are smaller.

Bellevue House, Kingston

This is a trip for people who want to slow things down. Most jump on Hwy 401 to speed to Ottawa, but they miss one of the best parts of Ontario. The drive hugs the St Lawrence River and you'll be tempted to stop in every little hamlet to see what is on offer. The area is a haven for small craft producers – think beer and whiskey rather than trinkets.

Link Your Trip

16 Lake Superior Coastline

Combine your drive north with a trip to the edge of Ontario. Sudbury is 250km from the northwest gate of Algonquin Provincial Park via Hwy 11/17.

19 The Kawarthas

Continue your drive up to the north of the province by heading northwest from Kingston for around 200km to Peterborough.

01 KINGSTON

Kingston was Canada's first capital for three years due to its strategic location, and this still rings true today. Pretty much in between Toronto and Ottawa, it's a lovely small city to grab a bite to eat and stretch your legs at the waterfront. It's also a Canadian historian's dream to visit **Bellevue House** (pc.gc.ca/en/lhn-nhs/on/bellevue), which was briefly home to the first prime minister, Sir John A Macdonald, or the **Fort Henry National Historic Site** (forthenry.com), a restored British fortification dating from 1832. If that bores you, then head downtown to Princess St and sample local beers at **Stone**

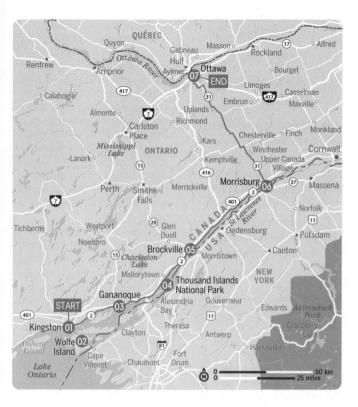

03 GANANOQUE

One of the largest towns in the Thousand Islands region, Gananoque is the perfect place from which to set out and explore. The more adventurous can choose a multiday kayak trip with **1000 Islands Kayaking** (1000islandskayaking.com), but we recommend traveling with the **Gananoque Boat Line**(ganboat line.com), which has several cruise options, including a trip to **Boldt Castle** (boldtcastle.com), where Thousand Island salad dressing was reportedly invented. If you do choose this trip, be sure to bring your passport as it is technically in the US.

Gananoque has several great places to sleep and even more places to eat and drink, but since you are here to see the Thousand Islands, you might as well stay as close as possible by renting a houseboat from **Houseboat Holidays** (house boatholidays.ca).

THE DRIVE

Continue east up King St E/Hwy 2 until you are out of the city. The highway will fork – go right to take the scenic route via the Thousand Islands Pkwy. It's a wonderful 32km drive to the next stop; be sure to get a panoramic snap up the 130m-high **1000 Islands Tower**, which is roughly 20km from Gananoque.

04 THOUSAND ISLANDS NATIONAL PARK

Just south of Mallory-town is the **Thousand Islands National Park** (pc.gc.ca/pn-np/on/1000), a collection of 20 small islands and a lush archipelago. Splurge and stay in the park's luxurious oTENTik roofed safari tents as you explore the area for

---

City Ales (stonecityales.com) or book ahead for a fusion meal at **Chez Piggy** (chezpiggy.ca) – you won't be disappointed. End with a stroll by the waterfront, embracing the charm of a city that cherishes its role in Canada's history.

THE DRIVE

Once in downtown Kingston, head north for several blocks until you see signs for the Wolfe Island Ferry – that's your next stop. The ferry is free for both pedestrians and vehicles. The 25-minute journey is best spent on the deck as the views of Kingston are spectacular. The ferry will drop you off on Centre St on the island.

02 WOLFE ISLAND

Wolfe Island is the largest of the Thousand Islands' 1800-plus islands. Much of the island is undeveloped and that is its attraction. The main town, **Marysville**, has a few restaurants and accommodations, but the main draw is the general feeling of remoteness despite being so close to Kingston. The 2009 installation of hundreds of wind turbines adds to the surreal feeling, rather than detracting from the peaceful drive around the island or the calm walk around the coast. Bring a picnic from Kingston's artisanal shops and enjoy a few hours of thoughtful pondering before getting back on the road.

turtles and rare birds. There is very little light pollution here so the stargazing opportunities are fantastic, as are the kayaking and hiking trails. It's also amazingly child-friendly and the **Mallory-town Landing Visitors Centre**, just before the park entrance, has a playground, live animal shows and a bike path.

THE DRIVE
Once you've recharged your batteries, hop back in the car and continue to meander east along the parkway. After around 11km you'll come to a large interchange. Hwy 401 is a slightly longer route but quicker and with more traffic, so we suggest taking Hwy 2, which continues along the St Lawrence River until you reach Brockville.

05 BROCKVILLE
Brockville, the 'City of the Thousand Islands,' is an attractive place with historical Gothic-style buildings and riverfront parks that will make you want to stay almost indefinitely. Head first for the riverfront for a short stroll and then take the children (or any young-at-hearts) to the **Aquatarium** (aquatarium.ca), an interactive museum detailing the history and ecology of the St Lawrence seaway. From here, head along Water St until you reach the **Brockville Railway Tunnel** (brockville-railwaytunnel.com), a 15-minute walk through a converted railway tunnel with a sound-and-light show. It's a great way to escape the heat in summer. You'll emerge at Pearl St, and we suggest turning left and walking 200m to Buell St, down which you'll find the highly rated **Buell**

TOP TIP:
Take the Scenic Route loop

Don't follow your GPS for this route – it will always send you to Hwy 401 to shave off time. Take Hwy 2, which skirts along the coast, and enjoy the drive – there's less traffic and, while the speed limit is slower, you won't want to travel too fast anyway.

Street Bistro (buellstreetbistro.com) for dinner.

THE DRIVE
When leaving Brockville, ignore the signs directing you to Hwy 401 – it's quicker but there is not much to see. Instead, stay on King St/Hwy 2 for 65km until you reach Morrisburg. The St Lawrence River will stay on your right the whole way, making you wonder why anyone would take a larger highway over this route.

06 MORRISBURG
Small and quaint, the stop in Morrisburg is really just for one thing – the preeminent historic attraction, **Upper Canada Village** (uppercanadavillage.com). Here costume-clad interpreters emulate life in the 1860s, never breaking character no matter what you try. There are around 40 historic buildings to discover, including a blacksmith, tavern, schoolhouse and a wool factory.

It's fun to stay over in **Mont-gomery House**, a historical log house, and try each of the four restaurants for authentic (but still modern and tasty) food.

The village is one of the best ways to learn about Canada's history without reading about it, so is an ideal visit with children (or adults with shorter attention spans). Try to come for a weekend in summer when it hosts special events, such as a haunted walk and musical celebrations.

THE DRIVE
Trace your steps back west on Hwy 2 for 11km until you see the turnoff to the right on Hwy 31. Travel north for 66km heading for Ottawa. You'll have a very short drive on Hunt Club Rd before heading into town on the Airport Pkwy/Hwy 79. This 10km will take you right to downtown Ottawa.

07 OTTAWA
The final stop of the trip encompasses multiple aspects into one city – lovely river views, grand historical buildings and artisanal cuisine. Ottawa is a city best explored through food so head to the **Rideau Centre**, just south of the famous **Byward Market** (byward-market.com). This market is the perfect place to stop when hunger strikes. Aside from the fresh produce and cheese, an array of international takeaway joints offers falafel, spicy curries, flaky pastries, sushi... the list goes on. Look for the stand selling beavertails, Ottawa's signature sizzling flat-dough dish. Once you park, get out and stretch your legs as you explore Canada's capital city.

View from 1000 Islands Tower (p147)

BUENA VISTA IMAGES/GETTY IMAGES ©

Le Château Frontenac (p152), Québec City

Québec

Explore

Québec

Exploring Québec by car is a richly rewarding introduction to Canada's francophone culture. Of course, the big-city excitement of Montréal and the captivating old-town charms of Québec City should not be missed. But it's the province-wide encounters with bright-painted villages, passionate artisanal producers and achingly beautiful landscapes that reveal even more about the backstory and latter-day vibrancy of French-Canadian life. The scenery alone is worth the trip. Depending on your route, you'll be stopping for countless panoramic photos of dense woodland swathes, snaggle-toothed ancient peaks, or gorgeous little coves overlooking tranquil, shimmering shorelines. Stay longer for the full effect.

Montréal

One of Canada's biggest cities, Montréal is an endlessly exciting fusion of art scenes, contemporary culture, adventurous gastronomy and vibrant ethnic diversity that goes way beyond French or English identities. Spend a few days here and it will never feel like enough, especially if you time your visit for one of the huge festivals where everyone seems to be partying in the streets. Start your trip with the cobbled charms of Vieux-Montréal (Old Montréal), then dive into a world-class art museum or two. And don't miss the chance to dine with the locals (summertime outside tables recommended) in foodie-forward neighborhoods such as Little Italy, Quartier Latin and Plateau-Mont-Royal, where you'll find everything from classic and modern French cuisine to highly authentic dishes from Africa, South America and beyond.

Québec City

The spiritual citadel of francophone Québec is the superbly scenic Old Town area of this city, a beautiful, stone-walled district that looks and feels like a transplant from medieval Europe. It's dominated by Le Château Frontenac, a steep-roofed grand hotel that no visitor can pass without photographing. Wandering the narrow streets and old squares that radiate from the château is all anyone needs to do here. But aside from the museums and important historical sites (guided walking tours are recommended), don't miss the chance to head beyond the Old Town walls and explore the wider city, including

WHEN TO GO

There are festivals and long, sunny days in July and August here. But it can also be hot and crowded at this time, with hotel vacancies hard to find, especially in Québec City. Better to visit in late spring or early fall, with the latter especially popular among traveling autumnal-foliage fans.

the vibrant St-Jean-Baptiste area with its indie restaurants, hip boutiques and inviting nightlife.

Trois-Rivières

Located on the north shore of the St Lawrence River between Montréal and Québec City, this historic community (one of the oldest in North America) is a handy pit stop for province-wide explorers. But it's not just about restocking your car cooler with drinks and snacks. If you have time, an overnight stay here is recommended so you can peruse some unique museums (including an old prison) and partake of local activities such as nature hikes and canoeing trips that take you into the superbly scenic Mauricie region.

Gaspé

The shoreline 'capital' of the breathtakingly scenic Gaspé Peninsula is a handy hub with places to eat and sleep. And it also has an excellent museum that illuminates the area's salty maritime past as well as profiling Jacques Cartier, a revered figure in French-Canadian history. But the wider peninsula will always be calling your name here, with coastal walks and dramatic cliffside views never far away.

TRANSPORT

Montréal and Québec City each have international airports (the former is much larger). Alternatively, you can reach both cities and beyond on Canada's VIA Rail train services; US Amtrak trains also arrive in Montréal from New York City. Long-distance buses arrive from neighboring provinces and the US; you can also drive here via highways from the US and across Canada.

WHERE TO STAY

Montréal has a huge and diverse array of accommodations, with everything from independent hostels to sleek boutique hotels. Québec City takes a different approach, especially in the Old Town area, where pension-style hotels and antique-lined B&Bs abound. Prices in these cities and beyond are highest during the summer peak (plus during the region's large winter festivals), but July and August availability is especially tight in Québec City. Book far ahead for the iconic **Fairmont Le Château Frontenac** (fairmont.com/frontenac-quebec) or Montréal's stylish **Hôtel Le Germain** (germainhotels.com). And check out **Camping Québec** (campingquebec.com) for campsite options throughout the province.

WHAT'S ON

Festival d'été de Québec
(feq.ca) Canada's biggest music festival is a multiday extravaganza of concerts in Québec City.

Festival de Montgolfières de Gatineau
(montgolfieresgatineau.com) Hundreds of hot-air balloons take flight, alongside a huge roster of live music.

Montréal International Jazz Festival
(montrealjazzfest.com) Huge and mostly free open-air concerts in downtown Montréal.

Just for Laughs Festival
(hahaha.com) Montréal's world-famous comedy showcase, with hundreds of acts around the city.

Resources

Bonjour Québec *(bonjour quebec.com)* Official tourist-information site for the province.

Cult Mtl *(cultmtl.com)* The inside track on Montréal events, arts, life and more.

Destination Québec Cité *(quebec-cite.com)* Specific visitor information for Québec City.

Tourisme Montréal *(mtl.org)* Planning resources for your Montréal visit.

22

Up to the Laurentians

DURATION	DISTANCE	GREAT FOR
2 days	120km/75 miles	Wine, Nature

BEST TIME TO GO	Winter for the region's best skiing; May/June for spring flowers; September/October for a colorful fall display.

St-Jérôme Cathedral, St-Jérôme

This straightforward road trip will take you through more than a half-dozen delightful towns and villages, from St-Jérôme, the acknowledged gateway to the Laurentians, and busy St-Sauveur-des-Monts to Val-David, perhaps the best place to put up your feet and chow down along the way, and Ville de Mont-Tremblant, la crème on your Laurentians gâteau. It will also introduce you to Québec province's oldest national park.

Link Your Trip

23 Eastern Townships

Drive an hour east of Montréal for charming villages and lakeside beauty.

24 Montréal to Québec City

From St-Jérôme, drive 85km northeast to the start of this memorable journey to Québec's oldest city.

01 ST-JÉRÔME

This sizable town, the largest in the region, may not overwhelm you, but it is officially recognized as the gateway to the Laurentians. It's also the southern terminus of the **Parc Linéaire du P'tit Train du Nord** (Little Train of the North Linear Park; laurentides.com/parclineaire), a trail built on top of old railway tracks for cyclists and cross-country skiers. Despite its administrative and industrial look and feel, St-Jérôme is worth a stop for its neo-Romanesque, Byzantine–style **cathedral** (paroissestj.ca/paroisse-saint-jerome), a castle-like structure built in 1897 with stunning stained-glass

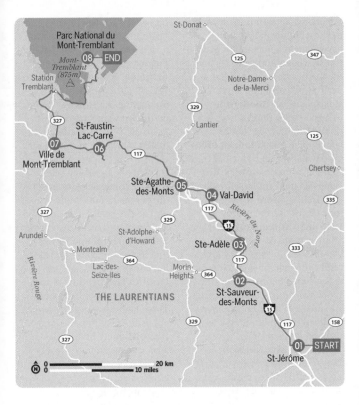

Parc Linéaire du P'tit Train du Nord

Should you see roadside signs directing you to the Parc Linéaire du P'tit Train du Nord (Little Train of the North Linear Park), don't think it's showing you the way to something that goes 'choo-choo.' It's a trail system built on top of old railway tracks that wends its way for 232km north from Bois-de-Filion to Mont Laurier, passing streams, rivers, rapids, lakes and great mountain scenery. In summer it's open to bicycles and in-line skates, and you'll find rest stops, information booths, restaurants, B&Bs and bike rental and repair shops along the way. In winter the system lures cross-country skiers to the 42km-long section between St-Jérôme and Val-David, while snowmobile aficionados rule between Val-David and Mont Laurier (49km).

windows and Venetian chandeliers. Nearby is the town's **Musée d'Art Contemporain des Laurentides** (museelaurentides.ca), a contemporary-art museum with small but excellent exhibitions of work by regional artists. St-Jérôme is about 50km northwest of Montréal. Reach it via Rte 15 Nord and take exit 43E.

THE DRIVE
Rejoin Rte 15 Nord and follow it for just under 20km to exit 60, which will lead to Chemin Jean-Adam (Rte 364 Ouest) then Ave de la Gare and lastly Ave de l'Église in the center of St-Sauveur-des-Monts.

 02 ST-SAUVEUR-DES-MONTS

Usually just called St-Sauveur, this busy village is often deluged with day-trippers due to its proximity to central Montréal, 70km to the southeast. A pretty church anchors Rue Principale, the attractive main street, which is lined with restaurants, cafes and stylish boutiques. The main draw here is Les Sommets, five major ski hills with about 100 runs for all levels of expertise. The biggest hill, **Sommet St-Sauveur** (montsaintsauveur.com), is famous for its night skiing. Thrill-seekers might also enjoy other attractions here like Le Dragon, a double zip line, the Viking, a scenic, dry 1.5km-long

toboggan ride through rugged mountain terrain, and, in summer, **Parc Aquatique** (Water Park; sommets.com/en/water-park-saint-sauveur). Cross-country skiers flock to the more than 150km of interconnecting trails at **Morin Heights**, 8km to the west.

The **Factoreries Tanger St-Sauveur** (tangeroutletcanada.com/saintsauveur/stores), factory outlets representing some 30 big-name brands from Reebok and Puma to Guess and OshKosh B'gosh, are another draw in St-Sauveur.

THE DRIVE

The easiest way to reach Ste-Adèle, some 10km to the north, is to follow Rue Principale east to Rte 117 Nord and take it to Blvd de Ste-Adèle and the center.

03 STE-ADÈLE

Ste-Adèle may not be as pretty as St-Sauveur, but there are plenty of things to keep families and outdoor enthusiasts happy, especially in and around picturesque **Lac Rond** (Round Lake). If you're traveling to Mont-Tremblant – the town and/or the national park – this might be a good place to stop awhile as it has some excellent accommodations. Go for **Au Clos Rolland** (auclosrolland.com), a B&B in a sprawling 1904 mansion with gorgeous public spaces and vast grassy lawns surrounding it. Au Clos Rolland is only 300m from the Parc Linéaire du P'tit Train du Nord recreation path, making this a great option for cyclists and cross-country skiers. A favorite place for a meal is the **Adèle Bistro** (adelebistro.ca), right on Lac Rond, with serious French dishes. Rue Morin, which runs from Lac Rond down to Rte 117, is lined with bars and other places to drink after dark.

THE DRIVE

To reach Val-David, head southeast on Blvd de Ste-Adèle to Rte 15 Nord. Follow that for about 6km when it merges with Rte 117 Nord. You'll reach Rue de l'Église in Val-David after about 4km.

04 VAL-DAVID

Arguably the most attractive village in the Laurentians, little Val-David offers great food, lovely wooded trails and views of the narrow

Rivière du Nord running through the heart of town. Its charms have made it a magnet for artists, whose studios and galleries line the main street, Rue de l'Église, where you'll also find a number of agencies like **Roc & Ride** (rocnride.com) that will get you skiing, climbing, cycling or canoeing. The town's **tourist office** (valdavid.com), in a cute old train station, is conveniently located alongside the Parc Linéaire du P'tit Train du Nord recreation trail. Check out the nearby **Val-David Summer Market** (Marché d'Été de Val-David; marchesdici.org/nos-marches/val-david/#marche-d-ete) if you're in town on a Saturday morning. You'll also find artisanal bakeries, jazz music in cafes on summer weekends and more than a few arts-and-crafts people.

Artsy **Le Mouton Noir** (bistromoutonnoir.com) attracts a very Val-Davidian crowd of beards – some hippie-esque, some hipster-esque, some lumberjack-y. Everyone enjoys the funky Canadian fusion on old LP menus; you gotta love a place that serves bibimbap alongside poutine. Open mike on Friday and live music on Saturday keep the 'Black Sheep' baaing till late on weekends.

THE DRIVE

To reach Ste-Agathe-des-Monts, just less than 10km to the northwest, head southwest on Rue de l'Église toward the Parc Linéaire du P'tit Train du Nord then turn right onto Rte 117.

05 STE-AGATHE-DES-MONTS

This mountain village, located about 9km northwest of Val-David, has a prime location

on Lac des Sables. By the beginning of the 1900s, it was a well-known spa town. Later, famous guests included Queen Elizabeth, who came here during WWII, and Jackie Kennedy. Ste-Agathe is a stopover point on the Parc Linéaire du P'tit Train du Nord recreation path, making this a great option for cyclists and cross-country skiers. If you'd like to get out on the water, **Croisières Alouette** offers regular 50-minute cruises on Lac des Sables between two and five times a day in summer. The large **Hôtel Spa Watel** (hotelspawater.com), overlooking Lac des Sables, has spa facilities plus treatments and an indoor and outdoor pool. Three lakeside beaches are just opposite, including the large **Plage Major**. There is also quite a good restaurant in a lovely dining room here with views out to the lake.

THE DRIVE

From Ste-Agathe-des-Monts join Rte 117 Nord and follow it for 20km to exit 107. Follow Chemin des Lacs for 3km into the center of St-Faustin-Lac-Carré.

06 ST-FAUSTIN-LAC-CARRÉ

The gateway to the region around Mont-Tremblant, St-Faustin has a couple of attractions in its own right, including a gorgeous slice of protected Laurentian wilderness at **Centre Touristique Éducatif des Laurentides** (ctel.ca), 20km by road to the south. This verdant park is a marvelous protected area and a great place to learn about local flora and fauna. The extensive trail network includes some wheelchair-accessible sections,

Parc Linéaire du P'tit Train du Nord (p155)

and there are also kayak and canoe rentals to use in the dozens of lakes around here. Another reason to visit St-Faustin is **La Tablée des Pionniers** (latablee despionniers.com), a seasonal roadside eatery serving top-notch traditional Québécois cuisine in rustic country surroundings. Multicourse menus, served during maple-sugaring and apple-harvest seasons, feature such delights as split pea, cabbage and bacon soup; smoked-trout soufflés; pulled-pork and mushroom puff-pastry pies; and maple-walnut tarts – all accompanied by cider and maple from the family's orchards.

THE DRIVE
From St-Faustin, follow Rte 117 Nord for 10km to exit 116 and Rte 327, which turns into Chemin du Village.

Photo Opportunity
The base of Mont-Tremblant as the skiers descend.

07 **VILLE DE MONT-TREMBLANT**

This village is the crown jewel of the Laurentians, lorded over by the 875m-high eponymous peak and surrounded by pristine lakes and rivers. It's a hugely popular winter playground, drawing ski bums from late October to mid-April. Founded in 1938, the **Mont-Tremblant Ski Resort** (tremblant.ca) is among the top-ranked international resorts in eastern North America and includes more than 100 trails and 14 lifts. Its state-of-the-art summer facilities and

activities include golf courses, water sports, cycling, tennis courts, hiking, yoga and zip lines.

Ville de Mont-Tremblant is actually divided into three sections: Station Tremblant, the ski hill and pedestrianized tourist resort at the foot of the mountain; **Mont-Tremblant Village**, a tiny cluster of homes and businesses about 4km to the southwest; and Mont-Tremblant Centre Ville, the main town and commercial center about 12km south of the mountain.

There's the full range of places to stay – from the basic-but-comfortable **Auberge Manitonga Hostel** (manitongahostel. com) to the uber-luxurious **Hotel Quintessence** (hotelquintes sence.com). In-between is the favorite, **Auberge Le Lupin** (le-lupin.com), a log house with nine themed and spacious rooms just 1km away from the ski station and

Mont-Tremblant Ski Resort

private beach access to sparkling Lac Tremblant. Among the best restaurants are **La Petite Cachée** (petitecachee.com) in a charming chalet halfway between the ski slopes and Mont-Tremblant Village, and **sEb** (seblartisan culinaire.com), where seasonal, sustainable local ingredients are turned into culinary works of art.

🚗 THE DRIVE

It's just under 30km from Ville de Mont-Tremblant to the Diable sector entrance of Parc National du Mont-Tremblant. Follow Chemin du Village (Rte 327) to Chemin Duplessis and Chemin du Lac Supérieur.

08 PARC NATIONAL DU MONT-TREMBLANT

Québec province's oldest **park** (Mont Tremblant National Park; sepaq.com/pq/mot), which opened in 1895, covers 1510 sq km of gorgeous Laurentian lakes, rivers, hills and woods. The park shelters rare vegetation (including silver maple and red oak) and is home to foxes, deer, moose and wolves. It is also a habitat for almost 200 bird species, including a huge blue heron colony.

You'll find fantastic hiking and mountain-biking trails as well as camping and river routes for canoes. The half-day **Méandres de la Diable** route from Lac Chat to Mont de la Vache Noire is particularly popular. You won't be able to drive this far into the park. Reserve a canoe and a place on the shuttle bus by calling the park reservations line well in advance.

🚗 THE DRIVE

From the Parc National du Mont-Tremblant you can return to Montréal via Rte 117 Sud and Rte 15 Sud (128km) and walk around Old Montréal.

MARIDAV/SHUTTERSTOCK ©

Maple syrup

MAPLE: AMBER NECTAR OF THE GODS

Québec is by far the largest producer of maple syrup in North America, with production exceeding 24.5 million liters, and the Laurentians are a major contributor. That's more than three-quarters of the world's maple syrup, which is perhaps why it enjoys such pride of place here, appearing on everything from meat and desserts to foie gras, blended with smoothies and, of course, in maple beer. It's a very big business and worth a lot of money. It was thus not entirely a surprise when, over the course of several months in 2011 and 2012, nearly 3000 tonnes of syrup valued at $18.7 million was stolen from a storage facility in Québec. The Great Canadian Maple Syrup Heist was the most valuable in Canadian history. In late 2012, 17 men were arrested.

French settlers began producing maples syrup regularly in the 1800s after learning from Indigenous people how to make it from maple-tree sap. Sap is usually extracted in March after enzymes convert starch into sugars over the winter. Once the weather warms and the sap starts flowing, the tree is tapped and the long process of boiling the raw sap down into syrup begins. It takes about 40L of sap to make 1L of syrup.

Québécois head to *cabanes à sucre* (sugar shacks) out in the countryside during this time. There they sample the first amber riches of the season and do the *tire d'érable* (taffy pull), where steaming maple syrup is poured into the snow and then scooped up on a popsicle stick once it's cooled.

23

Eastern Townships

☑

Antique-store hopping for a glimpse of another era.

DURATION	DISTANCE	GREAT FOR
1 day	153km/95 miles	Culture, Families, Nature

BEST TIME TO GO	June and July has sunny weather with less traffic than in August.

Musée du Chocolat de la Confiserie Bromont

This is a trip for people who like to take things at a leisurely pace, to experience local Québécois life with all its quirks – local produce, including cider and cheese made by monks, lakeside towns with duck festivals, and a treasure hunt of open-air murals. Between all the eccentricities, the ride is smooth and carefree.

Link Your Trip

22 Up to the Laurentians

After completing the trip, head two hours northwest to St-Jérôme for the start of a memorable ramble through the fabulous lake- and hillside scenery of the Laurentians.

24 Montréal to Québec City

From Sherbrooke, head northwest to Trois-Rivières, from where you can make a beeline for Québec City, or follow this itinerary in reverse to head back to Montréal.

01 **BROMONT**

From Montréal's Champlain Bridge take Hwy 10 for 75km and take Exit 78 to central Bromont. The ever-changing palette of Mt Brome is the highlight of stopping in this town. Its winter pines are laden with snow, luring skiers to **Ski Bromont** (skibromont.com) with its roughly 140 trails, including almost 100 trails open for night skiing. In warmer weather the resort hosts a water park with fun slides, and its 100km of marked trails, including 15 thrilling downhill routes, have made it a major draw for mountain-bike aficionados (Bromont has

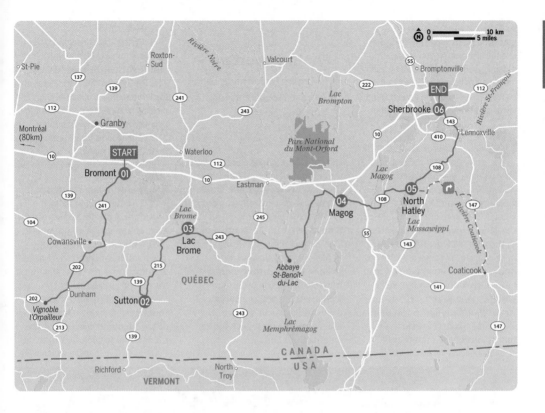

hosted world championships). Even if you don't stop for long, a cruise by the edges of the 553m-high mount is a fine start to the journey into the region and its hidden history – Mt Brome is what remains of an ancient series of volcanoes.

If that sounds too active, you might prefer to indulge with treats such as chocolate-covered cherries at the **Musée du Chocolat de la Confiserie Bromont** (lemuseeduchocolatdelaconfiserie bromont.com). Its museum covers the history and process of chocolate making. And vegans can enjoy the taste sensations at **Gaïa Resto Végan** (legaia.ca).

THE DRIVE
Head south for 35km through Cowansville to Vignoble l'Orpailleur, a flat drive through the region's wineries and the long-flat houses with pruned lawns. As you head east from the wineries to Sutton, the 60km of road rise and there are three crossroads without any large signage. Instead, look for the small street signs to decide which street to follow.

02 SUTTON
This is wine country and the most prestigious of them all, **Vignoble l'Orpailleur** (orpailleur.ca), has a quirky display on the history of alcohol in Québec and offers wine tasting year round. The vineyard was

established in 1982, but l'Orpailleur has pedigree – two of those in charge of the vines are sons of winemakers. The flat greenery is worth a peek, even if you are the designated driver. It has an attached restaurant, too.

Pause for a stroll through relaxed and beautiful Sutton and to linger at one of its cheery cafes. You might spot skiers getting warm after a trip on Mont Sutton during the winter, and hikers recovering from the climbs and rough camping on **Parc d'Environnement Naturel** (parcsutton.com).

THE DRIVE
The easy 18km drive northeast to Lac Brome is along Rte 215. In the

south, the trees are sparser with grasslands and lawns stretching out into the distance. As you approach the town, you'll know it because of the mansion-like homes beaming as if recently painted, and pine trees on large lawns as if every day were Christmas.

03 LAC BROME

The traditional village-life essence of the Eastern Townships is encapsulated in downtown Lac Brome, the name given to a town made up of seven villages that converge on a lake of the same name. The town is home to the well-heeled, and the stores here cater to fine tastes with boutique clothing and gift stores, and more than a dozen well-curated antiques. Many stores are in converted Victorian houses, so there is a British flavor of yesteryear that is part of the highlight of

Photo Opportunity

At Abbaye St-Benoît-du-Lac with Lac Memphrémagog in the background.

stopping here. Stroll the lake and pop in for the area's famous duck products at **Brome Lake Duck Farm** (canardsdulacbrome.com). Lac Brome's prettiest village, **Knowlton**, is in the south and has the nickname the Knamptons (a play on the Hamptons) for the swanky **19th-century country houses**, owned by Montréalers who use the town as a summer getaway. It's worth driving off the main road for a peek at the architectural heritage.

 THE DRIVE

On the 43km drive from Knowlton, Lac Brome, to Magog, you'll first pass the Abbaye St-Benoît-du-Lac. Take Rte 243 east for five minutes and the left turnoff at Chemin de Glen, passing picturesque ponds and some unpaved roads to the abbey after 23km. Then follow the lakeside road north 20km to Magog.

04 MAGOG

Just 20km before you enter Magog from the south, the **Abbaye St-Benoît-du-Lac** (abbaye.ca) is an unmissable highlight of the townships. The complex mixes traditional architecture, such as a tall church tower, with modern features, such as colorful tiling. The abbey is framed by the wide dark expanse of Lac Memphrémagog and the mountains, resplendent in trees,

Parc National du Mont Orford

which are particularly spectacular in the fall or dressed in winter snow. A visit is especially magical if you can coincide with the three-daily Gregorian chanting recitals. Drop by the abbey to buy products made by monks, such as blueberries dipped in chocolate, cider and cheese. Continue on with a drive through pretty downtown Magog and around Lac Memphrémagog to ogle the waterfront properties. You can even take a narrated boat cruise on the lake, if you have extra time up your sleeve and have booked a month in advance. The **Parc National du Mont Orford** (sepaq.com/pq/mor) is also nearby for winter skiing and summer hiking.

THE DRIVE
The short but hilly 18km drive east from Magog to North Hatley passes by drool-worthy redbrick and colorful stately houses in the loftiest section and then the road narrows and becomes surrounded by thick trees just before North Hatley. If you can make it to North Hatley's Farmers Market, enter by car along Capelton and park for free.

05 NORTH HATLEY
North Hatley is what first-timers to the region picture as the Eastern Townships and it is this beauty, easily one of the top stunners in Québec, that makes the town worthy of a stop. Admire the postcard-perfect aspects of the village – hugging the north of sparkling **Lac Massawippi**, populated with visitors in colorful bathers and kayaks in summer, and polished-up centuries-old houses flanking the streets. A cruise along the main street is the best way to spot the restored historic houses and antique stores, which are filled

DO MI NIC/SHUTTERSTOCK ©

Astrolab, Parc National du Mont-Mégantic

NATIONAL PARKS

There are four national parks in the Eastern Townships, each with a slightly different flavor and all worth making extended stops.

Plan Your Trip

If you plan to camp or stay in a hut, check ahead; some accommodations are quite basic and not all parks are open year-round. The trails leading to the national parks are gravel, so plan for your wheels to rough it a little.

Parc National du Mont Orford

This compact **park** (sepaq.com/pq/mor) is a delight in summer and a favorite with families for its gentle hiking trails, kayaking and canoeing in its lakes, and its small size, conveniently reached 8km northwest from Magog.

Parc National du Mont-Mégantic

The standout feature in this **park** (sepaq.com/pq/mme) at the eastern extremity of the townships, 80km east of Sherbrooke, is the **AstroLab** (astrolab-parc-national-mont-megantic.org/en) observatory and educational center. If you have kids in tow, finish the day's road trip with an astronomy tour (reservations required).

Parc National de la Yamaska

At the heart of this 12-sq-km park near Bromont is an arrow-shaped lake ringed by towering forests. Come here in warm weather to rent sailboards, canoes and rowboats and then stay in a comfortable nature cabin. Visit in winter for snowshoeing and Nordic skiing.

Parc National de Frontenac

Wildlife lovers should make the trek 100km northeast of Sherbrooke to Frontenac to spot more than 200 species of bird and 30 of mammal. The park borders **Lac St-François**, with lakeside campsites and cabins, and has good family water activities as well as hiking and cycling.

Parc de la Gorge de Coaticook

hiking. If you have kids (or you are a big kid at heart), aim to visit on a summer evening for one of the highlights of Coaticook, **Foresta Lumina** (foresta lumina.com), an outdoor light show where forest trails turn into colorful lit-up paths through the national park. At other times, there is an animal petting farm and winter snow-tubing. Be sure to stop off for a maple syrup ice cream at **Laiterie De Coaticook Ltée** at 1000 Rue Child.

From North Hatley head east on Rte 143 and then south along Rte 147 for 28km (30 minutes) to Parc de la Gorge de Coaticook. To rejoin the main part of the trip, head north on Rte 147, becoming Rte 143, for 33km (30 minutes) straight to Sherbrooke.

06 SHERBROOKE

More of a small city than a township, there are unusual but worthy attractions to make Sherbrooke, the last of the main Eastern Townships, your final destination for this trip. Hunt for the 11 **street murals** dotted downtown at the **Circuit des Murales de Sherbrooke** starting from the corner of Rue Frontenac and Wellington. Each piece tells a local story of the people and region, including painted life-size re-creations of shop facades that once stood in the area. From a distance, the facades are camou-flaged by the adjacent real stores, adding to the hunt-and-discovery fun, especially for tired kids at the end of a road trip. At **Bishop's University** (ubishops.ca/st-marks-chapel) original architecture abounds, with most of the two-dozen buildings dating from the 1840s. The most convention-ally attractive architectural sight is **St Mark's Chapel**, which woos visitors with stained-glass windows and decorative pews.

with local treasures. Catch the local buzz by planning a visit to coincide with the **North Hatley Farmers Market** on Saturdays in warm weather, held at River Park. Tasting the locally pro-duced honey, apples and pastries are part of the charm, but it's the buskers and the chance to chat with locals that makes it special. By night you can taste the local ingredients that go into four-course menus at **Auberge Le Coeur d'Or**.

THE DRIVE

The 20km drive northeast from North Hatley to Circuit des Murales de Sherbrooke is a mostly straight, flat trip whether you take Rte 108 or the

more southerly Rte 143, though the former does pass an asphalt plant, which might amuse those looking for a passing quirky sight. Traffic will get thicker as you enter Sherbrooke.

DETOUR
Coaticook
Start: 05 North Hatley

Cheese lovers will find the cheese map provided by the tourism office enough reason to detour to attractive Coaticook, a southern town of the Eastern Townships full of nature activities. The town's big magnet for outdoorsy types is the lush **Parc de la Gorge de Coaticook** (gorgedecoaticook.qc.ca) where you can explore the endless green space bordering the USA while horseback riding, mountain biking or

Abbaye St-Benoît-du-Lac, Magog (p162)

WHY I LOVE THIS TRIP

Phillip Tang, writer

This trip takes you into the heart of classic, slow Québécois life with wholesome, locally produced food. Many think that an abbey sounds like a dressed-up church, until they reach Abbaye St-Benoît-du-Lac and get to taste cheese and cider made by monks, who then break into Gregorian chanting. All this plus knockout lakes and mountains once you continue on your merry way.

24

Montréal to Québec City

BEST FOR

Delving into the minutiae of Québécois lives at quirky museums.

DURATION	DISTANCE	GREAT FOR
1 day	383km/238 miles	Culture, Nature, Families

BEST TIME TO GO	June and July has sunny weather, and less traffic than August.

Musée Gilles-Villeneuve, Berthierville

This trip is for people who want to explore Québec's lesser-known Mauricie region, reachable in a couple of hours from Montréal along the northern shore of the St Lawrence River, with stops at wonderfully weird museums. The backdrop is the ever-reassuring guiding line of the mighty waterway as well as a constant flow of quaint towns to pass through and compare.

Link Your Trip

23 Eastern Townships

From Trois-Rivières, head south to join this classic trip at Sherbrooke, then follow the itinerary in reverse for a picturesque route back to Montréal.

25 Around, Over & In the St Lawrence River

At this trip's end, continue to Île d'Orléans,' just north of Québec City, for island roaming, waterfalls and outdoor adventures.

01 BERTHIERVILLE

From Montréal take scenic Hwy 40 east on the northern side of the St Lawrence River for 80km (one hour), to pause at pretty Berthierville. Fans of race-car driving should make a pit stop at **Musée Gilles-Villeneuve**, which commemorates the eponymous Québécois motorsport legend, who grew up in Berthierville. The small museum housed in an old post has a surprisingly large collection of race cars (including the one with which his son, Jacques Villeneuve, won the Indy 500), a mini race track and memorabilia galore

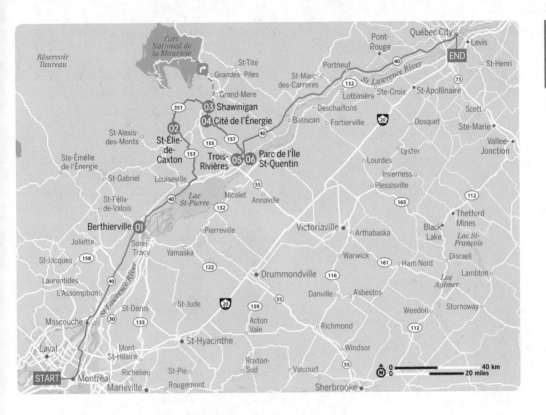

such as helmets, race suits and competition snowmobiles.

For something more tranquil, the free **Park Scirbi** has three nature trails from 2km to 4.5km in length, where you can spot more than 222 species of birds, grazing farm animals and wetlands. You can also participate in nature workshops. Parking is available.

Then drop by **Délices D'antan** (on Rang de la Rivière-Bayonne) for the local specialty, potato doughnuts.

 THE DRIVE
On the 70km drive northeast from Berthierville to St-Élie-de-Caxton, river-hugging Hwy 40 is quite flat until after Louiseville, where the road starts to climb away from the

St Lawrence River and up through neighborhoods of white flat houses sporting spacious green lawns.

02 ST-ÉLIE-DE-CAXTON

A town circled by mountains and decorated with lakes might be whimsical enough to make you break into song. Indeed Québécois folk musician and storyteller Fred Pellerin was born here and has famously sung its praise. It's worth a stop to see the charming houses and shops that inspired him. Head to the **Bureau d'Accueil Touristique** at 52 Chemin des Loisirs for the free two-hour (on foot; 30 minutes if driving) self-guided **audio tour** (from June to October) 'Le Caxton

Légendaire' narrated by Pellerin himself, which really brings it all to life, even if you have never heard anything by him. Pop into the **Rond Coin** for an iconic eatery in the village, a boutique 'gridchize' (grilled cheese sandwich). While it's wholesome and delicious, half the fun is the location. The convivial restaurant and general store is inside a large round yurt, and it has novel accommodations set in old milk wagons.

THE DRIVE
The 28km drive from St-Élie-de-Caxton to Shawinigan is extremely flat and easygoing on the northeasterly Rte 351, and a bit bumpier though slightly greener east on Rte 153 with narrower roads. Both take you by large

Québécois homes that will make you envious of the space they have.

 03 SHAWINIGAN

Shawinigan's orderly downtown is modeled on Manhattan and set in a convenient grid of streets. Unlike central NYC, Shawinigan still maintains cute small stores and has river views from its cafes. Factor in some playtime with **D'Arbre en Arbre** on four very thrilling **zip-lining** courses in Parc de l'Île Melville. There are varying difficulties, which can get pretty challenging. It's set around the river with commanding views across downtown Shawinigan. Head to the river for a stroll, and if you have a spare couple of hours, you can rent a boat there for a cruise along the river. Then, if you plan to be here in the evening, book tickets to watch the **Cirque Éloize** show *Nezha,* about an orphan girl stranded on a pirate island, at the covered insulated amphitheater.

🚗 **THE DRIVE**

It's a swift 4km drive south from downtown Shawinigan to Cité de l'énergie on Île Melville, where there is also Parc de l'Île Melville. There is free outdoor parking on the island.

🧭 **DETOUR**

Parc National de la Mauricie
Start: 03 Shawinigan

Moose foraging by an idyllic lake, the plaintive cry of a loon gliding across the water, bear cubs romping beneath a potpourri of trees waiting to put on a spectacular show of color in the fall – these are scenes you might possibly stumble across while visiting **Parc National de la Mauricie** (pc.gc.ca/mauricie). What may well be Québec's best-run and best-organized park is also among its most frequented.

Photo Opportunity

Gliding on a zip line at Parc de l'Île Melville.

The numerous walking trails, which can take anywhere from half an hour to five days to complete, offer glimpses of the indigenous flora and fauna, brooks and waterfalls (the **Chutes Waber** in the park's western sector are particularly worth the hike), as well as panoramic views onto delicate valleys, lakes and streams. The longest trail, **Le Sentier Laurentien**, stretches over 75km of rugged wilderness in the park's northern reaches. Backcountry campsites are spaced out every 7km to 10km. No more than 40 people are allowed on the trail at any time, making reservations essential. Topographic maps are for sale at the park.

The park is excellent for canoeing. Five canoe routes, ranging in length from 14km to 84km, can accommodate everyone from beginners to experts. Canoe and kayak rentals ($18/50 per hour/day; locationcanot.com) are available at three sites, the most popular being **Lac Wapizagonke**, which has sandy beaches, steep rocky cliffs and waterfalls. One popular day trip has you canoeing from the Wapizagonke campground to the west end of the lake, followed by a 7.5km loop hike to the Chutes Waber and back by canoe.

The park entrance is located about 25km north of Shawinigan. Reach it from Shawinigan by driving along Hwy 55 north and taking exit 226.

04 CITÉ DE L'ÉNERGIE

The City of Energy is a kind of science museum built around a 1901 hydroelectric power station, telling the story of how machinery is powered. It might sound dry, but the multimedia exhibits help to make it amusing and educational. Tours of the historic area, with a river crossing and a visit to the power plant itself, are worth doing to make even more sense of the whole mini-city's past. Be sure to climb to the top of the observation tower for some fine views of the area. If you can visit on a summer evening, be sure to catch a show by **Cirque de Soleil**, reason enough to stop in the region. The musicians, dancers and acrobats put on a performance with the broad theme of energy.

Stop for a bite to eat at the **Roulotte Beauparlant**. The biggest claim to fame of this 1940s trailer-turned-diner is that former Prime Minister Jean Chrétien often ate here.

🚗 **THE DRIVE**

The 35km drive southeast along Rte 157 from Cité de l'Énergie to Trois-Rivières runs downhill toward the St Lawrence River on an uneventful, easy trip. You'll pass by tightly packed houses that give way to low-level farmlands and then back to quiet suburban streets with detached houses.

05 TROIS RIVIÈRES

It's no surprise that this is the most common rest stop on the way to Québec, when you realize how much there is to see and do in the town of Trois-Rivières. The area has a small selection of museums, but the quirky **Musée Québécois de Culture Populaire** (museepop.ca) is by far the most engaging. Visit for the temporary exhibitions, which

Moose, Parc National de la Mauricie

Cité de l'Énergie (p169)

pick out lesser-known aspects of the social and cultural life of the Québécois. Known as Musée POP, themes are indeed pop, rather than highbrow, and in the past have included a quirky show on the social significance of garage sales, and one exhibiting woodcarvings of birds commonly spotted in the area.

Then visit the **Centre d'Histoire de l'Industrie Papetière Boréalis**, which focuses on the process and history of paper making. Kids particularly love the workshops, which take them through the process of making their own sheet of paper. They can then continue to the underground vaults for a **treasure hunt** using UV flashlights.

Finish off with a stroll along the attractive **riverfront promenade**, which leads to the oldest section of town along Rue des Ursulines.

THE DRIVE
This brisk 4km drive north and then east across two bridges from central Trois-Rivières to Parc de l'île St-Quentin is easy. You can see the forested island for much of the ride. There is a $5 charge per person (including vehicle entry).

06 PARC DE L'ÎLE ST-QUENTIN
The island just across from the central Trois-Rivières waterside promenade has a riverside **beach** with yellow sand and a **pool** that are both worth

visiting in warm weather for a splash about. City views form the backdrop. The park also has easy boardwalk trails dotted with black squirrels, picnic tables and a playground, making it a great stop if you have kids with energy to use up.

THE DRIVE
After spending the day at Trois-Rivières, you can head directly to Québec City, 130km east on Hwy 40, or head back to Montréal 142km on Hwy 40 west. A more scenic route to return to Montréal is via the charming Eastern Townships, taking Rte 55 southeast either 155km to bustling Sherbrooke or 175km to picturesque North Hatley.

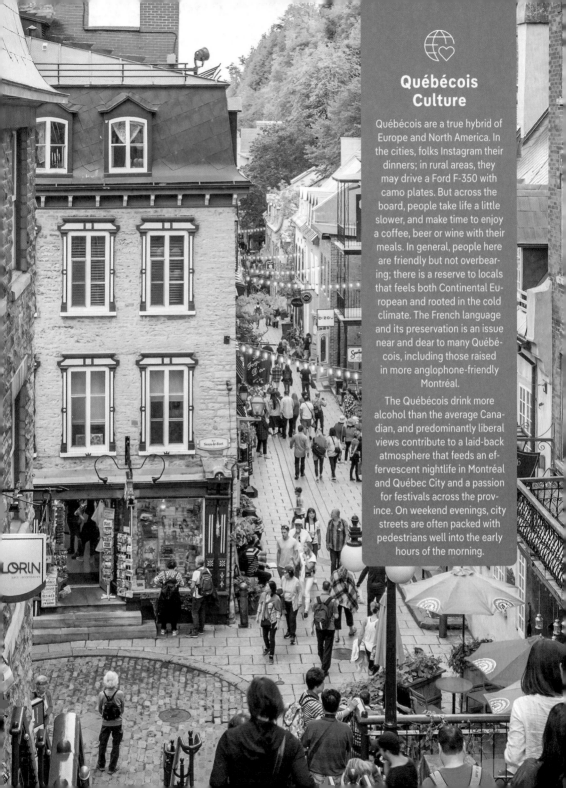

Québécois Culture

Québécois are a true hybrid of Europe and North America. In the cities, folks Instagram their dinners; in rural areas, they may drive a Ford F-350 with camo plates. But across the board, people take life a little slower, and make time to enjoy a coffee, beer or wine with their meals. In general, people here are friendly but not overbearing; there is a reserve to locals that feels both Continental European and rooted in the cold climate. The French language and its preservation is an issue near and dear to many Québécois, including those raised in more anglophone-friendly Montréal.

The Québécois drink more alcohol than the average Canadian, and predominantly liberal views contribute to a laid-back atmosphere that feeds an effervescent nightlife in Montréal and Québec City and a passion for festivals across the province. On weekend evenings, city streets are often packed with pedestrians well into the early hours of the morning.

25

Around, Over & In the St Lawrence River

DURATION	DISTANCE	GREAT FOR
3 days	383km/238 miles	Wine, Nature, Culture

BEST TIME TO GO	Visit May/June for springtime flowers and produce, September/October for magical fall colors.

La Boulange, St-Jean, Île d'Orléans

This drive, with the St Lawrence River at its heart, will circle you around idyllic Île d'Orléans, an island dotted with strawberry fields, apple orchards, windmills, workshops and galleries, across to the Côte de Beaupré, with a waterfall taller than Niagara Falls and Québec's largest basilica, and on to Charlevoix, a stunning outdoors playground with some lovely local towns crammed with artists' studios, galleries and boutiques.

Link Your Trip

24 Montréal to Québec City

It's less than a two-hour drive from the Île d'Orléans to Trois-Rivières, where you can complete this road trip along the St Lawrence in reverse.

26 The Saguenay Fjord & Lac St Jean

From Baie St Paul, continue another 138km northeast to a spectacular journey along the Saguenay Fjord.

01 **ÎLE D'ORLÉANS' NORTH COAST**
'Orléans Island,' 15km northeast of Québec City, with a population of just 6825, is still primarily a farming region and has emerged as the epicenter of Québec's agritourism movement. Foodies from all around flock to the local *économusées* (workshops) to watch culinary artisans at work.

To reach the island from Québec City, take Rte 440 Est to the Pont de l'Île d'Orléans, the huge suspension bridge leading to the island, then join Rte 368. This 60km-long road encircles the island, with two more cutting across it north–south.

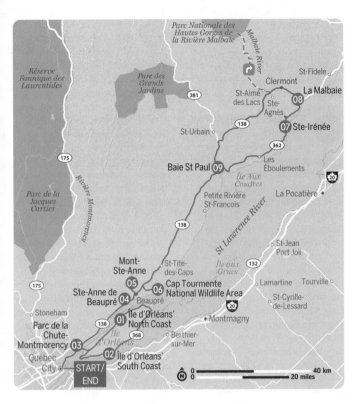

WHY I LOVE THIS TRIP

Steve Fallon, writer

This drive will introduce you to the best Québec has to offer: the agricultural delights and *économusées* (workshops) of the Île d'Orléans where artisans make everything from cider to nougat; the grandeur of Montmorency Falls; the awesomeness and spirituality of Ste-Anne de Beaupré; and the unspoiled beauty of Charlevoix with its pretty and very arty towns boasting a wide assortment of boutiques, galleries, cafes and restaurants.

02 ÎLE D'ORLÉANS' SOUTH COAST

The next three villages ahead of you on the island's southern coast are St-Jean, St-Laurent and Ste-Pétronille. Their edges are dotted with strawberry fields, orchards, cider producers, windmills, workshops and galleries. Some of the villages contain wooden and stone houses that are up to 300 years old.

If you're feeling peckish, stop off at **La Boulange** (laboulange. ca), a memorable bakery and a grocery store in St-Jean. Devour to-die-for croissants while taking in views of the St Lawrence and the 18th-century **Église St-Jean** next door.

Further along in St-Laurent, the little **Parc Maritime de St-Laurent** (parcmaritime.ca/ en) is worth a look to understand the maritime heritage of the region. At the nearby **La Forge à Pique-Assaut** (forge-pique-assaut.com), artisanal blacksmith Guy Bel makes and sells decorative objects at his *économusée*.

There are a half-dozen villages on the island. On the north side you'll find St-Pierre, Ste-Famille and St-François, each with its own attractions. Before setting out, though, stop in at the **Île d'Orléans tourist office** (tourisme.iledorleans.com/en), which you'll come to after crossing the bridge. Its very complete *Autour de l'Île d'Orléans* (Around the Île d'Orléans) brochure is well worth the $1 charged for it.

Then make a beeline to any of the many workshops and boutiques lining the road in St-Pierre, including **Cassis Monna & Filles** (cassismonna.com/en), where everything from mustard to liqueur is made from black-currants, and **La Nougaterie Québec** (nougateriequebec.com), where egg whites and honey are miraculously turned into nougat.

In Ste-Famille, the main draw is **Maison Drouin** (maisondrouin. com), a house dating back to 1730 that has never been modernized, while in St-François you can climb the wooden **Observation Tower** for views over the St Lawrence River and the brooding mountains beyond.

🚗 THE DRIVE

Nothing could be easier. Just continue on the only highway on the island – Rte 368 – which loops around the island and back to the bridge (33km).

Our last stop, in Ste-Pétronille, is the incomparable **Chocolaterie de l'Île d'Orléans** (chocolaterie orleans.com), where *chocolatiers* above a delightful shop in a 200-year-old house churn out tasty concoctions.

THE DRIVE
From Ste-Pétronille's center, continue along Rte 368 and back to the Pont de l'Île d'Orléans. Cross the bridge and join Rte 138 Ouest to the Blvd des Chutes exit and the Parc de la Chute-Montmorency (10km).

03 PARC DE LA CHUTE-MONTMORENCY
The waterfall in this national park just over the bridge from the Île d'Orléans is 83m high, topping Niagara Falls by about 30m (though it's not nearly as wide). What's cool is walking over the falls on the **suspension bridge** to see (and hear) them thunder down below.

Once you reach the park's entrance you have one of three choices: park the car and take the **cable car** (sepaq.com/destinations/parc-chute-montmorency) up to the falls; follow the Promenade de la Chute from the cable car's lower station and climb the 487-step **Escalier Panoramique** (Panoramic Staircase); or stay in the car and drive to the upper station and the **Manoir Montmorency**, a replica of an 18th-century manor house with an information counter, interpretation center about the falls and park, a shop and a terrace restaurant. To really get the adrenaline going, there's a zip line that shoots across the canyon in front of the falls and three levels of via ferrata (cable-aided protected climbing trails).

THE DRIVE
From Parc de la Chute-Montmorency, rejoin Rte 138 and this time travel east. The town and basilica of Ste-Anne de Beaupré are 25km to the northeast.

04 STE-ANNE DE BEAUPRÉ
The drive along the Côte de Beaupré to the **pilgrimage church** (sanctuaire sainteanne.org) at Ste-Anne de Beaupré is a delight in any season, including winter, when the ice floes in the St Lawrence shimmer in the sun under the bright blue sky. Approaching along Rte 138, the basilica tower's twin steeples dwarf everything else in town. Since the mid-1600s, the village has been an important Christian site; the annual pilgrimage around the feast day of St Anne (July 26) draws thousands of visitors. The awe-inspiring basilica you see today was constructed after a devastating blaze in 1922 and has been open since 1934. Inside, don't miss the lovely modern stained-glass windows (there are 214 of them), the impressive tilework and glittering ceiling mosaics depicting the life of St Anne.

A delightful spot to stop for lunch en route to the church is **Auberge Baker** (aubergebaker. com). It's 5km to the southwest in Château-Richer on Rte 360, which runs parallel inland to Rte 138.

THE DRIVE
Follow Rte 138 Est (also known as Blvd Ste-Anne in these parts) to the fork in the village of Beaupré and join the 360 Est (Ave Royale) to Mont-Ste-Anne.

05 MONT-STE-ANNE
This immensely popular **ski resort** (mont-sainte-anne.com) is just 50km northeast of Québec City so it gets a lot of weekend skiers, especially between mid-December and well into April. It counts nine lifts and 71 ski trails, nine of which are set aside for night skiing (from 4pm to 9pm). You'll find all sorts of other winter activities here, including cross-country skiing, snowshoeing, skating, ice canyoning and dogsledding. You can rent skis and snowboards too.

During the summer, the resort features mountain biking, hiking and golfing opportunities. This is also the time to hike to **Jean Larose Waterfalls** in a deep chasm to the south across Rte 360. With a drop height of 68m, it is one of the most beautiful (and least developed) waterfalls in Québec. You can walk around and across the falls via a series of steps (all 400 of them), ledges and bridges.

THE DRIVE
From Mont-Ste-Anne, follow Rte 360 Ouest (Blvd Beaupré) back to Rte 138 Est and exit at the signposted Chemin du Cap Tourmente (15km).

06 CAP TOURMENTE NATIONAL WILDLIFE AREA
Lying at the confluence of the upper and lower estuaries of the St Lawrence River, this **wildlife sanctuary** (canada.ca/en/environment-climate-change/services/national-wildlife-areas/locations/cap-tourmente.html) offers contrasting landscapes shaped by the meeting of the river, large coastal marshes, plains and mountains. It shelters

Photo Opportunity

La mer (the sea) that is the St Lawrence River from La Malbaie.

St Lawrence River, La Malbaie

a multitude of habitats that are home to a very wide diversity of animal and plant species. The wildlife area is home to more than 180 bird species, including flocks of snow geese that migrate to wetlands in spring and autumn. Many of these species are at risk, including the peregrine falcon, the bobolink and the butternut. In addition, there are 30 mammal species, 22 types of forest stands and 700 plant species. The sanctuary is beyond the villages of St-Joachim and Cap-Tourmente; there's a visitor center here and a network of marked trails.

THE DRIVE
Follow the Chemin du Cap Tourmente back up to Rte 138 Est. At Baie St Paul you have a choice, but we recommend following the Uoute du Fleuve along Rte 362 Est

to Ste-Irénée (88km) and La Malbaie (108km). On the way back you can drive the ear-popping hills of the Route des Montagnes (Mountain Route) along Rte 138 Ouest.

07 STE-IRÉNÉE
This stretch of the drive is particularly beautiful, with breathtaking views of the St Lawrence as you ride up and down the hills. The first major village is **Les Éboulements**, 'one of the prettiest villages in Québec,' the road signs tell us, with wonderful old wooden houses, an old mill and grazing sheep. Next up is Ste-Irénée, with full-frontal views of the river and its hilltop **Domaine Forget** (domaineforget.com), a music and dance academy with a 600-seat hall that attracts classical and jazz musicians and dancers

from around the world, particularly during its annual festival in summer. Just down the hill from the village as you approach La Malbaie is the **Observatoire de l'Astroblème de Charlevoix** (astroblemecharlevoix.org), an observatory that examines how meteors created the valleys on which Charlevoix sits through multimedia exhibits.

THE DRIVE
It's just 20km along Rte 362 Est to La Malbaie from Ste-Irénée.

08 LA MALBAIE
La Malbaie is a town on the St Lawrence River at the mouth of the Malbaie River. The river's so wide here that locals call it *la mer* (the sea). Formerly Murray Bay, it actually encompasses five once-distinct villages. The first you'll encounter

along Rte 362 Est from Ste-Irénée is Pointe-au-Pic, a holiday destination for the wealthy at the beginning of the 20th century and Canada's first seaside resort. To learn more about the town's history, visit the **Musée de Charlevoix** (museedecharlevoix.qc.ca). It's right on the water so you'll get some lovely views of 'the sea.' For more dramatic views, head up to the **Auberge des 3 Canards** (auberge3canards.com) for lunch or tea and take a seat on the sprawling verandah. It's not far from the **Fairmont Le Manoir Richelieu** (fairmont.com/richelieu-charlevoix), sister hotel to Québec City's Fairmont Le Château Frontenac, with almost as much history and prestige: it dates to 1899.

🚗 **THE DRIVE**
For a little variety, take the Route des Montagnes along Rte 138 Ouest to Baie St Paul (49km).

🧭 **DETOUR**
Parc Nationale des Hautes Gorges de la Rivière Malbaie
Start: 08 **La Malbaie**

This 225-sq-km **provincial park** (sepaq.com/pq/hgo) has several unique features, including the highest rock faces east of the Rockies. Sheer rock plummets (by as much as 800m) to the calm Malbaie River, creating one of Québec's loveliest river valleys. The park is located about 40km northwest of La Malbaie. To reach it, head northwest on Rte 138 toward Baie St Paul, then take the turn for St-Aimé des Lacs and keep going for another 30km.

There are trails of all levels, from ambles around the 2.5km loop of L'Érablière (Maple Grove) to vigorous hikes of up to 11km ascending to permafrost. A highlight is the boat cruise up the river, squeezed between mountains. The river can also be seen from a canoe or kayak, which are available for hire, as are mountain bikes. Boat tickets and rentals are available at Le Draveur Visitor Center at the park entrance.

09 **BAIE ST PAUL**
Arguably the most interesting of all the little towns along the St Lawrence, this unique blend of the outdoors and the bohemian – Cirque du Soleil originated here – may be the most attractive. Plan to kick off your shoes and stay awhile and, if you do overnight, book the delightful **Auberge à l'Ancrage** and have a meal at either the Alsatian **Le Diapason** or the very French **Le Mouton Noir** (moutonnoir resto.com). The architecturally arresting **Musée d'Art Contemporain de Baie St Paul** (macbsp.com), with contemporary art by local artists and some photographic exhibits from its own collection of 3000 pieces, makes a valiant effort to present the town as an artistic hub, though not entirely successfully. Instead, visit one of the local galleries such as the **Galerie d'Art Beauchamp** (galeriebeauchamp.com) just up from the helpful **Baie St Paul Tourist Office** (tourisme-charlevoix.com).

🚗 **THE DRIVE**
From Baie St Paul you can return to Québec City via Rte 138 Ouest (95km) and walk around the Old Town's historical buildings and museums.

Baie St Paul

26

The Saguenay Fjord & Lac St Jean

BEST FOR

☑

Whale-watching from Tadoussac.

DURATION	DISTANCE	GREAT FOR
3–4 days	526km/327 miles	Food & Drink, Nature

BEST TIME TO GO	Late August through mid-October for whale-watching, blueberry season and fall colors.

Whale-watching, Tadoussac (p183)

The Saguenay region's glories start outdoors with the dramatic scenery along the fjord. Hop on a boat to check out its cliffs and forests, or venture out on a whale-watching tour. Nearby, Lac St Jean has sandy beaches, lakeside cafes and shoreside trails to hike or cycle. Naturally, there's food, too, from blueberries that blanket the fields in summer, to locally made cheeses, chocolates and craft beers ready to sample.

Link Your Trip

25 Around, Over & in the St Lawrence River

Continue your road trip in Charlevoix. From Tadoussac, take the free ferry to Baie Ste Catherine, then continue south.

27 Circling the Gaspé Peninsula

Catch the ferry (Les Escoumins/Trois Pistoles, or Forestville/Rimouski) to the Gaspé Peninsula for more maritime scenery and excellent seafood.

01 PETIT-SAGUENAY

Coming from Charlevoix or points south on Rte 138, leave the coast at St Siméon and turn northwest onto Rte 170, where the road, lined with evergreens, begins to climb into the hills, winding around and beneath steep rocky cliffs.

At the town of Petit-Saguenay, detour for your first glimpse of the fjord. Following the signs to the 'Quai de Petit Saguenay,' the municipal docks, bear right from Rte 170 onto Rue Tremblay, which becomes Rue du Quai. Keep following this road as it narrows (it's closed to cars in winter) and continues

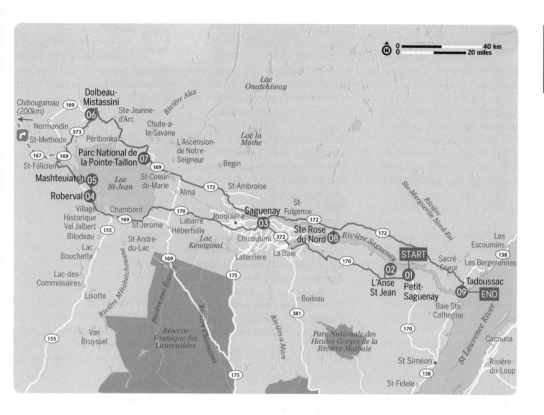

for 4km, where there's a small parking area at the edge of the rock-lined fjord. There's a lookout point and a small picnic area here, too, if you want to take a waterside break.

 THE DRIVE
Retrace your route back to Rte 170 and turn right to continue heading west on this highway. In about 13km, at the sign for L'Anse St Jean, turn right onto Rue du Coin, then make an immediate right onto Rue St-Jean-Baptiste, which will take you into the village.

02 L'ANSE ST JEAN
This pretty little village along the fjord is a great spot to get out on the water. Book a paddling excursion with

Fjord en Kayak (fjord-en-kayak. ca), or a cruise on the fjord with **Navettes Maritimes du Fjord** (navettesdufjord.com); both companies offer a number of different options to suit your time and experience level. Back on land, if you're ready for a bite, dig into a plate of poutine or a burger at **Bistro de L'Anse**, then stroll through the village and along the waterfront.

Drive west along the fjord to take in more scenic views at **L'Anse de Tabatière**. To get here, cross the covered bridge off Rue du Faubourg. Pause for a photo at the bridge, then follow Chemin St-Thomas to Chemin de l'Anse; it's about 5km to the beach.

Retrace your route to return to the highway, but stop along the way for a pastry and coffee at **Nuances de Grains** (nuances degrains.com), a boulangerie on Rue St-Jean-Baptiste next to the church.

THE DRIVE
Follow Rue St-Jean-Baptiste back to Rte 170, and head west toward Saguenay. Leave Rte 170 at La Baie (stop at Musée du Fjord to learn more about the fjord's ecosystem) and continue west on Rte 372. This increasingly urban road isn't the most picturesque, but it leads into Chicoutimi, Saguenay's largest borough. The drive is 1¼ hours in total.

03 **SAGUENAY**
Take a break from the fjord's scenic beauty with an urban interlude in Chicoutimi, Saguenay's largest borough. Hang out over coffee, a sandwich or a slice of cake at the cool **Cafe Cambio**, and take a stroll along Rue Racine, Chicoutimi's main street, to browse the boutiques. You can walk to the riverfront here, too, where you'll often find summertime outdoor concerts, along with the lovely water views.

It's less than a 10-minute drive to **La Pulperie** (pulperie.com), an interesting history and culture museum in the buildings that once housed Canada's biggest pulp mill. Inside the museum, look for the **House of Arthur Villeneuve**, too; it's the vividly painted former home of a former barber who became a prolific folk artist. His house was moved in its entirety to La Pulperie. From downtown Chicoutimi, go west on Rte 372/Blvd du Saguenay, turn left onto Rue Price W, then right onto Rue Dréan, which leads to the museum.

Head back to Rue Racine when you're ready to eat again for pizza jazzed up with local ingredients at **La Parizza** or a build-your-own burger at **Rouge Burger Bar** (rougeburgerbar.ca).

🚗 **THE DRIVE**
Leave Saguenay's more urban precincts and head for Québec's third-largest lake – Lac St Jean. Follow Rte 170 west until it intersects with Rte 169, which will lead south and then west along the lakeshore. Exit Rte 169 onto Rue Brassard toward Roberval, then turn left when it comes to a 'T' intersection onto Ave St-Joseph, which leads toward the marina.

04 **ROBERVAL**
As you head west from Saguenay, you'll get your first glimpses of the lake after Rte 169 splits off from Rte 170, but when you pull into Roberval, you can really take in the watery expanse.

Stop at the marina where you can climb the lookout tower for views across the lake. An office of **Maison du Vélo** (veloroutedesbleuets.com/en) has information about cycling in the area, as well as a snack bar and restrooms.

Roberval is a good place to stop for lunch on your round-the-lake tour. Try the home-style Québec fare at **La Bonne Cuisine de Roberval** (labonne cuisine.ca) along the highway or the good-value set menus at **Emporte-moi** in town; the latter also serves a large assortment of teas.

🚗 **THE DRIVE**
Continue along the lakeshore on Ave St-Joseph, then turn right onto Blvd Horace-J-Beemer, which becomes Rue Ouiatchouan as it enters the First Nations community of Mashteuiatsh.

05 **MASHTEUIATSH**
Stop to visit **Musée Amérindien de Mash-teuiatsh** (cultureilnu.ca), a small museum in a contemporary building above the lakeshore, where you can learn more about this indigenous community's culture and heritage. The exhibits highlight the cultures of the local Pekuaka-miulnuatsh people and of other First Nations in Québec. There are excellent vistas across Lac St Jean from this town as well.

BLUEBERRY LOVE

This is a place that loves its blueberries. More than 20 million kilos of the little blue fruits are harvested each summer in Saguenay-Lac St Jean, earning the region's inhabitants the nickname 'les Bleuets.' Its cycling route – a 256km network of bike trails through the area – is dubbed the **Véloroute des Bleuets** (veloroutedesbleuets.com/en) and an annual summertime fruit fest, **Festival du Bleuet de Dolbeau-Mistassini** (festivaldubleuet.com), includes concerts, activities for the kids and a giant blueberry pie.

You'll see farm stands selling fresh berries on local roads throughout the summer, and many local farms let you pick your own fruit. Late July or early August until early September is typically peak blueberry season. Strawberries, haskap berries (which resemble elongated blueberries but taste more tart) and raspberries also grow through the area. Strawberry season usually runs from late June through mid-July, haskaps ripen from mid-June until late July and raspberries peak from mid-July through August. Berries turn up in pies, jams and more at local markets, too.

A group of Trappist monks makes a particularly local berry treat: chocolate-covered blueberries, which are available only between mid-July and the middle of September. Get them at the shop on the grounds of their monastery, **La Chocolaterie des Pères Trappistes de Mistassini** (chocolateriedesperes.com). They make great road-trip snacks.

AWANA.JF/SHUTTERSTOCK ©

Photo Opportunity

The rocky cliffs along the fjord from Ste Rose du Nord (or from a boat).

Cliffs near Ste Rose du Nord, Saguenay Fjord

THE DRIVE

To continue your tour around the lake, leave Mashteuiatsh heading north and then west on Rue Oui-atchouan, which becomes Chemin de la Pointe Bleue. Turn right onto Rte 169, which will meander through the town of St-Félicien before heading northwest to St-Methode. From there, follow Rte 373 north along the lake and into Dolbeau-Mistassini.

DETOUR
A Taste of the Far North
Start: 05 Mashteuiatsh

Get a taste of Québec's Far North with a detour to Chibougamau, gateway to the Eeyou Istchee Baie-James region, and to the nearby Cree community

of Oujé-Bougoumou, where you can learn about this Indigenous culture.

You'll need at least an extra two to three days for this excursion. Chibougamau is 250km, or just less than a three-hour drive, northwest of Mashteuiatsh, toward the west end of Lac St Jean. And as you follow Rte 167 away from the lake, the terrain feels increasingly remote.

The Chibougamau region offers a variety of outdoor activities that introduce you to Québec's north, from fishing to hiking to canoeing on undeveloped lakes. The lovely water-side **Gîte de La Rivière** (gitedelariv ierechibougamau.com) would make an excellent base for outdoor explorations.

From Chibougamau, drive 45 minutes west (take Rte 167 south to Rte 113 west) to the Cree community of Oujé-Bougoumou. This young community, which was constructed in the 1990s, has an excellent cultural center, **Aanischaaukamikw Cree Cultural Institute** (creecultural institute.ca), where you can learn more about this First Nation, its history and its culture. Local outfitters like **Nuuhchimi Wiinuu Cree Culture Tours** (creeculturaltours@hotmail. com) offer other experiences that can introduce you to this Indigenous culture, while you have fun outdoors.

To return to the Saguenay-Lac St Jean region, take Rte 167 south and continue 230km to St-Félicien. Turn east onto Rte 169 to continue your tour around the lake. Alternatively, from Chibougamau, you can take Rte 113 west toward Val d'Or and the Abitibi-Témiscamingue region for more northern experiences.

06 DOLBEAU-MISTASSINI

The main reason to stop in this town near the west end of Lac St Jean is chocolate. Trappist monks run a chocolate shop, La Chocolaterie des Pères Trappistes de Mistassini (p180), on the forested grounds of their rural monastery outside Dolbeau-Mistassini.

The don't-miss confection? Chocolate-covered blueberries, which are available only in late summer and early autumn when the local blueberry season in the Saguenay-Lac St Jean region is at its peak. Even if you're not here at the right time for the blueberries, though, the shop sells a variety of other chocolate treats.

THE DRIVE
Return to Rte 169, which is now on the north side of Lac St Jean, and follow it as it snakes back toward the water near Péribonka. Stay on Rte 169 to the entrance for Parc National de la Pointe-Taillon.

07 PARC NATIONAL DE LA POINTE-TAILLON

On a peninsula jutting into Lac St Jean, this **provincial park** (sepaq.com/pq/pta) has sandy beaches and more than 40km of cycling paths. Stop to cool off with a swim or go for a paddle along the lake; the park rents canoes, kayaks and stand-up paddleboards.

For a longer stay, you can settle into a campsite here for a night or more. The park has 'ready-to-camp' tents, too.

THE DRIVE
Return to Rte 169 going east. When the road intersects Rte 172, follow Rte 172 to stay along the lake's north shore. It's 120km or about 90 minutes from the park to the turnoff for Ste Rose du Nord onto Rue du Quai, which leads into the village.

08 STE ROSE DU NORD

One of Québec's prettiest towns, the village of Ste Rose du Nord sits directly on the fjord. Explore the forests along the shore – there are walking paths in the woods near the quay – or drive up winding Rue de la Montaigne to a lookout point with expansive views. Have lunch at one of the cafes by the quay or pick up picnic essentials from the town's market to enjoy outdoors.

Above the fjord, off Rte 172 west of town, you can stay the night at **Pourvoirie du Cap au Leste** (capauleste.com), which has a collection of cute cabins and a well-regarded restaurant serving regional cuisine. There are more opportunities to go hiking or canoeing from the property as well.

THE DRIVE
As you leave the village, turn right (east) onto Rte 172. At the intersection of Rte 138, turn right (south) to Tadoussac. It's 85km, or about an hour's drive.

09 TADOUSSAC

Tadoussac sits at the mouth of the Saguenay Fjord, where the North Shore region of the St Lawrence River officially starts, and Rte 138 continues north to ever-more-remote coastal communities. But stay in Tadoussac for at least a day or two; it's one of the best spots in the region for whale-watching.

Learn more about the local marine life at the **Centre d'Interprétation des Mammifères Marins** (gremm.org), then head out on the water yourself. **Croisières AML** (croisieresaml.com) runs a variety of different whale-watching excursions from Tadoussac, while **Mer et Monde** (meretmonde.ca) leads guided sea-kayaking excursions.

Tadoussac has plenty of places to eat, so wrap up your road trip with a special dinner. Both **Chez Mathilde** (chezmathilde bistro.com) and **La Galouïne** (lagalouine.com) serve first-rate local seafood with plenty of produce from around the region.

If you want to stay in town, **Hôtel Tadoussac** (hoteltadous sac.com) is a good choice, looking out over the bay; you can't miss the white clapboard exterior and red roof of this historic property. Or you can camp nearby between the trees at **Domaine des Dunes** (domainedes-dunes.com). Reserve in advance for any accommodations if you're visiting in the busy summer months of July and August.

Before you leave the fjord region and its many maritime pleasures, head for **Microbrasserie Tadoussac** (microtadoussac.com) to raise a glass to your Québec adventures.

27

BEST FOR

Hiking to Land's End in Forillon National Park.

Circling the Gaspé Peninsula

DURATION	DISTANCE	GREAT FOR
7–8 days	900km/560 miles	Food & Drink, Outdoors

BEST TIME TO GO	Late June or early September draw fewer crowds than busy July and August.

Gannets, Île Bonaventure (p186)

Cue up the Québécois sea shanties and hit the road in this Francophone region, where each waterfront village is cuter than the next, and the landscape along the Gulf of St Lawrence varies from forested peaks to sea as far as you can see. Québec's first national park, plus several provincially protected beauties, offer excellent hiking. You can spot wildlife, too, from seabirds to whales (and lobster – on your plate).

Link Your Trip

25 Around, Over & In the St Lawrence River

For more riverside adventures and excellent eating, road trip through Charlevoix. Take the ferry to St Siméon, then turn south.

26 The Saguenay Fjord & Lac St Jean

Want more whales and maritime scenery? Ferry to St Siméon and loop the Saguenay Fjord.

01 STE FLAVIE
Kick off your trip with an unusual art installation – a line of stone figures marching out of the St Lawrence. *Le Grand Rassemblement* (The Great Gathering) was created by local artist Marcel Gagnon in this riverside village, on Rte 132, 350km northeast of Québec City.

Gagnon bought a cottage here in 1984, with the idea of opening a small art gallery. Two years later, he crafted the grand series of sculptures – installing them in the river behind his gallery – that would become his best-known work. That gallery, expanded

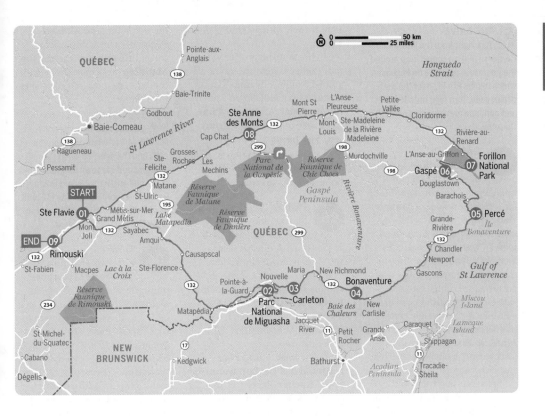

into the **Centre d'Art Marcel Gagnon** (centredart.net), showcases work by Gagnon and several family members; his son Guillaume now manages the business, which includes a restaurant and an upstairs *auberge* with several guest rooms.

Down the road, score your first lobster of the trip at **Capitaine Homard** (capitainehomard.com), a casual nautical-themed eatery, where you can choose whether you have your crustaceans boiled, grilled, in a tartare with local shrimp or in a *guédille au homard* (lobster-salad sandwich).

THE DRIVE
From Ste Flavie, turn inland onto Rte 132 and drive through urban

Mont Joli, following signs for Amqui, Causaspcal and Matapédia. The scenery gradually becomes more dramatic as you wind past inland lakes and forested hills. This 200km route takes you to an unusual national park; turn right at Escuminac, following signs for Parc National de Miguasha.

02 PARC NATIONAL DE MIGUASHA

As you follow the road along the Baie-des-Chaleurs, you get your first glimpse of Le Gaspésie's red cliffs, which give this park its name. Miguasha is a Mi'kmaq word meaning 'red earth.'

The region around what is now **Parc National de**

Miguasha (sepaq.com/pq/mig) is a geologic highlight. It's the world's top fossil site for illustrating the 'age of fish,' the Devonian period more than 350 million years ago, when sea creatures began evolving into tetrapods, which could walk on land. The park's collection includes more than 11,000 specimens, some of which are on exhibit in the informative **Information Center & Museum** (sepaq.com/pq/mig). Watch a short film to learn more about this heritage, and allow time for a guided walk with a park naturalist along the bay and cliffs where many of the fossils were unearthed.

THE DRIVE
Turn right from the Information Center to make a scenic loop around the peninsula on Route de Miguasha, which rejoins Rte 132 near the town of Nouvelle. Turn right onto Rte 132 and continue another 16km east to Carleton.

03 CARLETON
This waterfront town overlooking Baie-des-Chaleurs is a relaxing spot to stay for a night (or more) – **Manoir Belle Plage** (manoirbelleplage.com) is a comfortable updated motel – with good restaurants, a **craft brewery** (lenaufrageur.com), a contemporary arts and performance center, and a bayside quay to stroll. You can drive – or hike if you're really energetic (it's 555m above town) – up to **Mont St-Joseph** (montsaintjoseph.com), a chapel with expansive views across the bay.

Before getting back on the road, stop for coffee at the local roastery, **Brûlerie du Quai** (brulerieduquai.com), and pick up pastries or a picnic lunch at **La Mie Véritable**, a first-rate bakery-cafe.

THE DRIVE
Leave town heading east on Rte 132. The highway briefly climbs up from the coast, then, as you descend toward the town of Maria, the whole bay suddenly spreads out before you. Continue on Rte 132 into Bonaventure.

04 BONAVENTURE
Acadians founded this town back in the 1700s, and you can learn something about this heritage at the interesting **Musée Acadien du Québec** (museeacadien.com). Across the street, take a peek inside the stone **Église de Bonaventure**, an 1860 church with a grand gilded ceiling.

To break up your drive with a more active adventure, go for a guided paddle – by canoe, kayak or stand-up paddleboard – along Rivière Bonaventure with **Cime Aventure** (cimeaventure.com).

THE DRIVE
Continue following Rte 132 east along the coast. It's 135km – about a two-hour drive – to Percé.

05 PERCÉ
Stay alert as you approach this small town at the Gaspé Peninsula's east end. You'll come down a hill where – surprise! – you'll glimpse its famous stone landmark: **Rocher Percé** (Pierced Rock). Perhaps it's fitting that this stretch of coastline has been called 'La Côte-Surprise.'

Take a boat tour to **Parc National de l'Île-Bonaventure-et-du-Rocher-Percé** (sepaq.com/pq/bon), the protected area that encompasses both the arched rock and the nearby **Île Bonaventure** and together houses North America's largest migratory bird refuge. On the island, the highlight is a hike to see the colony of more than 100,000 gannets, a strikingly beautiful seabird. The boat operators all offer whale-watching trips, too.

Back on land, head for **Géopark de Percé** (Percé Unesco Global Geopark; geoparcdeperce.com) to hike in the hills above town or take in the views of the rock and island from a glass-floored lookout platform cantilevered over the cliffs.

The more you adventure, the more you'll appreciate your seafood dinner at one of the village restaurants overlooking the water. Both **La Maison du Pêcheur** (maisondupecheur.ca) and **Restaurant La Maison Mathilde** (aubergelestroissoeurs.com) are good options for dishes from the sea.

THE DRIVE
Leave Percé heading north on Rte 132, which twists between the cliffs and the sea. Pull off at the rest stop just outside town for great views of the gulf and back toward Rocher Percé. Then continue on Rte 132 until it meets Rte 198, which will take you north into the town of Gaspé.

06 GASPÉ
Get some culture at the **Musée de la Gaspésie** (museedelagaspesie.ca), which highlights the region's maritime heritage. Check out the museum's cool virtual-reality exhibit where you head out to sea with a couple of fisherfolk. Just beware if you get seasick – it's surprisingly realistic! Or visit **Site d'Interpretation Micmac de Gespeg** (micmacgespeg.ca) to learn something about the area's Indigenous culture.

Gaspé has a fun local eatery, **Bistro Bar Brise-Bise** (brisebise.ca), which serves excellent seafood and often hosts live music, while its craft brewery, **Microbrasserie Cap Gaspé**, is a popular spot for a beer. The town also has several hotels and inns, including the lovely **Auberge sous les Arbres** (aubergesouslesarbres.com), that could serve as your base for exploring Forillon National Park (your next stop), if you don't want to camp or stay in one of the hostels just outside the park.

THE DRIVE
Follow Rte 132 north out of town toward Forillon National Park. From

TOP TIP:
Which Way to Loop?

You can do this loop trip in either direction, but if you travel counter-clockwise around the peninsula, as we've suggested here, you'll always have the water on your right – where it's easier to pull over for photos or gawk at the views.

Mont-Saint-Alban, Forillon National Park

Gaspé, it's 20km to the park's Penouille Visitor Centre and about 30km to the south entrance gate.

07 FORILLON NATIONAL PARK

Plan at least a couple of days to explore this majestic national park, though there's plenty to do to fill a week or more.

There's a sandy beach near the **Penouille Visitor Centre**, where you can rent kayaks or paddleboards. After you've had fun on the water, continue east on Rte 132 to the park's south gate, where you can explore the heritage buildings at Grande-Grave, then gear up for the park's don't-miss hike: the 8km round-trip Les Graves trail from L'Anse-aux-Amérindiens to **Land's End**.

If you didn't go whale-watching in Percé, or you want another look at these massive mammals, book an excursion departing from Grande-Grave Wharf with **Croisières Baie de Gaspé** (baleines-forillon.com). Also at Grande-Grave is a heritage site where you can poke around a group of historic homes and a restored general store.

Up for another hike? Consider the Mont-St-Alban trail, which climbs to a lookout with a panoramic vista. Then continue driving north on Rte 132, where Canada's tallest lighthouse stands guard at Cap des Rosiers, and you have more views across the water and cliffs. The short Du Banc trail serves up more cliff vistas nearby.

THE DRIVE
The 200km drive on Rte 132 from Forillon to Ste Anne des Monts takes you through some of La Gaspésie's

most striking scenery, as the highway hugs the coast between steep cliffs and the sea. For a coffee break or local-produce menu lunch, stop at Auberge l'Amarrée, a colorful cafe along the main road in Mont Louis.

08 STE ANNE DES MONTS

This pretty town on the river is a good spot to spend the night. The town has several lovely inns; you can watch the sunset over a bowl of seafood chowder at **Auberge Château Lamontagne** (chateaulamontagne.com). Grab a beer at the local microbrewery or party till the wee hours at the riverside hostel, **Auberge Festive Sea Shack** (aubergefestive.com).

In the morning, you can learn more about the marine life of the St Lawrence at **Exploramer**

Photo Opportunity

Hiking to Land's End
in Forillon National Park.

(exploramer.qc.ca), the town's aquarium. If you have time, detour off the coast for some hiking in one of the peninsula's most spectacular mountain regions, **Parc National de la Gaspésie** (sepaq.com/pq/gas), where you can explore the trails for a day or more.

🚘 THE DRIVE

Continue west on Rte 132; it's 185km from Ste Anne des Monts to Rimouski. After Ste Anne des Monts, the

landscape starts feeling more urban. But just when you think you're done with the scenic part of your road trip, another expanse of river opens up beside the highway or you find one more cute beach town along the shore.

🧭 DETOUR

Parc National de la Gaspésie
Start: 08 **Ste Anne des Monts**

As you leave the coast and wind your way into this 800-sq-km park, the trees get denser and the mountains higher, with spiky peaks that almost begin to resemble those of the Canadian Rockies. If you'd like to break up your road trip with some hiking in the mountains, head inland to Parc National de la Gaspésie.

The park has more than two-dozen summits that top 1000m, including Mont Jacques Cartier, which at 1268m is Québec's second-highest mountain.

Pointe-au-Père National Historic Site, Rimouski

Several of the park's peaks are accessible to day hikers, and a section of the International Appalachian Trail runs through the park as well. All in all, there are 140km of hiking paths to explore.

You can easily day-trip to the park from Ste Anne des Monts. From Rte 132, turn south on Rte 299, which leads to the park's **Interpretation Center**. While it's only a 35-minute drive from town, if you want to stay longer, consider overnighting at **Gîte du Mont Albert** (sepaq.com/pq/gma), the comfortable park lodge.

09 RIMOUSKI
Whether you're heading back toward Québec City or going on to another adventure, wrap up your Gaspé Peninsula road trip in Rimouski. As you're following Rte 132 into the city, stop at **Pointe-au-Père National Historic Site** (shmp. qc.ca), where you can check out a historic lighthouse and visit the well-designed **Empress of Ireland Museum** (shmp.qc.ca) to learn about the worst maritime disaster since the *Titanic*.

Cheer yourself up with a pastry from **Pâtisseries & Gourmandises d'Olivier** or with an excellent sweet or savory pancake at **Le Crêpe Chignon** (crepechi-gnonrimouski.com). If you haven't had enough seafood, you can fill your crepe with local shrimp or cold-smoked salmon before you leave this maritime region.

Have time for one more stop? Continue south to **Parc National du Bic** (sepaq.com/pq/bic), off Rte 132, 20km south of Rimouski, for more hiking, kayaking or just exploring the shore. In the summer, you might even spot seals swimming or sunning on the rocks.

Rte 132

QUÉBEC'S HONEYMOON HIGHWAY

Rte 132, which circles the Gaspé Peninsula, celebrated its 90th anniversary in 2019, and many Québécois will tell you that the highway played a role in anniversary celebrations in their own families. By the mid-1900s, the road, which was completed in 1929 (it was originally called Rte 6), became one of the most popular destinations in Québec – for honeymooners.

The Québec government wanted to bring tourists to this newly completed roadway, which – with unfortunate timing – opened just at the start of the Great Depression. The province began producing a series of visitor guides, starting with an illustrated 32-page brochure, *Romantic Gaspé*, published in 1929, to introduce visitors to the peninsula's charms.

Apparently, this promotion – and many subsequent marketing campaigns – worked. The local tourism bureau estimated that in 1925, before the road was constructed, only about 100 tourists visited La Gaspésie. By the 1950s, the region was drawing nearly 100,000 road-trippers, including many newlywed couples, in an average summer, lured by the sea, the mountains and the Francophone *joie de vivre*. Today, that number is more than 700,000.

Of course, the Gaspé Peninsula has yet to approach the romantic popularity of Canada's 'Honeymoon Capital,' Niagara Falls, a region that draws more than 14 million annual visitors. But head for the La Gaspésie, instead, young lovers. Because, really, if you're on your honeymoon, you don't need 14 million other people hanging around.

ATLANTIC OCEAN

200 km
100 miles
0
0

NEWFOUNDLAND AND LABRADOR

Newfoundland

Northern Peninsula

Red Bay
Forteau
St Anthony
Main Brook
Roddickton
St Barbe
Port-au-Choix
Baie Verte
Springdale
Cow Head
Deer Lake
Rocky Harbour
Corner Brook
Stephenville
St George's Bay
Port aux Basques

Twillingate
Lewisporte
Gander
Grand Falls-Windsor
Grand Lake
Meelpaeg Lake
St Alban's
McCallum
Burgeo

Bonavista Bay
Bonavista
Dildo
Clarenville
Terrenceville
Marystown
St Lawrence
Placentia
St Mary's
Ferryland
St John's

Fogo Island

Cabot Strait

ST-PIERRE & MIQUELON (FRANCE)

32
17
15
18

Cape Breton Island
Chéticamp
Sydney
Louisbourg
Baddeck
St Peters
Port Hastings
Sherbrooke
30
105

Gulf of St Lawrence
Îles de la Madeleine
Sable Island

PRINCE EDWARD ISLAND
Summerside
Charlottetown
New Glasgow
NOVA SCOTIA
Truro
Amherst
Parrsboro
Wolfville
Annapolis Royal
Digby
Caledonia
Bridgewater
Liverpool
Shelburne
Barrington
Yarmouth
Halifax
31
28
29
104
102
7
101
103

QUÉBEC
Sept-Îles
Harve-St-Pierre
Pointe-Parent
Etamamiou
Île d'Anticosti
St Lawrence River
Matane
Amqui
Murdochville
Gaspé Peninsula
Mont St Pierre
Rivière-au-Renard
Percé
Cloridorme
Chandler
Bonaventure
Matapédia
Kedgwick
Carleton
132
138

NEW BRUNSWICK
Grand Falls
Woodstock
Fredericton
St Stephen
St Andrews
Saint John
Sussex
Moncton
Miramichi
Bathurst
Caraquet
Grand Manan Island
Bay of Fundy
Cape Sable Island
8
2
11
132

GARETH JANZEN/SHUTTERSTOCK ©

Peggy's Cove (p201)

The Atlantic Region

Explore

The Atlantic Region

This wild, salt-sprayed region fuses the raw beauty of jagged ocean cliffs with a string of hidden coves and the awe-inspiring sight of icebergs sliding past the shoreline like ghostly leviathans. But while the fierce, elemental scenery lures many camera-happy adventurers, it's the contrastingly warm and hospitable welcome that soon becomes the reason to slow down and stay longer. In bright-painted towns and villages that seem to rise from the sea here, it's easy to find locals with wry wit, great storytelling skills and some handy tips on how to crack open the best fresh-catch lobster you've ever eaten.

Halifax

Home to Atlantic Canada's biggest airport, the Nova Scotian capital is where many visitors to the region start their trip. Give yourself a couple of days to explore the city's excellent museums and historic sites, many of them within (sometimes steep) walking distance of the waterfront's downtown area. Also consider a boat tour to see the city from the water. Dining-wise, there are lots of independent restaurants to try out in Halifax; seafood and a pint of local Alexander Keith's India Pale Ale are recommended. Accommodations tend to be of the standard business-hotel variety here, but there are also some distinctive boutique properties and heritage B&Bs to consider.

Charlottetown

While the camera-ready downtown area of Prince Edward Island's historic capital is lined with handsome heritage buildings, it's not a mothballed museum artifact. These days, the small city that staged the 1864 Confederation Conference that led to the creation of Canada has a welcoming small-town vibe that bustles with bistro and bar action, especially in summer, when its streets are filled with visitors from across Canada and around the world. Take a historical tour for the area's nation-building backstory; stay in an antique-lined restored B&B property; and drink and dine (seafood recommended) on Victoria Row.

WHEN TO GO

July and August are the warmest times to visit this region. But while crowds are generally not an issue during this period, especially beyond major attractions and popular destinations such as Charlottetown, accommodations can be scarce. Consider June or September, when children are back in school and attractions are generally fully open but not overly busy.

St John's

North America's oldest city has a story stretching back to the 1500s. But the biggest settlement in Newfoundland, which rises in cheerful-looking row houses from the harbor, has an artsy, university-town vibe that belies its unusually long history. Spend a couple of days checking out the rich array of heritage sites here, and be sure to join the locals for dinner and an ale or three at one of the ever-hospitable bars: try George St if you're keen to party, or Water St for a slightly more sedate approach where you'll be able hold a conversation without shouting.

Moncton

New Brunswick's busiest center, Moncton is a handy stop-off for visitors driving through the region toward Nova Scotia. Perhaps because it lacks the scenic charms of other cities in Atlantic Canada, with their calendar-photo good looks, it's easy to find a place to stay here.

Options are concentrated around Magnetic Hill and on Main St. And while there are also some good restaurants to fuel up at, consider a visit to one of the city's popular indoor markets so you can stock up that cooler you have in your car.

TRANSPORT

Many domestic and international visitors arrive in this region at Halifax Stanfield International Airport. There are also smaller airports in Charlottetown, Moncton and St John's. VIA Rail offers scenic train services from Montréal to Moncton and Halifax. You can also drive here from Québec via Trans-Canada Hwy 2 or from the US via Maine, arriving first in New Brunswick.

 WHAT'S ON

Celtic Colours
(celtic-colours.com) Cape Breton's smile-triggering, foot-stompin' celebration of music from Scotland and beyond.

Festival Acadien de Caraquet
(festivalacadien.ca) A huge Acadian cultural celebration in Caraquet, New Brunswick.

Halifax Jazz Festival
(halifaxjazzfestival.ca) A multiday extravaganza of great concerts around the city.

PEI Fall Flavours Festival
(fallflavours.ca) Charlottetown's party-like celebration of regional seafood and toe-tapping live music.

WHERE TO STAY

The biggest hotels in Atlantic Canada's larger towns and cities are generally of the bland, business, sleepover variety. Instead, research smaller independent inns and unique B&Bs here. The latter may be your only options in tiny coastal communities, offering you the chance to sample the region's famously warm hospitality. Book ahead, though, since space is limited in these diminutive properties, especially in summer, where two-night minimum stays are often required. In Charlottetown, consider the lovely **Fairholm Boutique Inns** (fairholminn.com) and in Halifax go for the luxurious **Pebble Bed & Breakfast** (thepebble.ca).

Resources

Newfoundland and Labrador Tourism *(newfoundlandandlabrador.com)* Planning resources, including activity suggestions and itinerary ideas.

Tourism Nova Scotia *(novascotia.com)* Official destination website for the region.

Tourism Prince Edward Island *(tourismpei.com)* Ideas for accommodations, sightseeing and more around the island.

28

BEST FOR

Kayaking the islands and inlets around Tangier.

Central Nova Scotia

DURATION	DISTANCE	GREAT FOR
10 days	861km/535 miles	Families, Nature

BEST TIME TO GO	June to September

Fundy Geological Museum, Parrsboro

Sandwiched between the lighthouse-strewn South Shore and the wild roads of Cape Breton – it's easy to see why central Nova Scotia gets overlooked by many visitors. But that's such a shame, as the middle part of the province has so much to recommend it: wild white water, remote peninsulas, fantastic sea-kayaking, fossil-studded cliffs and no shortage of off-the-radar beaches.

Link Your Trip

29 South Shore Circular

You've done Nova Scotia's middle; now it's time to go west.

30 The Cabot Trail

Cut the trip in half at Antigonish, and head east onto Cape Breton.

01 DARTMOUTH

Eclipsed by its big-city neighbor across the harbor, working-class Dartmouth is fast becoming a hipster hotbed for young folk, creatives and commuters. Founded in 1750, it has plenty of history and an excellent foodie scene: try the **Battery Park Beerbar** (batterypark.ca) for craft brews, **Portland Street Creperie** (portlandstreetcreperie.com) for pancakes or the smart **Canteen** (thecanteen.ca) for bistro food. The best way across is aboard the Halifax–Dartmouth ferry, which runs several times an hour; Dartmouth's accommodations choices

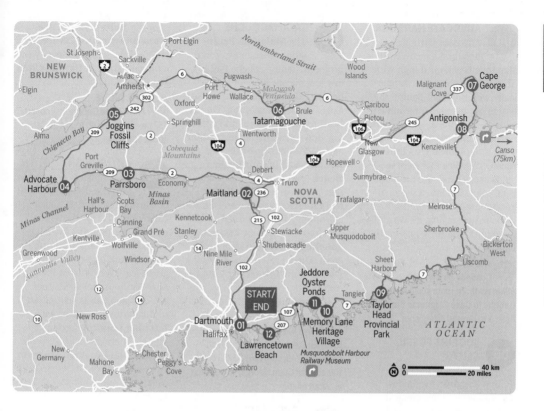

aren't great, but there are plenty of options in Halifax.

THE DRIVE
It's a fast drive from Dartmouth on Hwys 102 and 215 straight to Maitland, 80km north.

02 MAITLAND
Tiny Maitland is the place to brave the Shubenacadie River's legendary tidal bore, a mass of churning white water caused by the river's outflow meeting the blasting force of the incoming Fundy tides. Depending on the phase of the moon, the tidal bore can create wave heights of up to 3m, a wild, washing machine of white water that has to be experienced to be believed.

Shubenacadie River Runners (riverrunnersns.com) and **Shubenacadie River Adventures** (shubie.com) run trips on outboard-powered Zodiacs that plunge through the maelstrom for the two to three hours that the rapids exist.

THE DRIVE
The drive to Parrsboro around the Minas Basin is long: 122km. Take Hwy 236 to Truro, then turn onto Hwy 4, then Hwy 2 (the Glooscap Trail). Count on 2½ to three hours.

03 PARRSBORO
On the opposite side of the Minas Basin, Parrsboro is renowned among rock hounds for its geological deposits.

The best place to get a grounding is the **Fundy Geological Museum** (fundygeological.novascotia.ca), where you can view fossils and dinosaur skeletons dug out around the Fundy coastline, and peer into a working lab where new specimens are being processed.

THE DRIVE
Parrsboro makes an obvious overnight stop, with several B&Bs and hotels around town. The next stretch follows the coastal 209 from Parrsboro to Advocate Harbour, 46km west. Along the way, stop-offs include the Age of Sail Museum in Port Greville and a little lighthouse at Spencer Island.

04 ADVOCATE HARBOUR

Advocate Harbour is a breathtaking cove with a 5km-long beach piled high with driftwood that changes dramatically with the tides. Behind the beach, salt marshes – reclaimed with dikes by the Acadians – are replete with birds. Its best-known sight is the **Cape d'Or Lighthouse** (capedor.ca), where the old keeper's residence has now been converted into a seasonal guesthouse and restaurant. Even if you're not staying, it's worth the rough dirt road drive just for the Fundy views.

THE DRIVE

Continue on Hwy 209 to Joggins, 58km north. En route you'll pass turnoffs to Cape Chignecto Provincial Park, a renowned hiking area.

05 JOGGINS FOSSIL CLIFFS

Hidden in the cliffs around **Joggins** (jogginsfos silcliffs.net) is archaeological treasure: 300-million-year-old fossils dating from the coal age, aka the Carboniferous period, long before the first dinosaurs. Guided tours from the visitor center view fossils buried in the rock, including lycopsid trees, root systems known as stigmaria and shrimp-like creatures called pygocephalus. Tour times are tide-dependent; consult the website for schedules.

THE DRIVE

The next stage of the drive cuts across to Tatamagouche via the busy town of Amherst, 188km east via Hwys 242, 302 and 6. The coastal section from Port Howe to Tatamagouche is the most interesting; if you like, you can stop off at a wildlife reserve at Wallace Bay.

06 TATAMAGOUCHE

The **Malagash Peninsula**, which juts out into protected Tatamagouche Bay, is a low-key, bucolic loop for a drive or bike ride. Tatamagouche makes a great base for exploring. There's loads to see and do round here: top stops include a tasting session at **Jost Winery** (jostwine.ca), wildlife-watching at **Blue Sea Beach** (parks.novascotia.ca/content/blue-sea-beach) or **Rushton's Beach** (parks.novascotia. ca/content/rushtons-beach), and a visit to the excellent **Tatamagouche Brewing Co** (tatabrew. com). There are a few hotels and B&Bs around town if you want to overnight.

THE DRIVE

Take Hwy 6 for 55km to Pictou, then Hwys 106 and 104 to Sutherlands River for 32km. Here you'll turn off onto Hwy 245, then Hwy 337, around the edge of Cape George; this stretch is about 61km.

07 CAPE GEORGE

The jaunt to Cape George is a mustn't miss: with its remote beaches, cliffs and sea scenery, it's been compared in beauty to parts of the Cabot Trail. There are numerous beaches to stop off at – **Arisaig Provincial Park** and **Malignant Cove** are highlights – but the real pleasure here is the drive itself, all breezy bluffs and open ocean vistas.

The 110m **Cape George Point Lighthouse** (parl.ns.ca/lighthouse) overlooks the calm waters of St Georges Bay. The present light (the third) was built in 1961, but there's been a beacon here since 1861. If it's nearing lunchtime, head just around the cape to the fish-and-chip truck near the **Ballantyne's Cove Tuna Interpretive Centre**, then work off the fried goodness with a dip or a stroll at **Crystal Cliffs Beach**.

THE DRIVE

From Cape George, the coastal 337 meanders south to Antigonish, about 30km away.

08 ANTIGONISH

Antigonish is best-known for its well-regarded seat of learning, St Francis Xavier University, and for its Celtic roots: since 1861, the town has hosted an annual **Highland Games** (antigonishhighland games.ca) every July and it still attracts thousands of visitors. A 4km hiking and cycling trail to the nature reserve at **Antigonish Landing** begins just across the train tracks from the **Antigonish Heritage Museum**: you might see eagles, ducks and ospreys. If you don't stay in Tatamagouche, Antigonish is the next obvious place to take a break.

THE DRIVE

The cross-country journey to the Eastern Shore is via Hwy 7, which travels to Liscomb, then turns westwards and tracks the coast. Point-to-point, it's 155km from Antigonish to Taylor Head.

↗ DETOUR

Canso
Start: 08 Antigonish

One of North America's oldest seaports, Canso today stands as a lonely cluster of boxy fishers' homes on a treeless bank of Chedabucto Bay. Just offshore, **Grassy Island Fort** (pc. gc.ca/en/lhn-nhs/ns/canso/culture/grassyislandfort) was built in 1720 by the British to counter the French, who had their headquarters in Louisbourg. The fort was destroyed in 1744, but you

Cape George Point Lighthouse

can wander freely among the ruins. Boats run across until 4pm.

The most direct route is 115km southeast of Antigonish along Hwy 16. A slightly more circuitous route is to take the junction off Hwy 7 between Lochaber and Aspen onto Hwy 276 E, then follow signs to Hwys 316 and 16.

09 TAYLOR HEAD PROVINCIAL PARK

A little-known highlight of Nova Scotia, this spectacular **park** (parks.novascotia.ca/content/taylor-head) encompasses a peninsula jutting 6.5km into the Atlantic. On one side is a long, very fine, sandy beach fronting a protected bay. Some 17km of hiking trails cut through the spruce

Photo Opportunity

The view from Cape George Lighthouse.

and fir forests. The Headland Trail, an 8km round-trip, is the longest and follows the rugged coastline to scenic views at **Taylor Head**. The shorter Bob Bluff Trail is a 3km round-trip hike to a bluff with good views.

About 14km southwest of Taylor Head Provincial Park, **Tangier** is one of the best settings for kayaking in the Maritimes. Based at Mason's Cove, **Coastal Adventures**

Sea Kayaking (coastaladventures.com) explores the isolated '100 Wild Islands' nearby.

The **Liscombe Lodge Resort** (liscombelodge.ca) is the area's best place to stay, or you can pitch at one of a number of wild campgrounds dotted along the shoreline.

THE DRIVE

From Tangier, stick to Hwy 7; the twisting road carries you on toward Lake Charlotte, 43km west, with flashes of forest and coastline en route.

10 MEMORY LANE HERITAGE VILLAGE

A 20-minute drive from Tangier, **Memory Lane Heritage Village** (heritagevillage.ca)

LASZLO PODOR/ALAMY STOCK PHOTO ©

Psyche Cove Beach, Taylor Head Provincial Park

re-creates a 1940s Eastern Shore village in a series of lovingly relocated and restored buildings, chock-full of hands-on antiques, as if frozen in time. You'll find vintage cars, a farmstead with animals (great for kids), a school-house, a church, a miner's hut, a blacksmith, shipbuilding shops and much more.

Just to the south, in **Clam Harbour Provincial Park**, there's a fine beach for sunbathing.

◉ THE DRIVE
From Memory Lane Heritage Village, the Jeddore Ponds and Fisherman's Life Museum are 7km further west along Hwy 7.

11 JEDDORE OYSTER PONDS

The tiny **Fisherman's Life Museum** (fishermanslife. novascotia.ca), located 35km west of Tangier near a series of pools known as the Jeddore Oyster Ponds, paints a convincing picture of the tough lives of the people – particularly the women – who lived along the Eastern Shore at the turn of the century. The simple wooden house here belonged to Ervine Myers, his wife Ethelda and their 13 daughters; in summer, Ervine spent weeks away at his fish shack on Roger Barren Island, and worked at local lumber camps in winter, leaving his wife and daughters to look after the family home. The museum is dotted with family memorabilia, and costumed guides offer tea, tales and hospitality. It's surprisingly moving in its own homespun way.

◉ THE DRIVE
Hwys 107 and 207 traverse the deep inlets of the Eastern Shore. You'll reach Lawrencetown Beach after 42km.

FPI/ALAMY STOCK PHOTO ©

Memory Lane Heritage Village

↪ DETOUR
Musquodoboit Harbour Railway Museum
Start: 11 **Jeddore Oyster Ponds**

This wonderful little **railway museum** (mhrailwaymuseum.com), loved by train buffs and kids alike, looks a little incongruous in its surroundings: it's hard to believe there was once a passenger service through here. Housed in the 1918 railway station on its original site, the museum has train memorabilia inside and original rolling stock outside. It's near the small village of Musquodoboit Harbour, about 14km west of Jeddore Oyster Ponds on Hwy 7.

12 LAWRENCETOWN BEACH

Learning to surf might not be foremost in your mind when you plan a trip to Nova Scotia, but there are some surprisingly good swells (this is the Atlantic, after all). Surf central is Lawrencetown Beach, where Nova Scotia's only pro surfer offers lessons through his **East Coast Surf School** (ecsurfschool.com).

◉ THE DRIVE
Hwy 207 will carry you directly back to Dartmouth, 23km to the west.

29

South Shore Circular

DURATION	DISTANCE	GREAT FOR
10 days	734km/456 miles	Food & Drink, Culture, Outdoors

BEST TIME TO GO	June to September

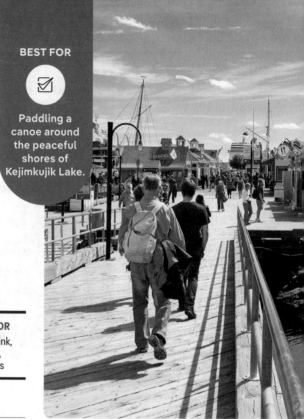

Waterfront boardwalk, Halifax

This trip makes a scenic circuit round the western half of Nova Scotia, meandering along the South Shore from Halifax (locally dubbed 'The Lighthouse Route'), before cutting inland to explore the forests and lakes of Kejimkujik National Park, circling back via the vineyards and orchards of the Annapolis Valley. It captures the essence of Nova Scotia in all its salty, sea-facing, good-natured glory: by the end, you'll feel like a true Maritimer.

Link Your Trip

28 Central Nova Scotia

From Halifax, hop across the harbor to Dartmouth for the start of this journey to dramatic coastal scenery.

31 Two Islands, Three Provinces

Extend the adventure from Halifax with a jaunt north on the Nova Scotia–Prince Edward Island combo.

01 HALIFAX

Big in Nova Scotian terms, titchy in Canadian terms, the port city of Halifax makes a fine place to begin. The city has some great museums, and the waterfront boardwalk has super views across the harbor to Dartmouth and Georges Island, plus pop-up food shacks and summer events aplenty. You'll need at least a couple of days in the city to explore.

THE DRIVE

The drive out of Halifax on Hwy 333 makes a pleasant start to the trip (so long as you manage to avoid any

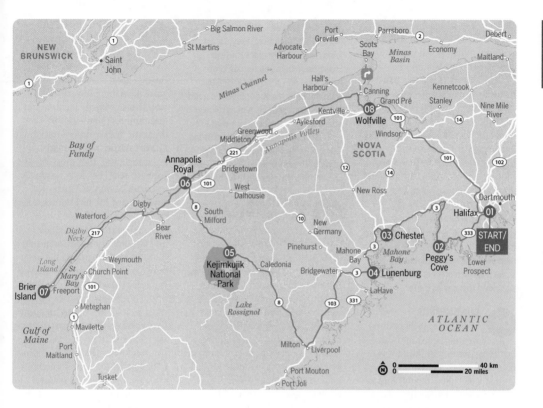

rush-hour traffic). This is the official beginning of the Lighthouse Route, for which you'll see plenty of signs. It's 42km to Peggy's Cove, a journey of 45 minutes to an hour depending on traffic.

PEGGY'S COVE

02 With its red-and-white striped lighthouse, colorful clapboard cottages and boulder-strewn shoreline, this tiny little fishing cove presents the classic picture that literally every visitor to Nova Scotia wants to snap. In summer you'll be doing battle with hordes of coach trippers for the prime spot, so it's much better to hit the cove very early or late in the day when it's

still relatively tranquil. Built in 1914, the **lighthouse** is apparently the most photographed in Canada, and rather bizarrely served as a post office for many years.

If the crush gets too much, you'll find the same kind of vibe at the cute-as-a-button cove of **Lower Prospect**, 30km to the east via Terence Bay. Admittedly, there's no lighthouse, but the tranquility more than makes up for its absence.

THE DRIVE

Head north from Peggy's Cove, following the coast through Glen Margaret and Tantallon; at Upper Tantallon, turn onto Hwy 3, which will take you on a scenic route along the coast via Boutiliers Point, Queensland and

East River (the alternative is the fast but dull main Hwy 103). It's a winding route of about 70km.

CHESTER

03 The seaside village of Chester is one of the prettiest stop-offs along the south shore. Established in 1759, it's had a colorful history as the haunt of pirates and Prohibition-era bathtub-gin smugglers, and it keeps its color today via the many artists' studios about town. It's also a popular place for well-to-do Haligonians to buy a summer home. Many visitors to Chester also take a day trip out to **Big Tancook Island** (tancookcommunitynews. com), the largest of the islets in

Mahone Bay, which offers some great walking and interesting settlement history. The one-way trip takes about 50 minutes.

Just along the coast is **Mahone Bay**, where you can wander along Main St, which is scattered with shops selling antiques, quilts, pottery and works by local painters. The town's seafront skyline is punctuated by three magnificent old churches that provide useful landmarks for sailors.

THE DRIVE
Skip the dull Hwy 103 in favor of Hwy 3 along the coast. It runs for 25km from Chester to Mahone Bay. Another 11km will bring you to Lunenburg. It's a pretty stretch of road, with plenty of sea views to enjoy en route.

04 LUNENBURG
With its brightly painted weatherboard houses, lawned squares and slate-topped churches, lovely Lunenburg almost looks like a model. And in some ways, that's exactly what it is: it was designed according to the standard British blueprint for colonial settlements in the 18th century, and seems barely to have changed since it was built. The old town's beautifully preserved architecture has earned it Unesco World Heritage site status, and deservedly so. The town's sea-going past is exhaustively covered at the **Fisheries Museum of the Atlantic** (fisheriesmuseum.novascotia. ca), and you might be able to take a cruise aboard the **Bluenose II** (bluenose.novascotia.ca) – successor to the original *Bluenose,* the fabled racing yacht that still graces the Canadian dime.

With plenty of B&Bs around town, it's also an obvious place to overnight.

THE DRIVE
From Lunenburg, Hwy 3 west joins Hwy 103 for a quick route to Liverpool, where you turn off onto Hwy 8, the only road into Kejimkujik National Park. It's about 134km, a good two- to 2½-hour drive. A much slower alternative are the coastal Hwys 332 and 331 via Crescent Beach and Broad Cove, offering views of the LeHave Islands. This route adds 25km to 30km and another 45 minutes to an hour.

05 KEJIMKUJIK NATIONAL PARK
Known as 'Keji' by locals, the vast 381-sq-km national park of Kejimkujik is home to the last tracts of true wilderness in Nova Scotia. Generations of Mi'kmaq people paddled, camped and hunted here, and the area is dotted with ancient camping sites, many marked by rock engravings known as petroglyphs: in summer you can take a fascinating guided hike in the company of native guides. Incredibly, even today, less than 20% of Keji's wilderness is accessible by car; the rest can only be reached on foot or by canoe.

Whynot Adventure (whynotadventure.ca) runs guided kayaking and canoeing trips from its base near Jakes Landing, on the shores of the enormous Kejimkujik Lake. The **national park visitor center** (parkscanada. gc.ca/keji) has details on local campgrounds where you can overnight in pre-pitched oTENTiks or cozy cabins.

THE DRIVE
The main national park visitor center is near Maitland Bridge, roughly halfway between the south and north coast. From the visitor center, it's 48km to Annapolis Royal on Hwy 8.

06 ANNAPOLIS ROYAL
There are many reasons to stop off in the well-to-do town of Annapolis Royal – great restaurants, lovely gardens, a fine brewery and a wondrous riverside location not least among them – but it's the dramatic 17th-century stronghold of **Fort Anne** (parkscanada. gc.ca/fortanne) that most visitors come to see. The town's strategic importance on the Annapolis River meant the fort witnessed many bloody battles between its construction in the 1630s and the end of hostilities in the mid-1700s; the battlements and bulwarks are now largely grassed over, but you can still get a sense of the imposing presence the fort must have presented to prospective attackers. There's an interesting museum in the old Officers' Quarters, with exhibits including a four-panel tapestry depicting 400 years of the fort's history.

Another couple of facts that might be worth retaining for a pub quiz: Annapolis Royal was the location of Canada's first permanent European settlement, and also served as the capital of Nova Scotia until the founding of Halifax in 1749.

THE DRIVE
Take the coastal Hwy 1 to Digby, then head toward Long Island and Brier Islands via Hwy 217. It's a super drive, with little traffic and brilliant views of the Bay of Fundy. The two car ferries run hourly (after midnight they're 'on call'). Each costs $7, payable only on travel toward Brier Island (the return fare is free); ferry times can be found at brierisland.org. From Annapolis Royal to Westport on Brier Island it's 101km: two hours if you time the crossings right.

Keji Seaside Adjunct

The main part of Kejimkujik National Park is supplemented by the smaller Keji Seaside Adjunct, 107km to the south, protecting an important coastal habitat of dunes, beaches and creeks between Port Joli and Port Mouton Bay. It's a popular place for backcountry hiking and kayaking. Most people camp, but if you prefer not, the nearby towns of Liverpool and Shelburne make the most obvious bases.

The Rum Runners Trail

Had enough of driving? Then take a break on this excellent bike route (rumrunnerstrail. ca), which runs from Halifax to Lunenburg via most of the main south shore towns, including St Margaret's Bay, Chester and Mahone Bay. It's 119km if you do the whole thing, but the website and route maps handily split the route into seven subsections that can each easily be done in a day. The 10km Mahone Bay to Lunenburg section is an ideal starter; you can hire bikes at Sweet Ride Cycling (sweetridecycling.com).

07 BRIER ISLAND

Some people might see it as a detour, but the there-and-back jaunt to Brier Island is an integral part of this trip. This huge basin is famous for its tides (which are the most extreme in the world), and also for its whales: plankton stirred up by the strong Fundy tides attract finback, minke and humpback whales, as well as the endangered and hard-to-see North Atlantic right whale. Several operators offer whale-watching trips from **Westport**, at the far end of Brier Island, including the excellent **Brier Island Whale & Seabird Cruises** (brierislandwhalewatch. com). It's a fairly long drive, so a stay at the old-school **Brier Island Lodge** (brierisland.com) is a sensible idea.

Getting out to the island is almost as much fun: you'll traverse two chugging ferries en route, and be treated to plenty of gloriously untouched island scenery. The workaday town of Digby makes a handy base before or after the trip: it's renowned for its scallops, which you can sample at restaurants all over town.

THE DRIVE
Backtrack to Annapolis Royal, then continue along the valley to Wolfville: Hwy 221 offers a more scenic route than main Hwy 101, passing through several small towns along the way. It's a pretty long drive of 208km and probably 3½ to four hours thanks to the ferry crossings; overnighting in Annapolis Royal makes it a more leisurely prospect.

Photo Opportunity

Standing next to the world-famous lighthouse at Peggy's Cove.

08 WOLFVILLE

If you mention the Annapolis Valley to Nova Scotians, one image is likely to spring to mind: a glass of ice-cold white wine, preferably served alongside a big pile of seafood. The area's nutrient-rich soils and temperate climate on the Bay of Fundy make it perfect for viticulture: in fact, the first vines in Nova Scotia were planted here way back in the early 1600s. The area's wineries are scattered around the university town of Wolfville and nearby **Grand Pré**, a National Historic Site steeped in Acadian history.

The valley is littered with world-class wineries, all of which offer guided tours and tastings, including the best-known local appellation, Tidal Bay. Among the oldest and most prestigious is **Domaine de Grand Pré**, whose vintages include a delicious spicy muscat and a nice sparkling Champlain Brut. The winery also has a renowned fine-dining restaurant, **Le Caveau**.

There's a slightly more contemporary vibe at **Lightfoot & Wolfville** (lightfootandwolfville. com), an organic, biodynamic vineyard producing a range of wines, from a bubbly rosé and Blanc de Blancs to a crisp Chardonnay and an ice wine. The tours ($15) are informative and last about 45 minutes, exploring the estate's ecofriendly approach and ethos, and including a taste of three wines. Afterwards you can lunch at its excellent bistro.

For a different taste, it's also worth stopping off in Wolfville for a visit to the **Annapolis Cider Company** (drinkannapolis.ca), which uses heirloom and heritage apples to makes all its brews.

THE DRIVE
Hwy 101 cuts directly across the island from Wolfville to Halifax: a distance of 93km, but you'll do it in less than 1½ hours if the traffic's OK.

DETOUR
Cape Blomidon & Around
Start: 08 **Wolfville & Grand Pré**

The area to the north of the Annapolis Valley is dominated by the high ridge of the North Mountain, which comes to an end at windswept Cape Blomidon. It's an under-explored area that's perfect for a detour. Key stops include the rustic **Halls Harbour Lobster Pound** (hallsharbourlobster.com), where you can gorge yourself on ocean delicacies straight from the source; the quaint town of **Canning**; and the renowned **Blomidon Estate Winery** (blomidon wine.ca). Another must-see is the **Look-Off**, a well-signposted viewpoint that has a panoramic perspective of the Annapolis Valley and, if you're lucky, bald eagles soaring overhead.

Hwy 358 ends in Scots Bay, where the dramatic 13km **Cape Split** hiking trail offers some of the finest views of the Minas Basin and the Bay of Fundy. If you're not up for the hike, nearby **Blomidon Provincial Park** (parks. novascotia.ca/content/blomidon) has a picnic area and plenty of easier walks.

Basalt cliffs, Brier Island

30

The Cabot Trail

BEST FOR

Taking a whale-watching tour to spot minke whales, pilot whales and fin whales.

DURATION	DISTANCE	GREAT FOR
3–4 days	420km/261 miles	Nature

BEST TIME TO GO	September and October for fall colors and fewer jams.

Fortress of Louisbourg, Sydney

This is the big one: the looping, diving, dipping roller coaster of a road that snakes its way around the northern tip of Cape Breton, with epic views of rolling seas, mountain passes, thick forests and the chance to spot a moose, eagle or even a whale en route. Take your time: this is a Maritime classic to relish.

Link your trip

28 Central Nova Scotia

You'll have to cut into the route halfway, but it's easy to join up Cape Breton with an exploration of central Nova Scotia.

29 South Shore Circular

It's a bit of a drive back to Halifax, but the spin along the South Shore is another mustn't miss.

01 SYDNEY

The trip begins in Sydney, Cape Breton's largest city, which built its fortune on coal mining and steelmaking, but suffered hard when those industries began to decline. It's a handy base for exploring one of Cape Breton's premier sites: the famous **Fortress of Louisbourg** (fortressoflouisbourg. ca), which sits on a peninsula 35km southwest of the city via Hwy 22. Built in the early 18th century, it was the site of numerous sieges and battles between the English and French armies, but finally fell for good following the conquest of Québec in 1760, when it was razed to the ground. It's since been painstakingly

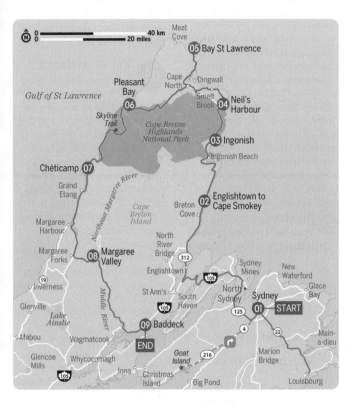

The Skyline Trail

The Cape Breton Highlands has some wonderful hikes, but none is better-known than the Skyline Trail, an 8.2km loop via boreal forest and windswept clifftops onto a spectacular ridge, ending at a stunning lookout: you might well spy bald eagles, moose and possibly whales swimming along the Gulf of St Lawrence from the viewing platforms. Several areas of the trail are boarded to allow for habitat regrowth: stick to the trail to avoid unnecessary erosion. The loop walk is fairly flat; allow two to three hours to complete it. If you don't follow the loop, it's about 6.5km return from the parking lot.

The trailhead starts near the top of French Mountain, about 22km north of Chéticamp, and 20km south of Pleasant Bay.

rebuilt as it would have appeared c 1744, with more than 50 buildings to explore, and costumed soldiers, cooks, orderlies, musicians, gardeners and artisans on hand to bring the place to life. Though the scale of the reconstruction is massive, three-quarters of the fort remains in ruins: a 2.5km trail winds through on its way to the Atlantic coast.

🛞 THE DRIVE

From Sydney, follow Hwy 125 and Hwy 105 for about 55km till you reach the junction with Hwy 312 toward Englishtown. A small 24-hour passenger ferry ($7) crosses the inlet to Jersey Cove, then leads north straight onto the main Cabot Trail.

🏁 DETOUR
Goat Island
Start: 01 Sydney

Forty kilometers southwest of Sydney, Goat Island is home to one of Nova Scotia's largest **Mi'kmaq communities** (eskasoniculturaljourneys.ca). Here local guides offer enthralling tours along a 2.4km trail that provide an introduction into Mi'kmaq culture, including the chance to weave baskets, learn traditional dances, hunting and cooking techniques, hear tribal stories and participate in a smudging ceremony (a cleansing smoke bath used for purification). You'll also get to try some bush tea and luskinigan, a bannock-style bread cooked over an open fire (sometimes known as 'four-cent bread' because it's so cheap to make).

02 ENGLISHTOWN TO CAPE SMOKEY

The stretch of road north from **Englishtown** gives you your first taste of the main Cabot Trail in all its forested, coastal glory. It's an easy drive, framed by thick woodland and rolling hills, with occasional flashes of ocean between the trees. There aren't too many reasons to stop, but if you're peckish, there are a couple of pleasant cafes en route: try the **Clucking Hen** for sandwiches, salads and fresh-baked cakes, or the **Dancing Moose** (thedancingmoosecafe.com) for Dutch-style pancakes. Eventually, you'll reach the dramatic point of

Cape Smokey, where the road climbs sharply up the mountainside; in bad weather it's wreathed in fog, but if it's clear you'll be treated to sweeping views over Ingonish Bay.

THE DRIVE
It's a straight-up drive of about 55km from Englishtown to Ingonish.

03 INGONISH
Up and over Cape Smokey, the trail leads you down into the broad bay of Ingonish, a collection of small seaside villages set around the shores of a sheltered lagoon. It's a scenic setting, and while there's not a huge amount to do in town (save for the big, sandy beach), it makes a useful staging spot to overnight, with plenty of B&Bs and motels around town, not to mention a famous golf course and one of Nova Scotia's plushest hotels, the **Keltic Lodge at the Highlands** (kelticlodge.ca). Even if you're not staying, it's well worth stopping in at the hotel for the chance to walk the **Middle Trail** out to the coast.

THE DRIVE
After overnighting in Ingonish, aim for an early start on the trail. You'll pass the National Park Information Centre as you drive north out of Ingonish: stop here to buy your park permit, review your route and get trail advice from park staff. It's a drive of about 27km from the park entrance north to Neil's Harbour.

04 NEIL'S HARBOUR
From Ingonish, you enter into the boundaries of the Cape Breton Highlands National Park. The road hugs the coast, dipping and diving around several scenic inlets where you can stop off for photo ops. After 27km, you'll spy the turnoff to Neil's

Harbour; here, you actually exit out of the park again, following a stunningly scenic stretch of road that hugs the coast, offering views of the restless Atlantic, clapboard houses and bobbing boats. It's well worth stopping at **White Point**, where a short 2km hiking trail leads out to a dramatic rocky headland, which has claimed many shipwrecks over the centuries; unfortunate sailors are said to have been buried around the point in unmarked graves.

THE DRIVE
From Neil's Harbour to White Point is about 7km; from here, the

TOP TIP:
Route Direction

The vast majority of drivers do the Cabot Trail from west to east, starting in Chéticamp and ending in Ingonish, but there's a good case for doing it in the opposite direction: there's less traffic this way, and you get to drive coast-side for the whole route, making for better views and easier stop-offs. It also means that if you do the trail in a day, you'll hit the west coast for sunset: cue photo ops aplenty.

Note that there are very few gas stations along the trail: be sure to fill up in Chéticamp or Ingonish before you set out.

road loops back round to rejoin the main Cabot Trail after about 15km.

05 BAY ST LAWRENCE
Not long after rejoining the main route, you need to keep your eyes peeled for another turnoff at North Cape, this time signposted for the remote Bay St Lawrence. The road dips down into a lovely green valley, passing **Cabots Landing Provincial Park** (parks.novascotia. ca/content/cabots-landing), where the globetrotting explorer is said to have landed in 1497 (becoming the first recorded European to set foot in North America) and where you'll also find picturesque beaches around Aspy Bay.

Another 7km brings you to the eponymous bay, still a working fishing harbor. Here you can take one of the best whale-watching trips in Nova Scotia in the company of the uber-experienced **Captain Cox** (captcoxwhalewatch.ca), who's been running expeditions since the 1970s. Sightings aren't guaranteed, but if anyone knows how to find you a whale or two, it's this man. You might see pilot whales, minke whales and dolphins without too much trouble; fin whales are much rarer.

THE DRIVE
From the turnoff at North Cape, it's about 18km to Bay St Lawrence and another 18km back. An optional detour is to take a rough, slippery gravel track for 14km to the unedifyingly named Meat Cove: it's about as far north as you can get in Nova Scotia by road, but unless you've got a sturdy SUV or 4x4, it's probably not worth the hassle.

Near White Point,
Cape Breton Highlands National Park

06 PLEASANT BAY

Once you've rejoined the trail again at North Cape, you'll begin climbing into one of the most dramatic areas of the national park, tracking along a deep 40km-long ravine known as the **Aspy Fault**, caused by the movement of tectonic plates. There are several places to stop en route to marvel at the scenery: look out for bald eagles soaring overhead. Eventually, you'll crest over the pass and drop down the other side into the aptly named Pleasant Bay. If you haven't already done a whale-watching tour, there are several operators

Photo Opportunity

Standing at the end of the Skyline Trail.

around town; alternatively, you can make the rather more surprising pilgrimage out to **Gampo Abbey** (gampoabbey.org), a Tibetan Buddhist monastery just along the coast. You're free to wander the grounds, or you can take a guided tour.

THE DRIVE

From Pleasant Bay, the road climbs again over Mackenzie Mountain and French Mountain, dropping down along the coast to reach Chéticamp after 43km.

07 CHÉTICAMP

The stretch of the trail leading south toward Chéticamp is a real eye-popper, looping and veering along the cliffs, with wonderful sea views around every bend: ideally, you want to hit this bit of the road for sunset, when the photo opportunities will have you stopping at every pull-out. You'll pass through the national park

Salmon-fishing, Margaree River

gate on the edge of town, then head on toward the distinctive profile of **Chéticamp Island**. The town itself is home to Nova Scotia's most vibrant and thriving Acadian community, owing much of its cultural preservation to its geographical isolation (the road didn't make it this far until 1949). It's a busy little fishing town, famous for rug-hooking; the **Trois Pignons** (lestroispignons.com) museum has a fine collection. You should be able to catch some live music over dinner at one of the town's lively restaurants and bars. There are plenty of accommodations too, making this the ideal place to stop overnight.

THE DRIVE
After a night in Chéticamp, spin 25km south along the trail to Margararee Harbour, then continue inland along the Margaree Valley.

08 MARGAREE VALLEY
The route veers inland along the course of the lovely **Margaree River**, renowned for its trout and salmon fishing. The **Margaree Salmon Museum** explores the history of fishing in the valley, with a collection of rods, reels, flies and vintage photos; you can also visit the **Margaree Fish Hatchery** to see how the river is kept stocked, and stop off at various points along the valley to explore riverside trails. It's well worth popping in for lunch at the cafe-bakery **Dancing Goat** (facebook.com/DancingGoatCafe), or if you're here in the evening, the quaint **Normaway Inn** (thenormawayinn.com) for some traditional fiddle music.

THE DRIVE
It's an easy drive along the valley of about 88km south to Baddeck.

Alexander Graham Bell National Historic Site, Baddeck

09 BADDECK
Our last stop is Baddeck, a small town hunkered on the shores of the majestic **Bras d'Or Lake** – which, at 1099 sq km, is the largest lake in Nova Scotia, more like an inland sea. The town's main claim to fame is its association with the pioneering inventor Alexander Graham Bell, who fell in love with the hilly scenery in the 1870s (apparently it reminded him of his Highland home). He built himself a grand summer residence on a peninsula nearby, and the town is now home to the **Alexander Graham Bell National Historic Site** (pc.gc.ca/en/lhn-nhs/ns/grahambell) – a fascinating museum that explores the great man's experiments in telecommunications, electricity, aviation, ship design, kite-flying and plenty more besides. Don't miss the scale model of his groundbreaking *Silver Dart* airplane, which made its first flight from the frozen ice of Baddeck Bay on February 23, 1909 (just over five years after the Wright Brothers).

THE DRIVE
From Baddeck, you can head back to Sydney, 78km east (perhaps to catch a ferry from nearby North Sydney to Newfoundland) or head west toward Port Hawkesbury and mainland Nova Scotia beyond.

31

Two Islands, Three Provinces

DURATION	DISTANCE	GREAT FOR
8 days	760km/472 miles	Food & Drink, Nature

BEST TIME TO GO	June to September

Swift fox, Shubenacadie Provincial Wildlife Park

This three-province loop is a great way to experience the diversity of the Maritime provinces, especially if you have limited time. On Nova Scotia, you'll visit the capital city and a superb wildlife park before catching a boat over to potato-crazy Prince Edward Island (PEI), home of some of the finest beaches in Atlantic Canada, as well as everyone's favorite flame-haired heroine, Anne of Green Gables. You'll finish in New Brunswick, with a walk among weird rock formations overlooking the incredible Bay of Fundy.

Link Your Trip

28 Central Nova Scotia

After crossing the Confederation Bridge, continue 115km southeast to Tatamagouche for the second half of this great ramble around Nova Scotia.

29 South Shore Circular

Since it begins and ends in Halifax, this Nova Scotian loop can be tacked on before this route.

01 HALIFAX
Maritime Halifax marks the start of this tripartite road trip. If you've only got limited time in the city, a great way to make the most of it is with a guided tour courtesy of **Halifax Free Tours** (halifaxfreetours.wixsite.com/halifaxfreetours), or hire a bike from **I Heart Bikes** (iheartbikeshfx.com) to take a scenic spin along the waterfront. Later on, you could take an evening cruise on the **Tall Ship Silva** (tallshipsilva.com).

THE DRIVE
It's a fast 61km up Hwy 102 from Halifax to Shubie; parallel Hwy 2 is arguably more scenic, but much slower.

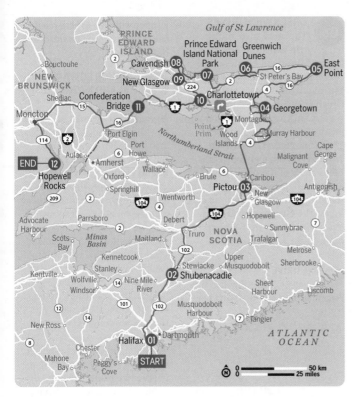

ings; unfortunately, the views are blighted by a giant smoking pulp mill on the opposite side of the estuary, which has long been slated for closure due to environmental concerns.

While you're in town, head for a swim at **Caribou-Munroes Island Provincial Park** (parks. novascotia.ca/content/cariboumunroes-island), which has a lovely beach less than 10km from Pictou.

 **THE DRIVE**
The ferry terminal is a few kilometers north of Pictou. Bay Ferries runs over to Wood Islands on PEI; there are around five sailings a day in spring and autumn, and up to nine per day in summer, so there should be no reason to have to overnight – but if you do, Pictou has several decent places to stay.

04 **GEORGETOWN**
The ferry will deposit you at Wood Islands, a strung-out settlement extending along the southern coast of PEI's eastern side. Make a detour for some wine tasting at **Rossignol Estate Winery** (rossignolwinery. com), stop in to see the historic lighthouse at **Cape Bear** (capebearlighthouse.com), which received the *Titanic's* first distress call, then head on via the artsy little fishing community of Murray Harbour to Georgetown, once an important shipbuilding center but now a sleepy seaside village with a lovely waterfront setting and several impressive mansions. Nearby **Montague** is the service center for Kings County; its streets lead from the breezy, heritage marina area to modern shopping malls, supermarkets and fast-food outlets. Georgetown and Montague both have a

02 **SHUBENACADIE**
To break up the drive north, kids (both big and little) will love a visit to **Shubenacadie Provincial Wildlife Park** (wildlifepark.novascotia.ca), where you have the chance to get up close to some of Nova Scotia's native fauna: moose, porcupines, timber wolves, lynxes, bobcats, cougars black bears and bald eagles. Contained within large enclosures, the animals were mostly born in captivity, but a few have been rescued from private ownership as 'pets' and thus cannot be released into the wild. Check out the website for feeding times and hands-on events.

 THE DRIVE
The easiest route to Pictou is on main Hwys 102 and 104. It's 105km but you should be there in a little over an hour, traffic willing.

03 **PICTOU**
The small seaside town of Pictou is mainly familiar to Nova Scotians as the terminus for ferries to Prince Edward Island; it's also sometimes known as the 'Birthplace of New Scotland' because the first Scottish immigrants to Nova Scotia landed here in 1773. It's an enjoyable base for exploring Northumberland Strait. Water St, the main street, is lined with interesting shops and beautiful old stone build-

handful of B&Bs if you want to break the journey.

🚗 THE DRIVE
From the ferry, head east on Hwy 4 along the coast for 18km to Murray Harbour, then take the scenic Hwy 17 through Gaspereaux and past the lighthouse on Panmure Island. This will bring you into Montague and Georgetown across the bay. To East Point, it's an easygoing 70km spin along Hwys 4 and 16 all the way.

05 EAST POINT
From Georgetown, it's a pleasant drive northwest up the coast toward Souris, with great views of the coast practically the whole way. The objective here is **East Point Lighthouse** (eastpointlighthouse.ca), an 1867 beacon which marks PEI's easternmost point, but there are a couple of interesting diversions along the way.

Elmira Railway Museum stands at the end of the island's short-lived railway (now the popular Confederation Bike Trail); the old station has been turned into a museum exploring the history of the line. Train nerds will love the miniature choo-choo, which winds its way through nearby forest.

Also worth a stop is **Basin Head Provincial Park** (tour ismpei.com/provincial-park/basin-head), which many PEIers think has some of the island's finest beaches – including the famed **Singing Sands Beach**, where the sand audibly squeaks underfoot when it's dry.

🚗 THE DRIVE
You can't get lost on the next section: just follow Hwy 16 west, tracking the north coast to Greenwich, which you'll reach after 58km.

06 GREENWICH DUNES
This next stage of the trip takes you west towards the small coastal community of **St Peter's Bay**. The highlight is the amazing Greenwich Dunes, a 6km wall of rolling, shifting sand overlooking an awesome, often empty beach. The avant-garde **Greenwich Interpretation Centre** details the ecology of the dune system and the archaeological history of the site; from the centre, you can follow the **Greenwich Dunes Trail** (4.5km return, 1½ hours) out into the sandbanks themselves.

🚗 THE DRIVE
Round St Peter's Bay, join Hwy 2 and then follow it for 45km to the

---

☑️

TOP TIP:

By Bridge or Ferry

You've got two options for getting to and from PEI: the Wood Islands ferry or the Confederation Bridge. The ferry is useful for heading onwards to Cape Breton and eastern Nova Scotia, while the bridge is handier for New Brunswick or central Nova Scotia, but there's another consideration: cost. Since you only pay the toll when you leave the island, it's actually about $30 cheaper to take the ferry to PEI, and leave via the bridge ($79 versus $47.75).

---

junction with Hwy 6; here you'll see signs to Prince Edward Island National Park.

07 PRINCE EDWARD ISLAND NATIONAL PARK
As you round the inlet of Tracadie Bay, and head north to Grand Tracadie, you're entering into the borders of **Prince Edward Island National Park** (pc. gc.ca/eng/pn-np/pe/pei-ipe/visit. aspx). For most Canadians, this is quintessential PEI – a sprawling expanse of dune-backed beaches and red sandstone bluffs, a landscape synonymous with summer. Established in 1937, the park runs in a narrow strip for 42km along the island's north coast, ranging in width from a few kilometers to just a few hundred meters. Backed by areas of wetland and woodland, the park provides an important habitat for plants, animals and birdlife, including the red fox and endangered piping plover.

In summer, this is sunbathing central – from east to west, the main beaches are **Dalvay**, **Stanhope**, **Brackley**, **North Rustico**, **MacNeills Brook** and **Cavendish**. If crowds aren't your thing, the beaches further east tend to be quieter – parking can be a real headache in July and August.

🚗 THE DRIVE
To get the most out of the views, follow the Gulf Shore Pkwy wherever possible; it dips in and out along the coastline, rejoining Hwy 6 at various points. Note that park entry fees are payable in summer. From Tracadie to Cavendish, it's about 45km via the coast.

EMILIE NGUYEN/SHUTTERSTOCK ©

Greenwich Dunes

08 CAVENDISH

Cavendish is famous across Canada as the home town of Lucy Maud Montgomery (1874–1942), author of the beloved *Anne of Green Gables* stories (round here she's known simply as Lucy Maud or LM). But far from being a quaint country village filled with clapboard houses and clip-clopping horses, modern Cavendish is a busy tourist attraction. The **Green Gables Heritage Place** (pc.gc.ca/en/lhn-nhs/pe/greengables) is the main point of interest; owned by Montgomery's grandfather's cousins, it's been painstakingly restored to reflect how it would

have appeared in Anne's day, including furniture, furnishings and decor.

A 1.1km trail leads through the 'Haunted Wood' to **Lucy Maud Montgomery's Cavendish Homestead** (lmmontgomery cavendishhome.com), which arguably offers a more authentic picture of LM's life and times: she lived here from 1876 to 1911 with her maternal grandparents Alexander and Lucy Macneill, after her mother Clara died of tuberculosis. It's here that she wrote books including *Anne of Green Gables* and *Anne of Avonlea*. There's a small museum and an Anne-themed bookstore.

THE DRIVE

From Cavendish, take Hwy 13 for 10km to New Glasgow.

09 NEW GLASGOW

Lobster suppers are a PEI tradition, and the old-fashioned **restaurant** (peilobstersuppers.com) in New Glasgow claims to be their spiritual home – it's been serving these indulgent shellfish feasts since 1958. Getting messy while you crack your crustacean is part of the fun – but leave room for chowder, mussels, salads, breads and a mile-high lemon pie.

THE DRIVE

Take Hwy 224 and Hwy 2 to Charlottetown, traveling through classic PEI countryside of fields, farmsteads and small towns. It's 28km and should take only 30 minutes when the traffic's good, likely longer in summer.

10 CHARLOTTETOWN

PEI's handsome capital, Charlottetown has stayed true to its small-town roots, with a lovely, low-rise downtown that still retains many of the redbrick facades and Victorian buildings of its late-19th-century heyday. Covering just a few blocks inland from the harbor, the old part of town was deliberately designed to be walkable, and it pays to wander around and soak up the sights – including the impressive mock-Gothic **St Dunstan's**

Photo Opportunity

Sunbathing on the beach at Brackley or North Rustico.

Basilica (stdunstanspei.com) and a surfeit of heritage homes, shops and colorful clapboard buildings. There aren't that many must-see sights – the real pleasure of Charlottetown is just having a good wander – but the town does have a wealth of excellent places to eat and drink. Sink some craft beer at **Craft Beer Corner** (upstreet craftbrewing.com), snack on a taco or two at **Sugar Skull Cantina** (sugarskullcantina.ca), and treat yourself to a slap-up dinner

at the **Brickhouse** (brickhouse pei.com).

THE DRIVE

Hwy 1 runs directly from Charlottetown to the Confederation Bridge, passing through the pleasant towns of Victoria and Crapaud en route. It's 56km, usually an hour's drive.

DETOUR

Point Prim
Start: 10 **Charlottetown**

Reaching out into the Northumberland Strait, this skinny spit of land makes a rewarding detour from Charlottetown. It's covered in wild rose, Queen Anne's lace and wheat fields through summer and has views of red-sand shores on either side. At the tip is the **Point Prim Lighthouse** (pointprimlighthouse.com): the province's oldest and, we think, the prettiest. If you're lucky, you'll be able to climb to the top to pump the foghorn.

Charlottetown

11 CONFEDERATION BRIDGE

Opened in 1997, and a marvel of Canadian engineering, the **Confederation Bridge** (confederationbridge.com) spans 12.9km linking Prince Edward Island and New Brunswick. It's the longest bridge that crosses ice-covered water in the world. Unfortunately, the 1.1m guardrails do a fairly good job of obscuring the view, but still, driving over the bridge is a PEI rite of passage.

THE DRIVE
The standard bridge toll covers travel to and from the island, and includes one car and all passengers (the toll is only charged on departure from PEI). Once you're over the bridge, it's a fairly long drive to Hopewell Rocks: 95km via Hwy 15 to Moncton, and another 40km to Hopewell Rocks Park on Hwy 114.

12 HOPEWELL ROCKS

On the far side of the bridge, you'll touch down in New Brunswick, your third Maritime province of the trip. A fine finish is provided by the Hopewell Rocks, a fantastical landscape of sandstone formations etched out by the awesome Fundy tides. They've been sculpted into a bewildering array of forms – arches, towers, ice-cream cones – and at low tide, you can get right in among them. From here, many more Fundy area adventures await, or you can loop back into mainland Nova Scotia; Halifax is around a three-hour drive away.

Confederation Trail, near Montague (p213)

THE CONFEDERATION TRAIL

Following the route of the railway that once cut across PEI, the **Confederation Trail** (tourismpei.com/pei-confederation-trail) is one of the best cycling routes in Canada. Winding through a varied landscape of fields, forests, rivers, valleys and coastline, it's a pleasure to cycle – not least because it's almost entirely flat. Some sections of the trail are completely canopied; in late June and the early weeks of July the trail is lined with bright, flowering lupines, and in fall, the changing colors of the foliage are a wonder.

The tip-to-tip distance from Tignish in the northwest to Elmira in the northeast is 273km, but it's easily done in sections, since the main trail passes through major towns including Summerside, Kensington and Mt Stewart, with branches to other towns, including Charlottetown, Souris and Montague. Since prevailing winds on PEI blow from the west and southwest, cycling in this direction is easier.

You can download a trail map and route guide from the Tourism PEI website, and information centers can help with route guidance, accommodations and bike hire.

32

Icebergs, Vikings & Whales

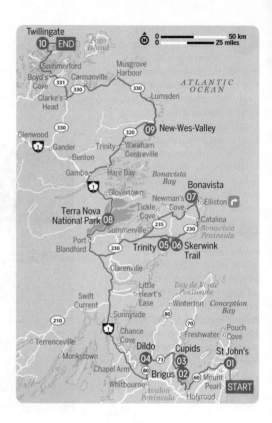

DURATION	DISTANCE	GREAT FOR
5 days	825km/513 miles	Culture, Nature

BEST TIME TO GO	July and August are busy, but the weather is great. May and June are colder, but have less crowds.

There are no straight roads in Newfoundland. Rather, this is a land that is off the beaten track seemingly by design. The province is cut through by winding loops of asphalt that connect the villages of remote peninsulas, several of which you'll explore on this journey, which gives travelers a taste of this province's warm hospitality and raw, severe beauty.

Link Your Trip

28 Central Nova Scotia

Take the ferry to North Sydney, and drive 185km southwest to Antigonish for the second half of this road trip.

30 The Cabot Trail

After exploring Newfoundland, catch the ferry from Port aux Basques to North Sydney for this classic Nova Scotia ramble.

01 ST JOHN'S

Newfoundland's capital is also its largest city, yet for many visitors St John's feels like a pleasant small town. Like all of the province, this is a neighborly, warm place, but it is a capital, meaning there's lots to do here. You can visit the **Rooms** (therooms.ca), the province's main museum, to get a sense of what makes this Rock tick. Take a spin up to **Signal Hill** (pc.gc.ca/signalhill), where the **North Head Trail** stands as one of Canada's great urban treks.

The dining options in St John's are varied and fantastic for a city of this size. You can't go wrong

BEST FOR

A refined meal at Bonavista's Boreal Diner.

Signal Hill, St John's

with fresh oysters on the half shell at **Adelaide** (facebook.com/theadelaideoysterhouse) or a premium handcrafted pizza at **Piatto** (piattopizzeria.com). Consider making a stop at the **Outfitters** (theoutfitters.nf.ca), a one-stop shop for all your outdoor needs. This town's famous for its nightlife, and while it's no fun driving with a hangover, consider at least catching some live music on George St, or a beer at the **Duke of Duckworth** (dukeof duckworth.com).

THE DRIVE
You can drive to Brigus by heading westbound on the Trans-Canada Hwy, and there is something to be said for starting that iconic road at its easternmost point. Still, we recommend taking NL 60 W, which hugs the coast and meanders through some attractive small towns.

02 BRIGUS
Brigus is so bucolic, in such a quintessentially English-cottage-y way, you half-way expect to see a cast member from *Downton Abbey* ride by on an old-time bicycle. This was once a prosperous port and a home for seafaring captains; now it's (more or less) a prosperous retirement community that attracts tourists who love tea, jams and a slow pace of life. You can kill a few hours here just walking around and appreciating how pretty everything is; make sure you get a scone at the **Country Corner** (thecountrycorner.ca), and don't forget to walk through the **Brigus Tunnel** – an artificially dug stone passageway that once connected the main part of town to a deep water berth.

THE DRIVE
It's an easy, short drive (about 4.5km) on NL 60 from Brigus to Cupids.

03 CUPIDS
Brigus may look like a stereotypical English village, but Cupids can actually lay claim to being the oldest continuously settled British colony in Canada. It's a small town – really,

more a strip of homes on Conception Bay than a town – and the main sights are associated with local history. The **Cupids Legacy Centre** (cupidslegacycentre.ca) is, for its size, a rather brilliant museum that explores the past of this settlement, as well as general Newfoundland culture, in great depth and detail.

If you want to get a little more hands-on with your history, check out the **Cupids Cove Plantation Provincial Historic Site** (seethesites.ca/the-sites/cupids-cove-plantation.aspx), which is not only a museum, but a working archaeological site. If you need to stretch your legs, the **Spectacle Head Trail** affords some excellent views of Conception Bay.

THE DRIVE
To get to Dildo, you can either cut across the Bay de Verde penin-

Photo Opportunity

From a clifftop on the Skerwink Trail.

sula on NL 73 W, or you can take the loooong (but pretty) way around and drive to the top of the peninsula, and then down.

04 DILDO
Dildo is far better known for its name then its actual physical beauty, which is a shame, because the phallic headlands the town is (supposedly) named for are quite gorgeous. This is a small settlement and there's not a heap to do besides

snap some nice sunset photos of the bay, pose with a statue of Captain Dildo at the **Dildo Dory** (dildodorygrill.ca), where the seafood is quite nice, or sink a beer at the **Dildo Brewing Company** (dildobrewingco.com), which has figured out you can sell anything if you brand it with the name 'Dildo.' If you really want to eat out like the locals do, leave Dildo and drive a few minutes north to **Pitchers**, a grocery store with a full-service kitchen to the side that dishes up very solid meals.

THE DRIVE
Time to hop on the highway. The Trans-Canada cuts through Newfoundland, but as you'll see, much of the province lives on the peninsulas that stick like amoeba arms off the TCH. Take NL 80 south from Dildo to the Trans-Canada, then take the highway north about 120km and exit

RAVI NATARAJAN/SHUTTERSTOCK ©

Dungeon Park, Bonavista

onto NL 230; drive this road about 70km to Trinity.

05 TRINITY

Trinity is another village with a preserved-in-amber vibe, largely because the main driver of the economy here is no longer fishing, but rather, tourism (and to a degree, the kind of tourism that indulges the idea that this is still a fishing village). This is an exceptionally pretty town, all heritage homes and narrow lanes. One of the foodiest food experiences in the province can be found at the **Twine Loft** (trinity vacations.com/our-restaurant).

The main thing to do here is tour historical properties via a multiuse ticket purchased at the **Trinity Museum** (trinityhistor icalsociety.com). If it's summer, make sure you pop by the **Rising Tide Theatre** (risingtidetheatre. com), which has a busy performance schedule of shows that engage the area's history and culture. Most of these shows are of the dramedy hybrid school of theater, so expect laughs and lumps in your throat.

THE DRIVE
Take NL 230 east/north out of Trinity, then turn onto Rocky Hill Rd and drive about 2km to find the trailhead to the Skerwink Trail.

06 SKERWINK TRAIL

The 5km **Skerwink Trail** (theskerwinktrail.com) is simply one of the best hikes in the province, if not Canada. If you're reasonably fit, it takes around two hours to complete this loop, although you'll want to factor in time to enjoy the views.

And oh, the views. The Skerwink winds past massive cliff faces and foggy coves and affords great views of Trinity and other small settlements clinging to the coast. It's just drop dead gorgeous, and the highlight of many a trip to Newfoundland.

If you're pressed for time, consider hiking the trail 'backwards' (it's a loop, so there is no front or back, but most people start by hiking toward **Dog Cove**). The other end of the trail terminates at **Sam White's Cove**, a rocky beach with some lovely sea stacks, so while you're cheating a little, you are getting a taste of some nice coastal scenery while putting in half the work.

THE DRIVE
Get back on NL 230 and head north; you'll want to follow it around 45km to the town of Bonavista.

07 BONAVISTA

Bonavista is nowhere as immediately beautiful as Brigus or Trinity. It's a working fishing village, or at least a fishing village that supports itself via a hybrid economy of fishing and, increasingly, tourism. You'll be hard pressed to find a friendlier place in Newfoundland. The big physical attraction is **Dungeon Park**, a dramatic sea arch that was carved out of the coast when Poseidon was apparently having a very bad day. You'll also want to spend a few hours poking around **Ryan Premises** (pc.gc.ca/en/lhn-nhs/nl/ryan) and **Ye Matthew Legacy** (matthewlegacy.com); the former is a reconstructed merchant warehouse complex that's now a museum of fisheries history, while the latter is a rebuilt version of the boat John Cabot sailed here in 1497.

The **Boreal Diner** (theboreal diner.com) is one of the best restaurants in the province; come

for local ingredients artfully massaged into Canadian contemporary cuisine that's delicious without being pretentious. If you want to tap your toes, the **Garrick Theatre** (garricktheatre. ca) is great for a show.

THE DRIVE
Take NL 235 back to the Trans-Canada, then take the highway westbound for 160km to reach Terra Nova.

DETOUR
Elliston
Start: 07 Bonavista

About 7km east of Bonavista, the little town of Elliston is famous for its sealing history and contemporary puffin-watching opportunities. Learn about the former at the **Sealers Interpretation Centre** (homefromthesea. ca), a modern museum dedicated to educating the public about this traditional hunting practice. Fair warning, this spot makes no apologies for the seal hunt. From here you can drive to a small parking area and walk a kilometer out to a small cliff. Across the water is a series of rocks and sea stacks where you can see hundreds if not thousands of puffins poking their heads out of their dens, seemingly prepping themselves for the cutest marine avian life photoshoot ever. Grab a meal at **Nanny's Root Cellar**, an excellent provider of hearty Newfoundland meals cooked in a fresh, innovative way.

08 TERRA NOVA NATIONAL PARK

Fantastic strands of spruce forest blanket this **national park** (pc.gc.ca/terranova) in a taiga-esque quilt year round. There are many trails to explore, but if you need a little break after the rigors of the Skerwink, **Sandy Pond** is an easy stroll over

View from NL 330, New-Wes-Valley

boardwalks and crushed gravel. This local body of water (way bigger than what you may think when you hear 'pond') is where lots of folks enjoy waterfront views and a slow pace of walking. If you're up for it, there are plenty more challenging trails in the park.

THE DRIVE
Continue on the Trans-Canada for about 35km, then hop on the exit for NL 320 north. Follow this narrow road past bays and forest for about 75km.

09 NEW-WES-VALLEY
This small town is a very Newfoundland kind of village – a friendly spot where there's not much to do but appreciate the stony shore, which is best done from **Pool's Island**, where you'll find walking

trails that wind over boulders and moorland. Just north of here, **Norton's Cove Studio** (nortons cove.com) is managed by a local artist; it's a cool spot for unique prints and embroidery, and the nearby **cafe** (nortonscove.com/pages/cafe) is a great spot for a waterfront meal of locally sourced goodness. At the very least, get yourself a cup of strong coffee, because there's a long drive ahead of you.

THE DRIVE
Jump on NL 330, and drive north about 170km to Twillingate. On the way, you'll pass some stunning coastal views and a range of tiny villages, each as scenic as the last.

10 TWILLINGATE
The town is composed of a series of islands, considered by many to be the tourism

jewel of the Central Coast. Many visitors come here to go on a whale-watching and/or iceberg tour by boat, an activity we highly recommend. Less known is the **Lower Little Harbour Trail**, which wends its way past ghostly abandoned fishing villages and rugged coastline. Be sure to grab some baked goods and excellent coffee (or a hot chocolate – or even better a mocha for the best of both worlds!) at the **Crow's Nest Caf**e (facebook.com/Crows NestCafe). If you need something stronger, the **Stage Head Pub** (splitrockbrewing.ca) is a very highly regarded local microbrewery. Pop into the **Artisan Market** (twillingateartisanmarket.com) for some locally produced art, a perfect and unique souvenir to mark the end of this epic road trip across the island.

Arriving

If you are arriving in Canada from another country, you will need to pass through customs and immigration at an airport, seaport or land crossing before continuing with your visit. It is a straightforward process for most travelers, and you should expect to be briefly quizzed by a polite border officer about the purpose and duration of your trip.

Car Rental at Airports

To rent a car in Canada, you typically need to be aged over 25 (some operators also rent to drivers aged from 21 for a higher fee). The major rental companies have counters at larger airports, and many also offer services at smaller airports. Book your vehicle before leaving home. This should ensure you get the car you need when you arrive, but it also gives you the best price options and vehicle selection.

You will need a valid driver's license to pick up your vehicle. If your overseas license is not in English or French, you will also need an International Driving Permit (IDP), which you can arrange before leaving home. Keep both your license and your IDP with you at all times while driving. Insurance is required to drive in Canada; if your credit card includes this coverage, this will save on the fees charged by the operator.

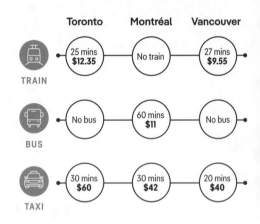

	Toronto	Montréal	Vancouver
TRAIN	25 mins $12.35	No train	27 mins $9.55
BUS	No bus	60 mins $11	No bus
TAXI	30 mins $60	30 mins $42	20 mins $40

VISAS

Most visitors to Canada require a digital eTA (Electronic Travel Authorization) or a visitor visa (typically valid for six months). US travelers only need proof of citizenship and identity such as a valid passport.

AIRPORTS

Most visitors who fly into Canada arrive at Toronto, Montréal or Vancouver airports. From each, you can connect to regional airports or collect a pre-booked rental car to start your driving adventure.

ROAD CROSSINGS

There are more than 100 official road crossings along the US–Canada border. Visit cbsa-asfc. gc.ca/bwt-taf for crossing locations, wait times and additional useful information.

LICENSES

Many visitors can use their foreign driver's license in Canada. But if it is not in English or French (or you are staying for more than 90 days), you may also need an International Driving Permit (IDP).

Getting Around

 Canada has a well-maintained highway network linking the nation from coast to coast. Provinces and territories also have their own highways, most with individual numbers plus more commonly used local names.

ROAD RULES

Driving is on the right-hand side and speed limits and distances are in kilometers. Using cell phones while driving is illegal and seat belts are compulsory. The national blood-alcohol limit for drivers is 0.08; some provinces have even lower limits.

Driving Conditions

The weather can quickly affect driving conditions in Canada, especially in winter and in mountainous areas. Check forecasts via the Environment Canada website (weather.gc.ca). And always have basic emergency supplies, such as water and snacks, in your car.

Parking

Small-town parking is often free and plentiful, but spots are scarce and expensive in big cities, with rates from $3 per hour. Follow posted parking rules to avoid a ticket, especially if you discover an apparently gratis side-street spot.

Fuel

Gas stations are easiest to find in suburban areas. Fuel is dispensed in liters. Prices vary widely but are highest in remote regions and lowest in oil-producing Alberta. Driving from the US? Fuel up beforehand at its cheaper pumps.

Right-turn Rule

Turning right at a red light after coming to a complete stop at a road junction is allowed in Canada. This rule does not apply on the island of Montréal or in specific areas where road signs state that it is prohibited. Be vigilant about pedestrians when exercising this rule; they have the right of way if a crossing light directs them to cross and they also have the right to cross forward on a green light.

Accommodations

NATIONAL PARKS

Aside from campsites and rustic cabins, some of Canada's national parks offer intriguing alternative accommodations. These can include yurts, sleek 'microcube' huts and a cool fusion of A-frame cabins and tents known as an 'otentiks.' You can also step back in time at some Parks Canada National Historic Sites with a sleepover in a heritage property.

HOW MUCH FOR A NIGHT IN A...

Parks Canada Yurt From $75

Campsite $40–50

Castle Hotel From $400

Campsites

Gazing from your camper van at a shoreline sunset or opening your tent to a morning panorama of glistening peaks are why campsites are so popular here. Check Parks Canada, provincial parks and private options, and book far ahead, especially in hot-spot areas and during peak summer periods. Alternatively, seek out remote sites where communing with nature can be utterly magical.

Heritage B&Bs

A subset of Canada's huge bed-and-breakfast sector (peruse your options at bbcanada.com), many handsome heritage homes across the country have been converted into highly inviting sleepovers. Often at the top end of the B&B market, these immaculate, antique-lined properties typically offer gourmet breakfasts, top-notch amenities, and owners who are proud of their properties as well as being great hosts.

Castle Hotels

From New Brunswick to Québec City and from Banff to Victoria, Canada's grand 'castle hotels' were built more than a century ago for 1st-class cross-Canada train travelers. Staying at a turreted landmark such as the Empress Hotel or Château Frontenac is a chance to dress for dinner, enjoy sweeping views from your window and pretend you're a visiting archduke.

University Accommodations

Hotel rates in many Canadian cities rise stratospherically in summer, but this is also the season when you can bag a bargain at a university. Post-secondary establishments often open their accommodations to summer visitors, with facilities from basic student rooms to spacious self-catering suites. Check the university websites in the cities you're planning to visit and book ahead.

TAXES & FEES

You might notice some unexpected additions to your bill when you check out of your accommodations, and we don't just mean that late-night room-service pizza. Inform yourself of these possible charges before booking to avoid an unpleasant surprise. Additions routinely include provincial sales tax (PST) and goods and services tax (GST). There might also be a local hotel tax as well as a destination marketing fee. Many hotels, especially in larger cities and resort towns, also levy parking fees of up to $50 per vehicle per night.

Cars

HOW
MUCH TO
HIRE A...

Economy Car
From $50/day

4x4/SUV
From $90/day

EV
From $125/day

Car Rental

Major companies dominate the rental market here. Their counters are easily found at airports and train stations, and they also have standalone outlets in most cities. Price-wise, book your rental before arriving rather than waiting until you get here. Rates usually include unlimited mileage, but surcharges are typical for one-way rentals, additional drivers, and drivers aged under 25 (not all rental companies offer vehicles to this younger demographic). Shop around, since rates and additional fees vary. Some car-share companies are also open to international visitors, but registration requires additional steps. Your own car-rental insurance (sometimes provided by your credit-card issuer) may be superior to the insurance provided by a rental company; research this before you arrive.

EVs

Canada's major car-rental companies are increasingly offering EV rentals, but they are generally behind their US counterparts. Hertz has one of the largest EV rental fleets in Canada, while some smaller independent operators also offer these vehicles, particularly in larger cities. The public-charging-station situation is annoyingly patchy but slowly evolving, with the highest concentrations in BC and Québec. Even in these regions, most stations (excluding Tesla's own proprietary stations) often do not have enough chargers, which means you may have to wait before you can charge up. Some hotels as well as Parks Canada sites offer charging facilities, while apps such as ChargePoint (chargepoint.com) and PlugShare (plugshare.com) can help you locate the nearest stations.

OTHER GEAR

Child and infant safety seats are required here; reserve them when you book your rental (rates are typically $10 to $15 per day). You can usually also rent ski racks, DVD players or GPS navigation systems. Drivers with disabilities can rent specialized equipment in advance of their arrival.

Safe Travel

Long-distance Driving

Canada is huge, which is why driving all day is second nature to many locals. But if it's new to you, plan ahead. Ensure your car is stocked with enough water and snacks/food for the journey. Plot the places you will rest or sleep over. Don't drive when you'd rather sleep, and consider a designated second driver to share the burden.

Wildfires & Weather

Canada's summer wildfires have worsened in recent years. Be aware of any potential flare-ups in the region you're driving around, and keep your radio tuned for local warnings of fires and evacuations. Winter driving can also be extremely challenging, with storms a major issue in some regions; keep tabs on weather conditions at weather.gc.ca/canada_e.html.

Animals

Outside its major cities, many of Canada's locals have four legs. And they may want to cross the road ahead of you without any warning. Keep your eyes peeled for road signs designating dense animal-crossing areas, but also stay vigilant wherever you are driving, especially in remote areas. Deer, elk, bears, skunks, raccoons and more are frequent road-crossers.

THEFT

Opportunistically breaking a car's side window and ransacking the prominently displayed contents inside is a common annoyance in some Canadian cities. Never leave valuables where they can be seen inside your vehicle and never leave your luggage or travel documents in your car overnight.

BREAKDOWNS

Canada's major car-rental companies typically include basic roadside assistance if your vehicle breaks down and needs a mechanical repair. If the issue is not your fault, a replacement car will be provided at no extra cost. Additional-assistance packages can be purchased at the time of booking; these usually include elevated service and cover a wider range of possible issues.

Responsible Travel

Climate Change

It's impossible to ignore the impact we have when traveling, and the importance of making changes where we can. Lonely Planet urges all travelers to engage with their travel carbon footprint. There are many carbon calculators online that allow travelers to estimate the carbon emissions generated by their journey; try resurgence.org/resources/carbon-calculator.html. Many airlines and booking sites offer travelers the option of offsetting the impact of greenhouse gas emissions by contributing to climate-friendly initiatives around the world. We continue to offset the carbon footprint of all Lonely Planet staff travel, while recognizing this is a mitigation more than a solution.

Happy Cow
happycow.net/north_america/canada
Vegan and vegetarian restaurant listings.

Birds Canada
birdscanada.org
Cross-country birding resource.

Destination Indigenous
destinationindigenous.ca
Local Indigenous experiences for visitors.

EAT LOCAL
Stop at roadside fruit stands and farmers markets to enjoy fresh-picked produce from Okanagan peaches to Niagara cherries and more. Check for options in BC (bcfarmersmarket.org), Ontario (farmersmarketsontario.com), Nova Scotia (farmersmarkets novascotia.ca) and beyond.

TRANSIT DAYS
Park up and explore major cities via public transit. Vancouver, Toronto, Montréal and more offer good-value transit day passes, and have extensive bus, train and even ferry services that encourage active exploration.

MEET CANADIANS
Tours By Locals (toursbylocals.com) offers guided private tours throughout the country, each hosted by a friendly local. Options range from Québec City walking tours to guided alpine hikes in Jasper and much more.

Nuts & Bolts

CURRENCY: CANADIAN DOLLAR ($)

Paying

Credit and debit cards are the primary form of payment in Canada, with Visa and MasterCard dominant and American Express less widespread. Cash is widely accepted (always ensure you have some with you) and can be particularly useful in smaller or more remote communities. Digital payments are increasingly available here.

ATMs

Bank branches routinely have ATMs and you'll likely also find them at airports and grocery stores. If you're planning to use your foreign credit card at ATMs here, check the potential fees and interest charges with your card issuer before you leave home.

Tipping

For restaurants, tip 15% to 20%, and for taxis 15%. Check your restaurant bill before paying since some places add gratuities automatically and you might pay twice. Food-court counters and even some stores are increasingly adding tipping options; remember that gratuities are always optional.

Taxes

Canada's goods and services tax (GST) adds 5% to most transactions. Most provinces also charge provincial sales tax (PST). Some provinces combine these into harmonized sales tax (HST). They're added to your purchase at the register.

Health Care

Travel insurance covering medical emergencies and treatment is essential here. Health care is generally excellent and accessible, but it can be very expensive for non-Canadians. Prescription medications can also be pricey without insurance.

Opening Hours

Banks operate 10am–5pm weekdays; some also Saturday mornings. Supermarkets are open 9am–8pm, some 24 hours. Restaurants serve breakfast from 8am, lunch from noon and dinner from 5pm.

ELECTRICITY 120V/60HZ

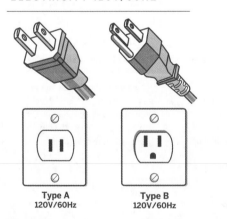

Type A
120V/60Hz

Type B
120V/60Hz

Index

Routes 000
Map Pages 000

Routes 000
Map Pages 000

THE WRITERS

This is the 3rd edition of Lonely Planet's *Best Road Trips Canada* guidebook, updated with new material by John Lee. Writers on previous editions whose work also appears in this book are included below.

John Lee

Born in the historic UK city of St Albans, John came to British Columbia to study at the University of Victoria in his early 20s and never went back. Now a Canadian citizen as well as a full-time freelance writer and a sought-after copywriter, his award-winning work has appeared in hundreds of national and international publications and digital outlets. He has also contributed to more than 40 Lonely Planet titles. Check out some of his work at johnleewriter.com. *@johnleewriter*

Contributing writers

Ray Bartlett, Oliver Berry, Gregor Clark, Shawn Duthie, Steve Fallon, Carolyn Heller, Anna Kaminski, Adam Karlin, Craig McLachlan, Liza Prado, Brendan Sainsbury, Regis St Louis, Phillip Tang

SEND US YOUR FEEDBACK

We love to hear from travellers – your comments keep us on our toes and help make our books better. Our well-travelled team reads every word on what you loved or loathed about this book. Although we cannot reply individually to your submissions, we always guarantee that your feedback goes straight to the appropriate writers in time for the next edition. Each person who sends us information is thanked in the next edition.

Visit **lonelyplanet.com/contact** to submit your updates and suggestions or to ask for help. Our award-winning website also features inspirational travel stories and news.

Note: We may edit, reproduce and incorporate your comments in Lonely Planet products such as guidebooks, websites and digital products, so let us know if you are happy to have your name acknowledged. For a copy of our privacy policy visit **lonelyplanet.com/legal**.

BEHIND THE SCENES

This book was produced by the following:

Commissioning Editor Darren O'Connell

Production Editor Joel Cotterell

Book Designer Fabrice Robin

Cartographer Julie Sheridan

Assisting Editors Sarah Bailey, Anne Mulvaney, Kate James

Assisting Book Designer Virginia Moreno

Cover Image Researcher Fergal Condon

Product Development Amy Lynch, Marc Backwell, Katerina Pavkova, Fergal Condon, Ania Bartoszek

Thanks to Ronan Abayawickrema, James Appleton, Karen Henderson

ACKNOWLEDGMENTS

Cover photograph

Rocher Percé, Québec; Instants/Getty Images ©